Congregational Transformation in Australian Baptist Church Life

New Wineskins Volume 1

National Library of Australia Cataloguing-in-Publication entry:
Cronshaw, Darren, editor.
Jackson, Darrell Richard, editor.

Congregational Transformation in Australian Baptist Church Life:
New Wineskins Volume 1 / Darren Cronshaw, Darrell Jackson.
ISBN: 9780992275525 (paperback)
Includes bibliographical references.
Baptists--Australia--History.
Baptists--Australia--Religious life.
Congregational churches--Australia.
286.194

Congregational Transformation in Australian Baptist Church Life

New Wineskins Volume 1

Edited by
Darren Cronshaw & Darrell Jackson

Morling Press
First Published 2015
120 Herring Rd Macquarie Park NSW 2113 Australia
Phone: +61 2 9878 0201
Email: enquiries@morling.edu.au
www.morlingcollege.com

© Morling Press 2015

This publication is copyright. Other than for the purposes of study and subject to the conditions of the Copyright Act, no part of it in any form or by any means (electronic, mechanical, micro-copying, photocopying or otherwise) may be reproduced, stored in a retrieval system or transmitted without the permission of the publisher.

Scripture quotations are from The Holy Bible, English Standard Version® (ESV®), copyright© 2001 by Crossway Bibles, a publishing ministry of Good News Publishers. Used by permission. All rights reserved.

ISBN: 978-0-9922755-2-5

Designed by Morling Press www.morlingcollege.com/morlingpress

Contents

Foreword
   Keith Jobberns...*vii*

Introduction
   Darren Cronshaw..*1*

Part A:
Case Studies of Transformation, Discipleship, and Missional Innovation **9**

It Started with a Parable
   Andreana Reale..*10*

Education as a Community-Creating Missional Platform
   Brian Harris *26*

Missional Rejuvenation of Historic Inner-City Churches
   Peter Francis *40*

Life in Community
   Robert Morsillo..*58*

Encounter Baptist Church's Journey with 3DM Discipleship and Mission
   David Wanstall..*76*

A Joining of the Ways
   Ian Hussey *97*

The Swan Island Peace Convergence
   Simon Moyle..*116*

Imagining a Renewed Story at AuburnLife
   Darren Cronshaw...*135*

Part B:
Theology and Tools for Congregational Transformation and Consultancy 153

Four Questions To Ask when Leading a Church into Change
    Gary Heard *154*

When the Wineskins Burst
    Alan Gordon *167*

From Stuck to Growing
    Ian Duncum *189*

The Work of Transformation
    Jeff Pugh..*206*

Giving Newcomers a Voice
    Ruth Powell *223*

A Contemporary Theology of Local Church Mission, in Global Perspective
    Darren Cronshaw, David Chatelier, Brent Lyons-Lee, Ryan Smith and Anne Wilkinson-Hayes..*251*

Conclusion
    Darrell Jackson *271*

Endnotes *278*

Foreword

Keith Jobberns

A surprising resilience but a need for new forms

Over the last decade the Australian Baptist movement has proven a resilience that has surprised informed observers of the state of the church in Australia.

Recent analysis of the 2011 Australian national census and the National Church Life Survey (NCLS) has underscored the continued growth of the Baptist movement in Australia.

Philip Hughes addressed Baptist state leaders recently and commented that, "Over the years, it has been interesting to see many of the other denominations shrink, but the Baptists have continued to grow at about the same rate as the population".[1]

Hughes suggests some probable reasons for the resilience. I have found it helpful to express these as our:

Christology ... the emphasis on personal commitment to faith — the lordship of Jesus as expressed in baptism. The centrality of baptism ensures that Baptists are highly committed: 63 percent of Baptists are at church once a month, compared with just 20 percent of Uniting, and 9 percent of Anglicans.

Ecclesiology ... flexibility due to the emphasis on the local church; flexibility to try different things, to be innovative, to adapt to the needs and interests of the local people; and to be flexible in finding the right leadership for the local congregation.

Hospitality ... more importantly and recently, Baptists have been hospitable to people of all races and all backgrounds. Migrant communities have made a huge difference over the years. They have been a major source of our growth and we have provided them a home.

NCLS Research estimates of weekly attendance at church services place the Baptists as the fourth largest denomination in Australia.[2]

The NCLS profiling of the Australian Baptist movement over the last decade has highlighted two significant trends. There has been an increasing engagement by Baptists within their local communities. The old paradigm of "come out and be separate" has been replaced by an effort to get beyond the walls of the church building.

All of this adds up to a positive news story. However, the NCLS survey also showed that in this increasingly pluralistic Australian society we seem to have lost our voice. Over the last decade Australian Baptists are less involved in faith sharing. The profiling seems to suggest that Australian Baptists have not only lost their confidence in Jesus as the way of personal and societal transformation but also their competence in sharing the good news. While the gathered research reflects that, as a movement we are in a better position than other denominations, the challenge for the future is the engagement with an Australian society that does not see the church as having any relevance to their life journey.

So here is the challenge facing the Australian Baptist movement: If the local church is God's instrument to change human history (Ephesians 3:10), then what new initiatives need to be encouraged? What are the shapes of the new wineskins that will be contextually relevant to the changing Australian population and society?

The Research Symposium that precipitated this publication purposed to draw together a group of Baptist practitioners, missiologists, and theologians who, with reference to our past experience, could point to what form the new initiatives might take. I am delighted that the outcomes of the very stimulating Symposium are now available in this volume.

I want to acknowledge the outstanding contribution of Darren Cronshaw and the leadership of the Baptist Union of Victoria in initiating and facilitating the Symposium. I am also delighted that the collaboration of Darren and Darrell Jackson at Morling College has enabled the papers presented at the Symposium to be published.

Keith Jobberns
National Ministries Director
Australian Baptist Ministries

Introduction

Darren Cronshaw

The church has a curious relationship with Australian society. Historically, it didn't get off to a great start. The first chaplain of the colony, Rev. Richard Johnson, got frustrated with the government's delayed delivery of the promise to build a church, so he built at his own expense. But some larrikin convicts burned it down — showing their distaste of its intent to force them into a more "orderly manner of spending the Sabbath day" that the chapel was designed for. Johnson was the first church leader in Australia, but was not the last to shake his head and wonder how to shape church in ways that fruitfully engage Australians.[1]

The inspiration for this book and the origin of most of its content was the National Baptist Research Symposium "New Wineskins: Exploring Transformation in Baptist Church Life". This was hosted at Whitley College, Melbourne, on 24 March 2014. Our theme was not a new idea. Baptists have been keen innovators in doing whatever we can — within the ethical bounds of the gospel — to make Christ known. In the lead-up to the Symposium, Darrell Jackson commented on Facebook, "Looking forward to joining a conversation that has been underway for quite some time (we can't take any of the credit for the 'new wineskins' metaphor!)"

Indeed, Jesus, at the end of one action-in-ministry-packed day, was asked by John the Baptist's followers why they fasted so much and he and his disciples fasted so little and ate so much, especially with certain sorts of people. In his reply, Jesus implied that there would be a time when fasting and abstinence would be more appropriate, but now while Jesus was still around it was most appropriate to focus on eating with the people Jesus loved. This is where we love Jesus' example: his imagination was not filled with spiritual exercises for their own sake, but exercises that connected with the mission of God. If that included eating, then he was all for it

(I think Simon Holt, in his recent book Eating Heaven, takes a leaf out of Jesus' book).[2]

To invite people to capture an alternative imagination for living on mission in all of life, Jesus paints a vivid image about making sure you put new wine, not into old wineskins (that would burst with the change, ruining everything), but into new wineskins ready for the new wine. Any move of God, Jesus implies, needs new forms and vessels, to bring out their flavours and make the most of them. Jesus' whole life, and this image he invoked, inspired me to ask what new wineskins might he be inviting Australian Baptists to imagine? How can we inspire and give permission for and train and empower a new generation of wineskin makers and out-of-the-box activists, and creative apostolic, prophetic, and evangelistic types? (Matthew 9:15–17).[3]

Many of us, and many in our churches, are convinced of the need for change, and fresh expressions and transformation — these are at the heart of the gospel. But where we are looking for help is HOW? We're convinced by the WHY, but want examples of WHAT and WHERE and HOW, to help shape and give inspiration to our own local contexts.

That is where I am most excited about the chapters in this book, and for the possibilities of our ongoing networking and writing together about our action and reflection with new wineskins and congregational transformation.

This *New Wineskins* volume comes in two parts. The first half offers eight case studies of transformation, discipleship, and missional innovation. We want to begin with stories of best practice — not to suggest these are the only or even the best ways to transform congregations and innovate in mission, but they offer wise lessons and inspiration for others.

Andreana Reale describes Urban Seed's journey of mission to people on the margins in Melbourne's inner city, and how helpful parables are for transforming and focusing mission initiatives. Urban Seed has invited residents to live in and work from their space, started Credo Café, and responded to the heroin crisis of the 1990s. They have navigated the resulting conflicts and renegotiated space as a mission organisation alongside the church. Urban Seed's stories offer helpful clues for others to be open to new countercultural parables.

Brian Harris, Principal of Western Australia's Vose Seminary and Pastor at Large of the Carey Movement, evaluates their missional initiatives in co-locating a church and a school, both named "Carey". He celebrates the attractional and incarnational aspects of their mission, and proclamation and presence, and explains how they have embodied Bosch's idea of mission as crossing of frontiers. Harris's reflections are helpful for any church seeking to use their existing missional platforms to help overcome barriers to belief and move people towards receptivity to Christian faith.

As people have been moving back into inner-city precincts, historic inner-city churches have often continued to decline, so Malyon College Field Education Director, Peter Francis, is determined to explore what factors help or hinder city churches engage their exponentially growing, neighbouring residential communities. He offers an analytical framework that can help diagnose a church's missional engagement and identify what cultural and theological aspects of their church life need strengthening.

Also from Queensland, Ian Hussey reflects on his own experience of the successful merger and subsequent revitalisation of two Baptist churches into the North-East Baptist Church. He discusses theological background and processes for mergers, and helpfully identifies factors that led to its success and issues that almost hindered the effort. North-East's story and the lessons Hussey describes are a useful reference point for any church considering whether they might be able to foster the kingdom of God better together with another church.

An antiwar activist and pastor who is taking mission beyond the walls and normal expectations of church, Simon Moyle narrates his experience of interventional, nonviolent direct action and resulting public awareness (and arrests and court appearances). He discusses the Swan Island Peace Convergence as a model for prophetic activism but also forming socio-politically aware and engaged disciples and communities. He appeals for a movement of churches who will "get in the way" of things that hinder the kingdom of God as catalysts for change.

This first section finishes with three specifically local church case studies in Melbourne. Robert Morsillo unpacks the new possibilities emerging in the transformation of inner-urban Moreland Baptist Church as a network of communities. Inspired by Rodney Stark and Ann Morisy, the church is offering open hospitality to external groups such as Merri Community Health Service and the Studio, and taking an adoptive interest in local community events. Their worshiping life is also growing in participatory and interactive directions, and with growing online connections.

David Wanstall describes Stonnington that became Encounter Baptist Church and their journey with the 3DM discipleship and mission system. They have downplayed the reliance on church programs, simplified church for the sake of mission and discipleship, and markedly increased community engagement. The 3DM lessons about discipleship processes, balancing rest and work, looking for "people of peace", and hosting mid-sized "missional community" groups of 15–30 people around a missional vision are transferable for churches of all sorts of shapes and sizes.

Locally at AuburnLife Baptist Church, I explain how we have recently engaged a congregational timeline and church history mapping exercise that have helped us understand our story and values. Appreciative inquiry helped us identify that the church has been at its best as a leadership farm and multicultural hospitality space — which are the two features the church of today most wants to foster as expressions of mission. Looking at history and a local church's story, such as with a congregational timeline, are powerful sources of inspiration for imagining a renewed story.

Part B offers seven chapters of theological frameworks and practical tools for congregational transformation and consultancy.

Melbourne-based pastor and Dean of Whitley College, Gary Heard introduces four pertinent questions to ask for leading a church into a process of change: (1) Do I love these people? (2) Do I understand my context? (3) What theology guides me? (4) What things "need" to be changed? Illustrated by his own experiences, Heard assumes the need for cultural and missional change, but argues that careful processes, a clear pastoral identity, and clear vision for the future are essential to navigate what can otherwise be a minefield for churches.

Alan Gordon advocates updating the five developmental tasks of Intentional Interim Ministries (IIM) with frameworks for "turnaround" leadership that he has found successful with IIMs. He discusses his principles and examples of how to help a church address its history, especially any conflict, exercise leadership and decision-making, discover a new identity, foster supportive and resourcing networks for a church, and commit to the future with a new pastor. Gordon demonstrates best practice of IIM and points in new directions for making the most of it.

Another proven interventional framework for congregational transformation is the client-driven and process-based Church Consultancy model developed by John Mark Ministries and used by Baptist Churches of NSW and ACT. Sydney-based pastor and consultant, Ian Duncum, investigated ten churches who have undertaken consultancies. From interviews and analysis of the National Church Life Survey (NCLS), he identified ways the consulted churches progressed in health and growth, and offers hopeful advice for consultants and churches struggling with viability.

Ruth Powell, NCLS Director, analyses the perspectives of newcomers to church life, which is 6 percent of church attenders. From responses to the NCLS 2011 survey, Powell explores what denominations they join, why they first attended, how they came to faith (often over time), how they find a church, whether they church shop (they don't), why they stay (usually friendliness of the people), newcomers' beliefs and experiences, and how they get involved and belong. For example, they are less likely to attend regularly but more likely to invite others. This chapter promises to open your eyes to some surprising insights from this group of Australians: those who are new to church. Let's be prepared to hear a prophetic challenge from their experience of joining church life, and consider how their experience might challenge us about how and where we need congregational transformation.

Jeff Pugh offers a deep-level description of the influence of church culture and its capacity to subvert or foster missional transformation. He explores the art and craft of how to discern the influence of God's Spirit when culture does shift in positive directions, utilising the complementary frameworks of trinitarian theology and organisational psychodynamic lenses. Consultants and leaders need to give their best thinking to consider theoretical frameworks and their most careful attentiveness to the agency of God in reshaping congregations for mission, and Pugh models both of these postures.

Finally, following a denomination-wide review process called "Reimagining the BUV", the Baptist Union of Victoria Mission's newly formed Mission Catalyst team was tasked with articulating a contemporary theology of local church mission for our work in resourcing churches for mission. Framed around our answer to the question "of what earthly use is the church?", we explore local church mission as spiritual and attentive to what God is saying; local church mission as inclusive and embracing people of diverse cultural and other backgrounds; and local church mission as transformational resulting in peace or shalom in our neighbourhoods.

In introducing this book, we appreciate and honour that it was birthed by the vision of Keith Jobberns, National Ministries Director of Australian Baptist Ministries (ABM), to invite together Baptist leaders from around Australia who were involved or interested in research and missional strategising. Baptist Union of Victoria and our Mission Catalyst team partnered with ABM and Crossover Australia to convene the day. Whitley

College generously offered to physically host the day and allow us the free gift of their space. We appreciate the partnership of other state Baptist Unions and colleges in promoting the day, and the partnership of Global Interaction, Baptist World Aid Australia, National Church Life Survey, Christian Research Association and the financial sponsorship of Baptist Financial Services.

Part of congregational transformation is to invite our churches to imagine and advocate not just for a different approach to church, but for a different future for our world. Bono challenged people to "dream up the world you want to live in. Dream out loud, at high volume". That sets the scene about why we want to see our congregations transform. We are not just interested in church for us ourselves. New wineskins are not primarily for the "consumers" who come — or church members who have been in church for years, or even burned-out Christians who need something new and tantalising to draw them back to church. We want to ask, instead, how can we help our people not just to dream about how to change church, but how to transform society? How do we "bring heaven to Hawthorn" and our other respective neighbourhoods?

I trust and pray that this first volume in the New Wineskins series, *Congregational Transformation in Australian Baptist Church Life*, will give you fresh encouragement and ideas for cooperating in the mission of God through your local church and beyond.

Darren Cronshaw
February 2015
Hawthorn, Melbourne

Part A:
Case Studies of Transformation, Discipleship, and Missional Innovation

It Started with a Parable
Understanding the Dynamics of New Church Missions

Andreana Reale

New church missions can be enormously prophetic, creative, and energising. Yet in time, often this initial energy ebbs away. This chapter follows the journey of Urban Seed — a mission birthed out of Collins Street Baptist Church, who sought to respond with love to marginalised people in their own neighbourhood. The chapter utilises the gospel and story-telling concepts of myth and parable, and the anthropological notions of structure and liminality to analyse changes in Urban Seed's journey across 20 years. Drawing primarily from John Dominic Crossan and John Hoffman, the chapter illustrates how stories, people, and situations that come from outside of the established social structure can generate new, exciting, and prophetic missions. Yet their very lack of structure can cause danger and conflict. The chapter concludes uncomfortably by calling for church missions to seek out unsettling stories, while also putting in place appropriate structures that can ensure stability and longevity. There are many ways that this story can be told; I have chosen one way of telling it. No authoritative claims are being made.

Upsetting stories
First — a story. This was told to a people long ago.

One day Israel will regain her sovereignty where we will appoint our own rulers. This is the way YHWH intended us to live. This is the kingdom of God, and it looks like a big majestic tree on a hill.

Here is another, quite different story.

The kingdom of God is like a mustard seed, which someone took and planted in their garden. It grew and became a large, sprawling garden plant, where many a bird found a home.

This second story is upsetting. It is spoken to an audience who is subjugated by Roman rule. They no longer even own the land on which they live their lives and eke out their livings. This story's audience yearns for the time when they were a self-determined people: abundant and prosperous like a fig tree. Instead, a story is told about a bushy old mustard plant that sprawls across the garden floor and offers its homely branches for birds and animals. There's not a fig or an olive in sight.

You will have recognised the mustard seed story as one of Jesus' parables. I would like to offer a way of thinking about parables as being a very particular kind of story, told from a particular perspective.

Here I draw on the work of John Dominic Crossan.[1] Crossan says that all the stories of the world can be lined up across a spectrum. At one end of the spectrum are stories that set up social worlds. These are called "myths", and they resemble the dominant narratives that were exemplified above. Myths are stories that tell us not only what reality is like, but what reality should be like. They are stories that are integral to the social fabric.

At the other end of the spectrum are the stories that upset social worlds. They are the stories that make us question things that we have taken for granted all our lives. Once spoken, these stories are as easy to ignore as a stone in the shoe. They are as powerful to the social structure as an earthquake is to an immaculate home.

It is the upsetting nature of such stories that Crossan says is the essence of a parable. What a myth sets up, a parable upsets.

Here is another story.

A grand church stood in the centre of a wealthy city. On its steps sat a very poor woman, who smelt bad and muttered to herself. Seeking God, people would walk past the poor woman to enter the church. Little did they know that they had passed God on their way in.

This story is a parable. It turns a world on its head: a world that says that God is to be encountered inside the church. This story upsets this world, by suggesting that in your determination to seek God in church, you may actually rush straight by.

This is a story that is responsible for the birth of Urban Seed.

Parables come from liminal places

There is an anthropological concept known as *liminality* that is helpful to understand, when considering the dynamics of parables. Arnold Van Gennep coined the terms *liminality* and *liminal* in his 1909 *Rites of Passage*.[2] The words are derived from the Latin *limen*, meaning "threshold", and were used to describe a period during a ritual when one was moving between stages (e.g., unmarried à married) but not a part of any. As Victor Turner describes it:

> During the intervening period the state of the ritual subject… becomes ambiguous, neither here nor there, betwixt and between all fixed points of classification.[3]

At the heart of liminality is the inability to classify within the social structure. The term has since been expanded beyond the original context of rituals. Liminality can describe, for example:

- a state of "outsiderhood" where people or groups sit outside the social structure, e.g., shamans, mediums, revolutionaries, and even priests, or counter-cultural groups like the hippies from the 60s and 70s, and the Romani (or "gypsies") in Europe;

- a position of "structural inferiority" — that is, occupying a devalued or rejected place in society, e.g., people who are poor, weak, or despised;
- an "in-between" period of history, where a group or society moves from a stable, well-established social order into a state of flux.

Liminality sits in stark contrast to social structure. Social structure is that which guards the norms of society. Key to social structure are social *institutions*, including family, government, economy, education, and religion, which protect and pass on custom, language, values, and other kinds of norms. "[I]t is impossible to live a human life apart from such a structure."[4]

In a Western, postmodern world, the social structure is in a certain state of flux. Social norms are not as regulated as they once were, and in multicultural places like Melbourne, are very diverse. We are, you could say, in a collective state in liminality. Yet not all is up for grabs, as we tend to find when we do things like break into a military base to protest a war, or try to hold our same-sex partner's hand in public, or display odd behaviour because of mental illness, or even hold very fervent Christian beliefs. In certain settings, these are uncomfortable things to do, because they "bump up" against the powerful forces of social structure.

In fact, liminality is a powerful threat to the social structure. Especially for those most committed to the norms of society, people and corporate structures occupying liminal spaces are seen as dangerous. There is a fear that if the liminality persists, chaos, meaninglessness, and anomy will ensue.[5] The liminal state creates a kind of "anti-structure" — the very opposite of social structure.

Yet for those occupying the place of anti-structure, the experience of liminality may not be negative at all. Anti-structure can be experienced as a kind of "generative center".[6] When standing "betwixt and between" (or "outside"), we have the opportunity to step back from the social structure and reflect on it. What are the limitations of the social structure, and what do I think of its values? What alternatives might we imagine? Liminality, or the place of anti-structure, can be immensely creative. It is an open field of free play, where our creative minds and hearts, unhampered by the grip of social structure, can conceive new ideas about life, purpose, and values.[7]

It is unsurprising, then, that our poets, writers, and prophets tend to have an element of liminality about them. The stereotype of an eccentric artist is well known to us, and we are unsurprised when great thinkers live unusual lives. These are liminal people, who seem not to be comfortable with a life lived wholly within the social structure. Biblical prophets often led itinerant lives, or lived in places removed from the social world. People have often retreated to wilderness areas — the liminal spaces untouched by the fixtures of human society — to seek the word of God.

Jesus was one of these people, and during his ministry lived within an atypical community removed from the customary family ties. He counselled people to "hate" their family in becoming his disciple (Luke 14:26), and to "let the dead bury the dead" (Matthew 8:22) to come and follow him. In other words, the life that Jesus lived and the words that he spoke turned the world as it was known on its head.

From the prophets in their wilderness places come the stories of liminality. These stories can be refreshingly new, casting light on a structure that was impossible to see because we were living inside it. These stories conceive of new possibilities, new ways of being. These stories can be devastating in their critique, strangely opaque, and have a ring of unnerving truth. These stories can make people so angry they want to kill. These stories are parables.

Here I credit the work of John Hoffman, who shows that myths and parables are analogous to structure and liminality.[8]

Parables in church missions

Collins Street Baptist Church heard a deeply unsettling story. It suggested that God might be found on the doorstep of the church and that, in our rush to encounter God within the church, we missed that God was residing in the street. Now that this story had been breathed, it could not be taken back.

In a quest to grapple with the notion that God might be dwelling beyond our four walls, Collins Street Baptist Church invited some fairly liminal people to live inside the church. These were three young men: post-school, pre-marriage and career. They were tasked to be church caretakers, but were also challenged to see if they couldn't connect with some of the marginal figures on the streets of Melbourne. By inviting some liminal types into the heart of their structure, Collins Street Baptist Church was seeking out the God beyond. The parable was being embraced. This movement was a key one in forming what became Urban Seed and what, at the time, was known simply as the Urban Mission Unit of CSBC.

The three young men found a leader in an intense, monastic figure who lived in the bowels of the Presbyterian church next door. This man, whom they called "Chappo", studied the Bible deeply and invited the people he met on the streets into his inner-church dwelling, for lunch. Lunch was bread — and jam if they were lucky.

Inspired by the example of Chappo and the structure-shattering parables of Jesus, the three young men began to invite the people *they* met on the street into their inner-church dwelling, as well. And because they were young and full of energy and ideas, they put on great banquets — not just bread and jam. The three young men met many of their guests in the laneway at the back of the church — a significant site for intravenous drug use in the Melbourne CBD, and a long, long way from the Paris End of Collins Street.

Next came a new force, in the form of the Reverend Tim Costello. Tim had been a pastor at St Kilda Baptist Church, and was formerly a lawyer and the mayor of St Kilda. Tim was a fervent anti-gambling campaigner when he was nabbed by the Collins Street Baptist Church to look after its new and emerging Urban Mission Unit. Tim promptly moved his operations into the church office on Level 6 of Central House, and resumed his anti-gambling campaign there. With him came hoards of young people, keen to join in the fight against a new casino that the maverick Jeff Kennett, Premier of Victoria, was set to build. At one point in the second half of the 90s there were around 20 people working with Tim in the church office, which up until then had accommodated two pastors and a receptionist.

Now the original three Urban Mission Unit residents had expanded to 15, and there were scores more young people working in the church office. People were attracted to some radical new energy at the heart of Melbourne, which transformed a tired gospel and showed how it could change the world. Suddenly the church had moved from a largely middle-class congregation that travelled in from the suburbs, to a place full of the noise and energy of Tim Costello's young followers, who were becoming accustomed to going downstairs to check the mail in their pyjamas.

The residents cleared out the church basement and turned it into an edgy space that they called Credo Café. This was to become the headquarters for a new community, who believed that *real* church happened not in the hard-pewed Baptist church sanctuary, but in a church basement lit by a naked light globe and separated from our back laneway by only a set of frosted windows. The pews were pulled apart and re-fashioned into furniture that suited the *new* way of doing church.

From Credo Café came a searing critique of middle-class Christianity, which was miles away, in distance and in consciousness, from the gritty, real lives of the people *this* community cared about. Young people, fed up with the domesticated Christianity of their parents, were flocking from the suburbs to the centre of the city, to join a radical new community.

This scene was the product of many stories from many liminal spaces. Liminality — or anti-structure — came onto the scene of Collins Street

Baptist Church in the following ways:

- Young people, in a liminal phase of life (post-school, pre-marriage/career), taking the reins on a new movement;
- Urban Mission Unit residents living in an unusual setting, away from family and friends;
- Marginal figures included within this new community;
- Liminal spaces used for the foci of community — the basement (not the sanctuary), the caretaker's apartment (not the suburban home);
- Leadership from the liminal, monastic figure of Chappo;
- Charismatic leadership from Tim Costello, which has an energy aside from pre-existing church structures; and
- An emerging movement inspired by the ultimate leader, the liminal and radical Jesus.

From this place of liminality and anti-structure, a new story was being lived out, which set itself as a challenge to the structures of Christianity that had birthed it. The newly formed mission of Collins Street Baptist Church was a living parable.

Danger and conflict

In the late 90s the heroin crisis hit. The Asian financial crash brought a flood of the drug into Australia, and on the streets of Melbourne you could now get a hit for $20. Heroin, of course, is related to morphine, and hence is a very effective painkiller. For those feeling the pain of abuse, loneliness, and homelessness, heroin offered cheap, effective relief. The laneway behind CSBC became the number one spot to hit up in the Melbourne CBD. The heroin at that point was pure and strong, and a couple of times each week Urban Mission Unit residents would go downstairs to find people comatose or dead.

The heroin crisis took its toll on the newly formed Urban Mission Unit. As the crisis wore on, and pressure on the residents mounted, infighting broke out. People fought about the best way to deal with a situation that was, frankly, beyond them.

There is a reason why social structure exists: it teaches values, passes on important lessons and wisdom, and guides the inexperienced. The Urban Mission Unit had very little of this. What it possessed in parabolic edginess it lacked in clear leadership and process. The Urban Mission Unit was a newly formed entity of anti-structure; a parable that answered back at a world, with few of the structures of the world it indicted. Many people who were involved in the Urban Mission Unit became hurt and burnt out; ironically, many who came to the Urban Mission Unit to fight for justice failed to find it for themselves.

In addition, it was only a matter of time before the nebulous spirit of the new mission rubbed up against the 170-year-old traditions and structures of the rest of Collins Street Baptist Church. It all seemed to come to a head over the issue of a tap.

The tap was controversial because it enabled people to inject using clean water, which was mixed with the drug before injection. The alternative would be to draw up from a puddle or some other dirty source. Many in the church felt that by having the tap there, it was enabling and condoning drug use. Residents with the Urban Mission Unit felt that people were going to shoot up anyway, and it was better that they did so in a place with caring people living upstairs, and that they were at least using clean water. The tap was removed, then replaced; removed, then replaced.

The tap issue represented differing attitudes within the church about our response to homelessness and drug use. Other issues soured the relationship also, like the checking-the-mail-in-pyjamas thing, as well as certain immature incidences that included young, disrespectful residents playing golf in the sanctuary (I think one of them got a "hole in one" in the organ). In 2002 it all got too much, and the Urban Mission Unit split from the rest of the church. It became a separate legal entity called "Urban Seed".

It turned out that inviting a parable into the heart of a 170-year-old institution was never going to be easy.

Rediscovering myth

When the universe burst forth from God, it was an expanding boom of gas and light. It quickly began to develop structure: gravity brought atoms together, which exploded into stars, which produced more complex atoms, which developed into planets and water and plants and people. Likewise, new ideas from liminal places quickly roar to life, before taking on more and more complex structures. Just as the Jesus movement became the church, new missions become incorporated.

The reality is that the stories told from the liminal places — the parabolic narratives that bite back at our myths — cannot exist on their own. They exist *within* the worlds that they subvert. Human life is not possible without our myth-created worlds; humans cannot do anything that lasts longer than a summer without a level of social structure. Jesus knew this better than anyone, which is why his mission was held very much in the palm of Judaism.

When we find ourselves as the main actors in a parabolic narrative, one of two things tends to happen: (a) we revert back to the dominant myth and its accompanying structure, or (b) the parable becomes a myth — i.e., forming the basis of a new "social order" of sorts — with our goals, objectives, programs, and decisions becoming less parabolic over time.

Urban Seed went with option (b). We realised that living in an unfixed, liminal space was not a tenable future plan. It was dangerous and lacked processes that would sustain us. We needed something of the institution from which we were birthed.

As an organisation, Urban Seed has responded by becoming far less liminal, and far more structured. As a result we have come to define ourselves by what we *are*, not what we *are not*. We have become a proper organisation, with a CEO who is generally around to manage important processes, and a coordinator who manages the residents who still live inside the church. We have policies and procedures and a certain level of professionalism.

Importantly, Urban Seed has decided that it is not a church. There is no longer a power struggle with Collins Street Baptist Church, because Urban Seed is allowing the church to be the church, while it settles into a strong identity as a mission organisation.

In other words, Urban Seed is now more than a parable that critiques and bites back: it now has its own myth and its own structure. As such, Urban Seed has a capacity to sustain its mission into the future.

Rediscovering parables

Urban Seed developed a myth — one that was as beautiful as it was necessary. It went something like this:

God is found in the basement of a church, within a community of people who gather around spaghetti bolognaise and re-fashioned church pews. We plod along in the light of God, committed to waiting out for transformation in the context of solid, long-term relationships.

This wonderful myth has sustained a growing mission organisation. We reinforce it each day as we pass the steaming bowls down the table to each other, as liturgical and solemn as the Nicene Creed.

But to any myth there is a parable, which answers back and shines the light in uncomfortable places. Lately we have heard this parable whispering in our ears; tripping us up as we walk. It goes something like this:

A young Urban Seed resident rushes down the stairs, late to lunch in Credo Café because of a meeting. She breathes the familiar smells (baking cheese, a soft linger of blown-out candles) and shares a meal and an animated conversation with a Credo regular. After the meal she wipes the tables and mops the floors, and then rushes to the shops before her afternoon meeting. On the way she passes someone she doesn't know — beanie on the pavement, waiting for coins. Busy and exhausted, the young Urban Seed resident thinks, "Surely today I have given enough", and she quickly passes him by.

She arrives at her afternoon meeting on time, unaware that she's rushed by God today.

Credo Café has used the same model for over a decade, and there is much to celebrate. However, we are beginning to confront a new parable, which is telling us that in our quest for God inside Credo, we have been paying less attention to seeking God outside of Credo as well. We have realised that Credo regulars have largely become people with whom we connected 15 years ago, who are doing a lot better now, rather than the most vulnerable people sleeping rough or struggling with hardcore drug addictions. We have become a vaguely inward-looking organisation; a tad suspicious of newcomers.

Perhaps this movement is familiar to other church and missional contexts.

Urban Seed's response has been to re-invest in outreach. It is when we venture beyond the four walls of our place of comfort that we open our ears to new stories, which can jolt us to new consciousness. This year we are extensively re-structuring our Melbourne CBD-based programs, such that we are focusing on spending a lot more time engaging with new people on new turf, and doing different things on familiar turf. We are hoping to discover parables that will set us alight in a similar way as 20 years earlier, and spur forth a new, prophetic voice that will shake us outside of the myth we are so comfortable in.

Myths and parables in creative tension

Getting out of one's comfort zone is uncomfortable. We find ourselves caught in a tension: between the desire to reinforce the structures that put concrete meaning around our lives, and the desire to get caught up in something unexpected. In fact both the myths that contain our reality and the parables that challenge it are equally important. Remember that Jesus stood firmly in his Jewish tradition and identity, while also travelling to the liminal spaces outside of his immediate world. We must hold myths and parables uncomfortably in one hand.

At Urban Seed we have learnt to hold tradition and structure, as well as make room for spontaneous response. One way we do this is through our residential program. From the very beginning, our work has been characterised by Christians who live in community and engage with their context in a whole-of-life way. Community is certainly not a site of anti-structure; yet the live-in nature of residency leaves space for venturing outside of the bounds of an institution. Urban Seed residents have tended to be in a space of vocational exploration, and have had the freedom to wander the streets of Melbourne, hang out with people in their squats, engage in stencil art, stage public witnesses, busk, write, and spend time in prayer and reflection. The residency program at Urban Seed, both in the Melbourne CBD and Norlane (Geelong), is something of a liminal incubator, nurturing to life new possibilities.

We know the importance of holding the residential program loosely, yet the reality remains that it sits at the centre of an organisation, with all of its structures, processes, and traditions. As such, we tend to oscillate between keeping residency unstructured, so that residents can dictate their own schedules; and a highly structured program where timetables are made on behalf of residents and there is a significant level of organisational accountability. We want structure and we want freedom. There is no way of solving this tension, without dispensing with the program itself. However, we will never do this, because the idea of Christians living together in missional community — open to the parables of the spaces they inhabit — is the lifeblood of Urban Seed.

One way that we might open ourselves to new parables, while still valuing our structures and traditions, is to give liminality a place within our structure. The residential program at Urban Seed is a good example of this. Other ideas include:

- Make sure we actively include and welcome liminal people in our organisations: people who are young, poor, GBLT, non-Christian, from non-dominant cultures.
- Schedule times to actively listen to these people. What does this organisation need to do differently? Take the suggestions seriously; act where necessary.
- Spend time reading the Bible with the group, and make space to hear from the non-dominant members of the group.
- Have scheduled "down time" as a group, where we can reflect, dream, and try new things.
- Share meals together — because the act of sharing a meal is equalising, and places a temporary pause on the hierarchies that tend to come with structure.
- Ensure that our groups are actively listening to the external prophetic voices. Encourage people to listen to our indigenous leaders and leaders from non-dominant groups. Invite challenging speakers to our meetings.
- Schedule times for our groups to walk silently through our neighbourhoods, to see if we can hear some of the stories from the liminal places.

Victor Turner wrote: "Man is both a structural and an anti-structural entity, who *grows* through anti-structure and *conserves* through structure".[9] It is clear that both are needed.

Conclusion

A final story:

An indigenous man, who had come to the city to sort out his demons, sat at the bottom of the front steps of Collins Street Baptist Church on a Sunday morning. Each Sunday he would progressively move up a step, until one Sunday he found himself inside the church sanctuary. He felt uncomfortable at first, but quickly met some friendly people who put him at ease.

A few weeks later one of the churchgoers was handing out ice and water with Urban Seed, during a heat wave. She ran into the man, who was camping out by the river, and introduced him to her friend, who happened to run the art program at Urban Seed. It turned out that the indigenous man was also an artist. Now the man comes to church on a Sunday, and has become a teacher to the art group in Credo Café. For him, both the sanctuary and the basement are integral parts of the one community.

This story is both myth and parable. Elements of this story are held firmly in the hands of a solid social structure: not only of a 170-year-old church tradition that continues to welcome and transform, but also of a 20-year-old church mission that extends a steady hand and has a structure to invite someone into. And yet this structure has ample room for that which is liminal: church-goers welcome with open arms a homeless man standing awkwardly in the sanctuary; church members and Urban Seeders, together, leave behind the cool walls of the church to seek out people excluded from air-conditioning. And a figure no less liminal than one who is both homeless and indigenous is not only included, but invited to the centre, by becoming a teacher.

It is a good story — a mythic-parable at its best. And yet stories such as these always have fallouts around the edges, because the parables that myths make room for are inevitably unsettling. They must be, or else they would not be parables.

This is the necessary and uncomfortable challenge for our church missions. We must have the stability of a myth — a guiding story that tells us who we are and where we are going. At the same time, we must make room for unsettling stories that cause us to question those very containers in which we pour our lives and missions. Trying to live inside a parable is like trying to live inside an earthquake. And yet living in the immaculate house is only viable if we allow ourselves, every now and then, to get seriously shaken.

And so:

If we are a missional start-up, temporarily riding the parable, let's remember not only the story that set us on this course but also the fact that we had to go out of our comfort zone to get it. This will be important for later.

When we have conflict with more established institutions, let's remember that they were the ones that gave us life, and have stood the test of time. Let's draw on their wisdom when we face crisis ourselves.

When the conflict has subsided and our original parable solidifies into a myth, let's celebrate all that structure can offer, and then go with God to seek out more unsettling stories.

And then, may we be always ready to hear those parables, and let them turn our world on its head.

Andreana Reale works at Urban Seed and is a Deacon at CSBC. She is a community development practitioner, committed to inner-city incarnational mission. Andreana has degrees in Arts and Law, has almost completed a Master of Arts (Theology) and has published in the areas of disaster risk reduction, religion, and land tenure.

Education as a Community-Creating Missional Platform
The Carey Story

Brian Harris

Conscious that it is extremely difficult to engage unchurched Australians in church life, a group of Perth-based young adults simultaneously planted and co-located a church and school in the 1990s, with the school providing a community-creating missional platform within which the church could be incarnated. They named both the school and church "Carey", and as they are now about to plant a second campus, this chapter explores the Carey story. It outlines Carey's understanding of mission and the questions that have arisen as the church contemplates its missional effectiveness. The article raises questions about both attractional and incarnational models of mission. It interacts with Bosch's concept of mission as a crossing of frontiers, and explores how this has worked out in the Carey context, whilst suggesting that the underlying principles might be more widely applicable.

About Carey and its mission

Ask most people what they remember of the 1989 movie "Field of Dreams" and there is a fair chance they will misquote Kevin Costner as saying, "If you build it they will come".[1] The sentiment has been used to justify a bias towards building and action in business and other fields. However, it is a conviction that appears to have little validity when it comes to church buildings. Too many large and impressive church complexes are underutilised — often to an alarming degree. Attractional models of church assume that a comfortable church building supplemented by an engaging and busy program will lead to solid church growth. The evidence to support this assumption is underwhelming and becomes increasingly so as suspicion of the institutional church in Australia grows. Finding ways to engage unchurched Australians in church life has become very difficult and, while church attendance figures are no longer haemorrhaging, they are not keeping up with the overall population growth, and in real terms have been declining for decades.[2]

It was against this background that a group of around thirty Perth-based young adults decided to embark upon a church-planting project in the mid 1990s. They were armed with a firm conviction that, if the church were to be relevant in a rapidly changing context, they would have to plant a church that would be "turned inside out" — to quote their oft-repeated mantra. Instead of expecting the community to make their way to the church, they would ensure that the church was incarnated in the community in such a way that residents could not help but bump into it over and over again. They decided to start a school, and via providing outstanding education, they hoped to win the trust of the community and the right to speak about the deeper matters of life.

Inspired by the missionary zeal of pioneer Baptist missionary William Carey, the group named the church and school "Carey",[3] and adopted as their own his slogan, "Expect great things from God. Attempt great things for God". It has been an apt choice, for this has never been anything less than a faith-stretching journey. To quote a founding member: "This has been far and away the most difficult and painful journey I have ever embarked upon. It has also been the most satisfying, and the one through which I have grown the most."

Walk onto the Carey campus today and you step onto a thriving campus that houses a college of 1335 pupils, a bustling childcare centre, a growing church, and an ever-expanding range of community projects. To accommodate the latter, a large community centre is nearing completion, and will open within a few months. The Carey movement employs around 200 people, and that number will soon double as an additional 55-acre site has been purchased on which to duplicate everything being done at the founding site. This campus in Forrestdale, Perth, about seven kilometres from the original Carey site in Harrisdale, is due to open in 2016.

With the second campus set to open in 2016, Carey is working through the implications of morphing from "Carey the Campus" to "Carey the Movement". The transition sparks more than a few questions, but the overall conviction that Carey has been called to build community-creating missional platforms that, via excellent service provision and incarnational presence, win the right to speak, is an unchallenged given. Carey has seen much fruit from its ministry. The years have birthed thousands of significant conversations, and there have been many conversions and baptisms. A Sunday night service has been started for youth and young adults, most of whom have come to faith as a result of the close work between the school and church.

Several churches in Australia run schools. Sometimes this has very obviously enhanced the mission and ministry of both the school and church; at other times it has proved problematic. An obvious question is, "Why has this model worked in the Carey context, when it hasn't in many others?" A study of Carey can perhaps help to highlight some ways in which education can be an effective community-creating missional platform in contemporary Australia.

As it has developed and grown, Carey has engaged in many discussions on its understanding of mission and its underlying ethos and vision. The convictions that have emerged from these discussions have been seminal, and are discussed below in the hope that they might prove helpful in other contexts.

Carey: attractional or incarnational?

An obvious question Carey had to answer was whether it planned to adopt an attractional or incarnational model of mission. While the models are often presented as contrasting opposites, Carey has concluded that it is possible to embrace a model that sits somewhere between the two.

It is attractional in the sense that the school acts as a magnet, drawing thousands of people onto the church/ school site every week. Given the co-location of the school and church, it is only logical that the church leverages its contact with the school by running a busy program of events. At times the youth group has over 300 teenagers from the school at its Friday night activities. Likewise, there is a flourishing children's club. Over 80 percent of attendees do not come from church families, so whilst the evangelistic opportunities must be dealt with sensitively, they are significant.

In addition, as the church has tried to leverage its connection with the school community, it has needed to ensure that its worship services are fresh, winsome, and sensitive to those who do not often attend church. Much time goes into "making Sunday happen" — and to happen in a way that is likely to open people to the love and grace of God. Every church service is carefully evaluated; the regular question being, "so how can we raise the bar a little higher next time?"

Whilst the above sounds classically attractional, the group would argue, I think accurately, that it can as accurately be described as providing an incarnational model for church growth. After all, a family with three children who all attend the school from kindergarten to year 12 could journey with the school for over 20 years — perhaps even longer depending on the spacing of their children. It provides a lot of time in which to make a difference in the life of a family. The church–school duo is there when a grandparent dies, when marriages collapse, when teenagers rebel, when a cancer diagnosis is announced, when tragedy strikes. It is there in celebrating moments, graduations, sporting triumphs and end-of-year functions. If it is there in these more dramatic moments, it is also there in the more ordinary day-after-day moments — there for casual conversations in the parking lot, and the hundred and one little ways that a school intersects with family life. For many families this act of simply "being there" continues for over 20 years; clearly that is incarnation.

While Carey requires all their school staff to profess a credible Christian faith and to be actively involved in a local church, it does not require that local church to be Carey. The church does, however, consider itself to have a role in helping to pastor the school staff, who in turn are viewed as front-line missionaries as they pour themselves into the lives of their students. Teachers are encouraged to consider each child in their care as providentially placed in their class, and to view teaching as a vocation — a sacred trust to be treasured deeply. When church and school are on mission together, there is no place for pettiness or the second rate. Educational excellence is the non-negotiable baseline and the outstanding pastoral care of each pupil is simply par for the course.

In short then, even though the church tries to woo people to programs it runs, the level of engagement with the community is high, regardless of whether church programs are ever attended or not. The incarnational and relational aspects of mission are thus deeply embedded in all that is done.

So what does mission mean in the Carey context?

One of the slogans kicked around at Carey is that "Carey builds and occupies community-creating missional platforms". As the movement expands and grows, it increasingly asks itself, "but what do we mean by this and what is mission in our context?"

It is common to differentiate between mission (a more inclusive term) and evangelism (a narrower term). Evangelism revolves around helping people come to a personal faith in Jesus. It is a subset of the much larger term, mission, which is usually about an outward movement into the world — though it can be about an inner journey of personal transformation (a mission to the self).

Mission embraces all that is involved in the Christian faith as it intersects with and impacts the world. Thus mission can include working for justice, creating a work of art that celebrates the goodness of God, spending time with a lonely person, offering excellent education, finding ways to work through differences in a Christ-honouring way, caring for children in the name of Christ, and so much more.

Ultimately the mission of the church is to be a co-worker with God in the *missio Dei* — the mission of God in the world. Discerning what God is doing in the world, and then accompanying God on God's mission, is one of the major reasons for the existence of the church.

For its part, the local church needs to discern the particular piece of the *missio Dei* that it is called to be involved in. Carey operates from the conviction that God is always active in the world, and the task of the church is to work together with God. In the Carey context it means that Carey regularly asks, "Of all the things that God is doing in the world, which ones carry Carey's name?" It has developed some filters to help in the required discernment process, and has identified four chords (or cords, both are seen as valid) that characterise the movement. These are hope, learning, compassion, and family. In practical terms, before Carey commits to any new program it asks, "In what way will this help foster hope, learning, compassion, or family?" At times a program might strengthen one or two of these chords. Better programs will develop all four.

But we are running ahead of ourselves. Let's look at David Bosch's now classic understanding of mission, which has deeply impacted Carey's understanding of mission.[4]

Mission as crossing barriers to receptivity to the Christian faith...

The word "mission" can have many different meanings. One definition is that "mission is an important assignment carried out for political, religious, or commercial purposes, typically involving travel".[5] Noted missiologist David Bosch suggests that Christian mission, while usually assumed to involve physical travel, more commonly involves *travelling across frontiers or barriers to receptivity and implementation of the Christian faith*.[6] Sometimes these frontiers are geographic, but this is not necessarily the case. There are many non-geographic frontiers that serve as barriers to the reception of the Christian faith. This is as true in the Carey context as it is in others, but six which are of special relevance to Carey are:

1. *Ignorance* of the Christian faith (people cannot be receptive to that which they do not know).

2. *Negative caricatures* of the Christian faith (we should not underestimate the damage done by negative and often satirical reporting of Christianity in the media).

3. *Intellectual barriers.* These sometimes flow from a muddled understanding of Christianity leading to a negative response to it: for example, the assumption that if you don't believe the world is about six thousand years old and that it was made in seven days, you can't be a Christian.

4. *Religious fundamentalism.* There is a growing misconception that all forms of religion will ultimately lead to fundamentalism and intolerance. There is a desperate need for a nuanced understanding of faith that differentiates between forms of faith that are likely to have toxic outcomes and expressions of faith which are life-serving.

5. *Experiential barriers.* Some are disappointed with God and find it impossible to reconcile belief in a loving God with the pain they endure or see others experience.

6. *Moral barriers.* Many think of Christianity as a moral creed, and are conscious that they have violated its principles — typically in areas of sexual morality, though often in other areas as well. They therefore assume that they would be unwelcome or pressurised to change their behaviour.

If ignorance, negative caricatures of the faith, and the like serve as blocked frontiers, it is important to ask how Carey helps to move into these zones. In doing so, it affirms that it is important to embrace mission both as proclamation and as presence.

Beyond the "Mission as Proclamation" versus "Mission as Presence" stereotype...

There is a debate about the effectiveness of mission as proclamation as opposed to mission as presence. Carey affirms the importance of both and indeed goes further to suggest that one without the other falls short of genuine mission.

St Francis is famously, but probably inaccurately, quoted as saying: "Wherever you go, preach the gospel, and if necessary use words". While a superficially attractive sentiment, it doesn't hold up to scrutiny. Paul in Romans 10:14 poignantly asks, "And how can they believe without hearing about him? And how can they hear without a preacher?" While preaching does not have to be done by a professional at a pulpit, incarnated faith needs to be supplemented with words of explanation that clearly point to Jesus and the teaching of Scripture.

Proclamation without presence or incarnation lacks credibility. Incarnation without proclamation is obscure and is often misunderstood. Rather than choose one or the other, Carey has asked in what way it should serve as a sign of the truth of Christian faith (the incarnational aspect) and in what ways Carey, like Paul, must proclaim the "whole counsel of God" (Acts 20:27).

Incarnational aspects of Carey's mission

John's gospel highlights the incarnation of Jesus. Incarnation is about being present — being earthed in a particular context. In John 1:14 we read, "The Word became flesh and dwelt among us. We observed his glory...". Incarnational presence makes observation possible. That is both its strength and risk. If people like what they see, they will be attracted to it. If they are not convinced by what they see, they will avoid it. When you are present, it is impossible to hide or to pretend to be what you are not. This is especially true for Carey where the incarnational mission that has been adopted is to offer excellent missional education, however that is defined, to the community. This is a long journey. A family with three children might well be involved with the school for over 20 years. This is a lengthy time span, and any artificiality or superficiality will be spotted.

Many aspects of Carey's mission are incarnational.

1. Carey provides a wide range of tangible, incarnated services. These include an early childhood service, K–12 schooling, after-school care, and holiday care. The community centre currently being built will house a coffee shop, several community halls and seminar rooms, a youth centre, a range of consultancy services, the church offices, and space for additional ventures. The church program includes a group for young mothers, a club for children, a large youth group, and a program for the elderly. The church often hosts seminars, and these are sometimes held together with the school. Each program offers a tangible and credible service. Excellence is the intentional baseline. The hope is that people will spot Jesus behind what is offered. The goal is that a sentiment will lead to a question. The sentiment: "Wow — that was impressive." The question: "I wonder why they go to so much trouble?"

2. Every staff member at Carey is seen to carry the "Jesus label". Carey makes it clear that it only employs Christian staff. This is a weighty responsibility. If one stumbles, all are compromised. A pastoral responsibility for the church is to ensure that all staff members are helped in their faith journey. At a board level, this means that enough time and resources must be released to help facilitate this. Investing in the spiritual development of staff is thus a priority.

3. Carey is a highly relational community — and rightly so. Perhaps

more than anything, it is the calibre of relationships that is likely to convince or dissuade observers of the genuineness or otherwise of the faith proclaimed. Jesus was realistic about this, pragmatically noting: "By this all people will know that you are my disciples, if you have love for one another" (John 13:35). It is all conditional on the *if* you have love. Sometimes this is stretched. It can be difficult to be a loving community when staff members find themselves competing against others for limited promotional positions, or being annoyed at the limitations of some staff members, or just having very different personalities. More significantly, as Carey contemplates the significant growth in the number of staff it is likely to employ (a probable growth from 200 to 500 in less than a decade), these challenges will increase. In principle, the issues are not dissimilar to those faced by a church that moves from being medium-sized to large. There are new challenges just as there are new opportunities, but work must be done to ensure that structures change to allow for good relational outcomes in an enlarged setting.

Proclamational aspects of Carey's mission

While the Christian faith is not limited to a set of coherent propositions about God, it has a cognitive dimension. Just as Carey evaluates the adequacy of what it teaches about science and history, it has started to evaluate what it teaches about the Christian faith. Questions being asked include whether it is possible to map what a student will learn about Christianity in a similar manner to the way learning outcomes are mapped in maths or English? The questioning also includes what these outcomes will be and what version of the Christian faith will be promoted. Naturally Carey is not alone in asking these questions. They are pertinent for all who are involved in Christian education, and given the rapid increase in the number of students now enrolled in this sector of the Australian educational market, it is important that satisfying answers are found.

Proclamation in Scripture is usually accompanied by invitation. Knowing about God is one thing. Actually knowing God is another. While directly inviting students to accept Jesus into their life is tricky in an educational context, it does not mean that appropriate evangelism cannot take place in a school environment. Creating highly emotional contexts where students feel pressurised to invite Jesus into their life would be an abuse of the power and trust conferred upon Carey by parents and educational authorities. However, the extreme end of the spectrum is not the only option available. Just as teachers share their passion for music or English or drama with their students, it would seem appropriate for them to share why they find following Jesus to be meaningful and how they came to have a relationship with God. In principle this is not fundamentally different from a physical education teacher enthusing about footy, or a music teaching discussing why they love Bach. Some might argue that when a music teacher discusses Bach, the topic is legitimate as it falls into their discipline area, but that discussion of the Christian faith does not, and therefore has no place in a music class. However, Carey makes it perfectly clear that it only employs Christian staff and the Christian character of the school is signposted to all prospective school families. They are therefore fully aware that their child will not simply be taught by an English teacher but by a Christian English teacher. It is only logical to assume that this distinctive will make a difference — if it doesn't, why bother to highlight it?

Not that discussion about faith will always be focused on the teacher's experience of faith. When a music teacher discusses Bach's music, their discussion is genuinely incomplete unless they mention Bach's controversial conviction that music's only purpose should be the glory of God. Be it in literature, science, music, art, or history, the fingerprints of the past were shaped by a conviction of the goodness of God. Sound education invites a genuine discussion of and exploration of the themes that have helped to shape and mould contemporary society.

A Carey student should therefore both witness faith in practice through the lives of the school staff, but also have the faith clearly unpacked and explored. Should they decide to embrace the Christian faith, they should understand how to make a commitment to Christ, and have a realistic understanding of the likely journey of discipleship that lies ahead. They should also find support and resources from Carey to help them mature in their faith. Should they decide against embracing faith, their decision should be on the basis of solid information and observation, rather than on the usual caricatures and stereotypes that fuel the disinterest in Christianity in the secular marketplace.

Evaluating Carey's missional effectiveness

The Carey organisation currently employs around 200 people. Many are full-time employees, some are part-time, and the number is set to grow significantly over the coming years. It represents one of the highest concentrations of Christian staff in Western Australia. It is therefore reasonable to expect a significant missional dividend from the work and time commitment of such a large contingent of Christians. In short, if there are not tangible results from the work of 200 Christian people, a large Christian resource has been wasted. All Christians are called to be salt and light to the world. Every person working at Carey could be salt and light somewhere else. We need to ask if the missional outcome from drawing this concentration of Christian people together justifies the fact that each staff member employed at Carey means one less Christian person to work at one of the public schools down the road.

While numbers do not reveal everything, the Carey Board is keen to start mapping the impact of Carey on the families who journey with it. Many possible questions spring to mind, but two seem especially important. What percentage of pupils arrives at Carey already linked to a Christian church? What percentage is linked to a church by the time they leave? If the latter figure is not significantly higher than the former, the missional effectiveness of Carey should be queried. In the third century Cyprian put forward the wildly debated maxim, "No salvation outside of the church". While often contested, the Bible knows nothing of churchless faith. If families who pass through Carey do not at some point make some credible connection with a Christian faith community, any claim at missional effectiveness is compromised.

Not that we should evaluate Carey's missional effectiveness purely by the number of converts flowing from its ministry. We should not underestimate the missional impact Carey makes by:

1. Serving as a sign of Christian concern, compassion, and engagement in society. Simply being in the market place is its own statement and makes a difference.

2. Creating happy memories for all its students. When many look back at the "good old school days" the link between those memories and the Christian faith will not be forgotten.

3. Strengthening the faith of those who are already Christians. While Carey staff could easily be employed elsewhere, together they strengthen and support each other and help to bring out the best in each other. Likewise, about 20 percent of pupils arrive at the school as part of a Christian family. We should not underrate the importance of passing the faith on from one generation to the next, and Carey's role in aiding this should not be overlooked.

4. Its strong overall performance. Carey bolsters the credibility of Christian education, thus helping other Christian schools in their mission.

5. The impact of Carey's Christian values on society. Though some students might elect not to follow Christ, many will be impacted by the broader values that flow from a Christian vision of life. This in turn will have a positive impact in society.

6. Staying the course. If their experience is positive, many families will send later generations to Carey. Even if the first generation did not

respond to the Christian message, their children or grandchildren might.

New wineskins

We have just overheard Carey's internal conversation with itself on its understanding of mission and missional effectiveness. It does not require too much imagination to see how comparable questions can, and should, be asked by many churches about their effectiveness. Each church has missional frontiers waiting to be crossed. They should be clearly identified, and then linked with a strategy — a strategy that will usually involve both incarnation and proclamation. Indeed, many churches have already built effective missional platforms that reach deep into their community. Occupying those platforms with a clear missional mindset is often the next challenge, but when this challenge is met, it might well help birth the next generation of Christ followers.

Dr Brian Harris is the Principal of Vose Seminary, Perth and Pastor at Large for the Carey Movement, where he also chairs the Board.

Missional Rejuvenation of Historic Inner-City Churches

Peter Francis

The past two decades in Australia have witnessed an unprecedented re-urbanisation of the inner-city precincts of many of our major cities. However, during this same period of time many of our historic inner-city churches have been slowly dying. This chapter reflects upon the findings of a research project undertaken in 2012, in which four historic inner-city churches from one of Australia's major cities were examined with a view to determining what, if any, were the internal church cultural and theological determinants which could either impede or impel such churches in their missional engagement with the residential communities which surround them. From this research an analytical framework is posited which may prove helpful either as a diagnostic tool assisting churches to identify their current position in terms of their missional engagement with their local community or as a remedial tool in helping churches to determine which aspects of their corporate life need strengthening if they are to become increasingly effective in their missional engagement.

Introduction

Since the turn of the century Australia has witnessed an unprecedented growth in inner-city residential dwelling. This rapid growth, which was first identified in Sydney back in 1993, was soon to be replicated in a number of other capital city centres throughout Australia. The Australian Bureau of Statistics 2002 Census[1] revealed the strength of this trend when it provided analysis of the dwelling approvals for inner-city communities over the period 1968 to 2002 as illustrated below.

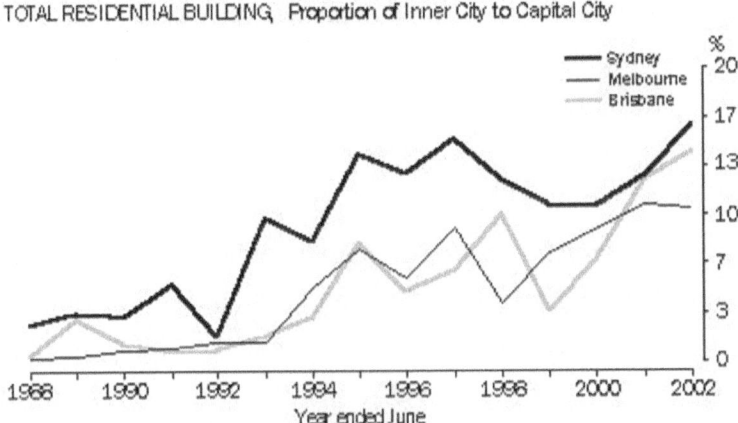

Figure 1–Australian Bureau of Statistics 2002

More recent statistical data from the Australian Bureau of Statistics reveal that this trend has continued strongly since the turn of the century, as more and more people are attracted to the perceived benefits of inner-city residential living. However, at the precise time in which our major cities have witnessed an exponential growth in their inner-city residential communities, there appears to have been an alarming decline in the number of congregants in many of our historic inner-city churches[2] and in the strength of their engagement with and witness to the burgeoning residential communities which surround them.

Nature of the challenge

The problems confronting historic inner-city churches around the world, in particular those being encountered within the Western world, are well expressed by the report which came out of the FIEC (Fellowship of Independent Evangelical Churches) twenty-four hour consultation in May 2012. In this report, Archer describes the challenges confronting evangelical inner-city churches in London as follows:

> The larger churches are in the suburbs, and those in Inner-City and Central London struggle with inadequate resources and

often a sense of isolation, whilst facing the challenges of multi-ethnic areas. Many churches don't reflect the ethnic diversity of their communities — and their pastors and leaders don't reflect the ethnic and cultural diversity of London. Also many congregations are ageing and struggle for cultural connection with their communities.[3]

The challenges of which Archer writes are not unique to the FIEC churches in London. The challenge of ageing and dwindling inner-city congregations, which in turn are often confronted by limited material and human resources, is a reality for many inner-city Australian churches. In reflecting upon the 2011 Australian Bureau of Statistics census data, Hughes observes that "as some churches decline in number and age in years, there is a tendency to focus in on themselves. With few resources, conserving what exists seems to be the best approach".[4] However, such an inward focus only serves to perpetuate and accentuate the marked disconnect between many of our inner-city churches and the rapidly growing and ethnically diverse residential communities that surround them.

While this may be the more comfortable option for the present time, the end result of such a stance is almost guaranteed to bring about the eventual demise of the local congregation. Yet, it is my contention that historic inner-city churches which embrace a fundamental belief in and commitment to the missional responsibility of the local church are well placed to rise to the challenge of missional rejuvenation and renewed missional engagement with the rapidly changing residential communities which surround them.

Motivated by this conviction, in 2012 I undertook a study of four historic inner-city churches within the heart of one of our major cities in Australia, with a view to distilling the key internal church cultural and theological determinants which could impede or impel historic inner-city churches in their missional engagement with the residential communities which surround them. Each of the four churches included in this study had been founded more than one hundred years earlier and was established by people who had a strong belief in and commitment to the church's missional mandate.

Literature review and development of a conceptual framework

While scholarly literature dealing specifically with the challenges faced by older inner-city churches is limited, a synthesis of a range of material addressing the challenges of inner-city ministry, and the challenges of revitalisation and community engagement for older congregations, draws attention to at least two main categories of concern which may significantly impact upon the willingness and capacity of such churches to missionally engage their residential communities. These are the church's theological convictions about its mission, and the internal organisational cultural and leadership culture of the church. Gornik captures the essence of these two categories when he contends that the inner-city church's style and level of connectivity with its community will depend on "an individual church's internal dynamics, its understanding of its mission and evangelism, and its relationship to the community".[5]

In view of this, a conceptual framework was posited as a way of examining the correlation between the internal theological and cultural determinants which may impede or impel historic inner-city churches in their missional engagement with their residential communities. It was further posited that a comparison between these two categories of concern, as illustrated in Figure 2, would help to plot the likely level of missional engagement of inner-city churches with their residential communities.

Figure 2 – Conceptual Framework – illustrating likelihood of missional engagement

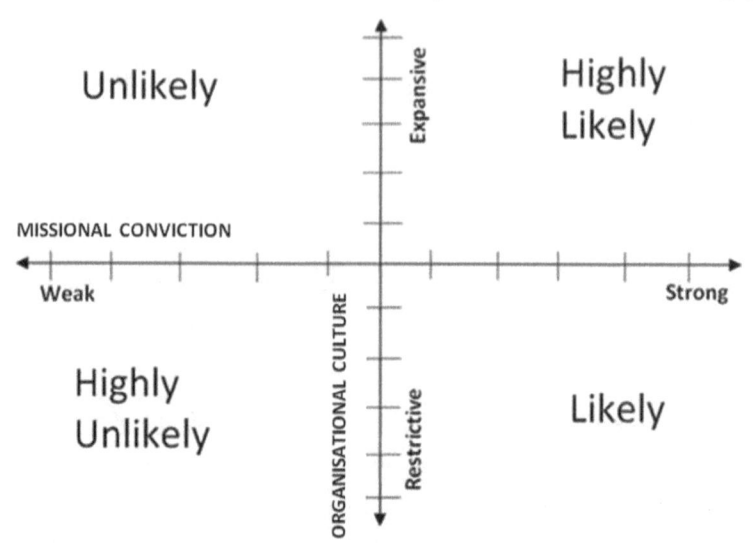

The two axes represent the strength of the local church's theological conviction about its missional purpose, and the nature of their organisational culture, be it more inwardly focused and restrictive or more outwardly focused and expansive.

Research question and methodology

While recognising the multitude of external challenges which confront historic inner-city churches, the focus of this research was upon the internal factors which impact upon the church's willingness and capacity to engage its community missionally. Thus, the research focused upon two essential questions:

1. Are there internal church cultural and theological determinants which may impede or impel historic inner-city churches in their missional engagement with the residential communities which surround them?

2. If so, what are these determinants?

In addressing these questions, the research explored the ways in which the complex matrix of such phenomena as church culture, past experiences in church life and community engagement, present priorities, and theological convictions concerning the church's mission, both espoused and lived, potentially converge and impact upon the willingness and capacity of historic inner-city churches to engage missionally with their local communities.

This research employed a modified form of rapid ethnography as a means of investigating the lived experience of the leaders and members of the four historic inner-city churches and then theorised about the theological convictions and internal organisational cultural realities which may either impede or impel them in their missional engagement with their residential communities. Elements of Hopewell's narrative inquiry[6] and Thuma's[7] congregational study method were employed with a view to pursuing two streams of investigation: direct observation and "deep listening" by engagement with a range of focus groups.

The direct observation required the researcher to spend time sharing in the life of each of the four churches which were included in this study, noting carefully such things as: the demographic makeup of the congregation; the physical setting in which they gather; the ways in which they worship together; their internal patterns of relationships; the language (both written and verbal) which they use to describe themselves and their purpose for existence as a community.

The "deep listening" was undertaken by engaging in a series of semi-structured, focus-group interviews with representatives of both the leadership and the congregational members of each of the churches included in this study. All interviews were recorded and later transcribed to facilitate a careful analysis of the perspectives and convictions held by the participants.

Findings of the research

The two tables which follow identify the key internal church cultural and theological factors which appeared either to impede or impel the churches studied in their missional engagement with their own inner-city residential communities. These factors were identified from the recurrent themes which emerged from focus-group interviews and were in many cases reinforced by direct observation. The research method(s) which expose these factors are noted against each church and coded as follows:

> MO = Material Observation (Physical Artefacts —e.g., Buildings and Written Materials)
> PO = Participatory Observation (e.g., Worship Forms and Personal Interactions)
> FG = Focus-Group Interviews (Perspectives offered by Focus Group Participants)

Table 1 – Factors which potentially impel missional engagement

Factors which potentially impel missional engagement	Church and Research Method
Church's Understanding of its Mission	
Significant focus on gospel outreach	Church B (MO, PO, FG)
	Church D (MO, PO, FG)
Clearly articulated mission and vision	Church B (MO, PO, FG)
	Church C (MO, FG)
	Church D (MO, FG)
Shared priorities in mission	Church D (PO, FG)
Convergence between espoused and lived values	Church B (PO, FG)
	Church D (PO, FG)
Church's Internal Culture	
Visionary leadership committed to gospel outreach	Church B (PO, FG)
	Church D (PO, FG)
Inclusive and empowering leadership	Church B (PO, FG)
	Church C (PO, FG)
	Church D (PO, FG)
Committed to the future	Church B (MO, PO, FG)
	Church D (MO, PO, FG)
	Church C (MO, PO, FG)
Accepting of change	Church D (MO, PO, FG)
Church's Community Engagement	
Welcoming of newcomers	Church A (PO)
	Church B (PO, FG)
Possibility focused	Church B (MO, PO, FG)
	Church D (PO, FG)
Understands local demographics	Church B (MO, FG)
	Church C (FG)
	Church D (PO, FG)
Development of missional engagement activities	Church B (MO, PO, FG)
	Church D (MO, PO, FG)
	Church C (MO, FG)
Church's Commitment to Missional Prayer	
Prayer linked to community engagement	Church B (PO, FG)

Table 2 – Factors which potentially impede missional engagement

Factors which potentially impede missional engagement	Church and Research Method
Church's Understanding of its Mission	
Primary focus on building up the church	Church A (PO, FG)
	Church C (PO, FG)
Unclear sense of mission and vision — not articulated	Church A (PO, FG)
Lack of shared priorities in mission	Church A (PO, FG)
	Church B (PO, FG)
	Church C (PO, FG)
Some disparity between espoused and lived values	Church B (PO, FG)
	Church C (PO, FG)
Church's Internal Culture	
Major focus on meeting internal needs of church	Church A (PO, FG)
	Church B (MO, PO, FG)
	Church C (FG)
Strong commitment to past traditions /forms	Church A (MO, PO, FG)
	Church B (PO, FG)
	Church C (PO, FG)
Reluctance to embrace change	Church A (MO, PO)
	Church B (PO, FG)
	Church C (PO, FG)
Church's Community Engagement	
No demonstrable commitment to missional engagement	Church A (PO, FG)
Problem Focused	Church A (FG)
	Church B (FG)
	Church C (FG)
Limited awareness of local demographics	Church A (PO, FG)
Church's Commitment to Missional Prayer	
Lack of prayer for local community	Church A (PO)
	Church C (PO)
	Church D (PO, FG)

In the tables it will be seen that some churches are identified as possessing seemingly contradictory features which both impel and impede them in their missional engagement. This is perhaps representative of the internal struggle that accompanies the quest for transition from being a church which is committed to primarily maintaining its heritage and forms to a church which is committed to missionally engaging its own residential community.

Analysis of the findings

This research suggests that there was no one single internal church characteristic which would impel historic inner-city churches in the missional engagement with the residential communities which surround them. Rather, it appears that a constellation of vital characteristics which pertain to both the church's missional conviction and its organisational culture need to be appropriately aligned for churches to be more effective in their missional engagement. The findings of this research suggest that historic inner-city churches which will have the most significant missional impact upon their inner-city residential communities will be those which exhibit the following broad characteristics: a strong missional conviction and an expansive organisational culture. These two characteristics are represented in the conceptual framework posited in Figure 2.

Five characteristics have been identified as strong impellers to the church's missional commitment: a significant focus on gospel outreach; a clearly articulated mission and vision; shared priorities in mission; a convergence between espoused and lived values; and a commitment to missional prayer. It is further noted that whilst there is often a tangible linkage between some of these characteristics, a lack of one or more of these characteristics can effectively counteract the more positive impact of others. For example, a church may have developed a clearly articulated mission and vision statement, but the impelling nature of this characteristic may be negated by the reality that the stated aims of missional engagement do not represent the shared missional priorities of the church members.

Figure 3 – Locating the missional conviction of the church

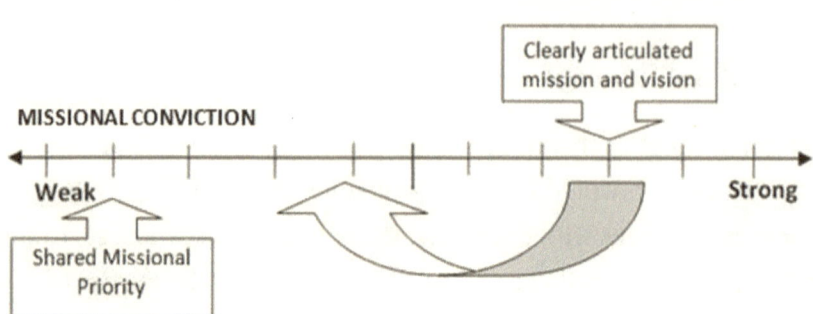

When considering the organisational culture of the church a range of eight characteristics have been identified which, together, may create an expansive culture which impels missional engagement. However, a lack of any one or more of these characteristics may create a restrictive culture which impedes missional engagement. These characteristics, positively framed are: visionary leadership that is committed to gospel outreach; inclusive and empowering leadership; a commitment to the future; an acceptance of change; a welcoming of newcomers; an understanding of the local demographics; a possibility focus; and a commitment to the development of missional engagement activities.

Once again it is to be noted that a lack of one or more of these characteristics can effectively counteract the more positive impact of others. For example, a commitment to missional activities may be counteracted by a resistance towards change in the communal life of the church which prevents those who are being reached by those missional activities from becoming integrated members of the community of faith. In this case, the potential is for churches to be relevant in their missional engagement, but then prove to be irrelevant in the way in which they express their faith communally. Rainer, in his extensive examination of the factors which contribute to the demise of local churches, observes that "the most pervasive and common thread of our autopsies was that the deceased churches lived for a long time with the past hero".[8] This strident commitment to "the past hero", which was regularly enshrined in past practices and forms, was one of the key ingredients which accelerated the process of the expiration of the local church.

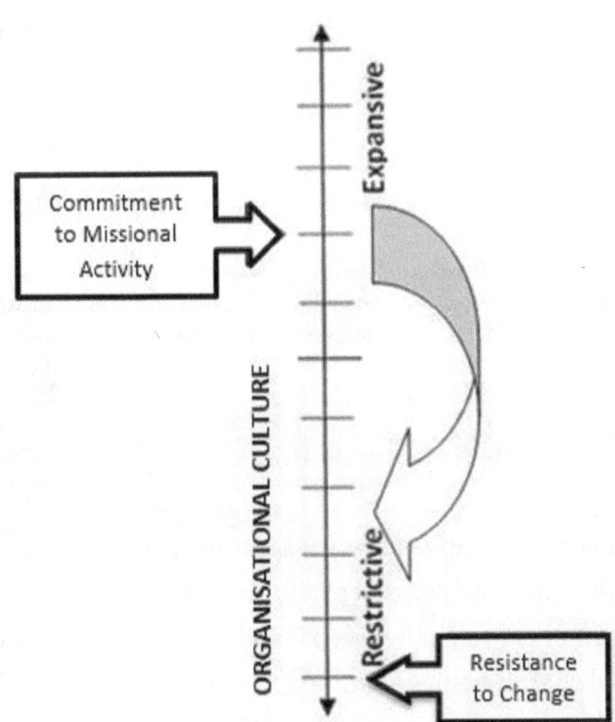

Figure 4 – Locating the organisational culture of the church

In identifying a church's specific location along each of these axes, it is important to recognise the interconnectedness between the range of characteristics which together will determine their precise location. Thus, it was important to develop some mechanism whereby the range of characteristics associated with each axis could be assessed in order to establish a composite positioning on each axis.

The mechanism employed in this study to establish a composite positioning of each church on the "Missional Conviction" axis was to simply ascribe a numerical value (between 0 and 10) for each of the five missional characteristics identified in this study and then to determine the average of these values (as illustrated in the Table below). It is acknowledged at this point that the process relied on a subjective evaluation of each characteristic and is thus not an exact science. However, this research would suggest that this has been a reasonable process for determining the general positioning of churches on the two key axes represented in the conceptual framework.

Table 3 – Assessing the missional conviction of the church

Church	Gospel Focus	Articulation of Mission and Vision	Shared Priority in Mission	Convergence –Espoused & Lived Values	Commitment to Missional Prayer	Average Score
Church C	4	7	3	4	2	4

A similar process was employed when seeking to establish a church's position on the axis which represents its organisational culture. By ascribing a numerical value (between 0 and 10) for each of the eight organisational characteristics identified in this study, and calculating the average of these scores, it was possible to provide a reasonable assessment of a church's organisational culture. Such a process is illustrated in Table 4.

Table 4 – Assessing the organisational culture of the church

Church	Visionary Leadership	Inclusive & Empowering Leadership	Committed to the Future	Accepting of Change	Welcoming Newcomers
Church A	0	2	4	2	7

Church	Understand Local Demographics	Possibility Focused	Develops Missional Activities	AV
Church A	3	2	1	2.6

In much the same way that a weaker representation in one or more of the characteristics on either of the two major axes may significantly diminish the overall strength of that broader characteristic (i.e., missional conviction or organisational culture), it is evident that a similar relationship might be observed between the two major axes. A church may demonstrate the characteristics of a relative expansive organisational culture, but this may be negated by a conversely weaker missional conviction.

Ministry implications

Using the conceptual model posited in Figure 2 and reflecting on the categories set out by Hopewell[9] and Becker[10] I propose the following taxonomy of descriptors which will assist in predicting the likelihood of a historic inner-city church's missional engagement with its own community. Along with each cultural typology is a description of the internal convictions and corporate characteristics which identify and consolidate that particular style and an assessment of the likelihood of each to engage their own residential communities missionally.

Table 5 – Proposed church missional/cultural taxonomy

Cultural Typology	Cultural Distinctive	Likelihood of Missional Engagement
Missionally Engaged	Strong, shared missional conviction which is clearly articulated and lived out, along with an expansive organisational culture which is committed to the future and empowers its members to be active participants in the *missio Dei*.	Highly Likely
Missionally Aware	A genuine awareness of the missional responsibility of the church and a relatively expansive organisational culture that invites participation, but lacks unified commitment to the task of missional engagement.	Unlikely
Missionally Open	Strong awareness of the missional responsibility of the church and a willingness to support mission activities. Strong commitment to the building up of the present congregation and a strong commitment to its forms and traditions.	Likely
Missionally Closed	Limited commitment to the missional calling of the church. Strong commitment to the maintenance of the present congregation and the historic forms of the past.	Highly Unlikely

It is posited that the application of this analytical framework may prove helpful as a diagnostic tool in assisting churches to identify their current position in terms of their missional engagement with their local community, and also as a remedial tool in helping churches to determine those characteristics which need strengthening if they are to become increasingly effective in their missional engagement.

It was not within the scope of this study to examine the ways in which a church may be led in transitioning from one quadrant to another. However, it appears likely that the most difficult transition would be diagonally across from the position of a missionally closed to a missionally engaged style as a series of major organisational and missiological shifts would need to be made at the same time.

In regard to the application of this analytical framework, the mechanism for establishing the precise location of churches on the two axes posited in the conceptual framework may be worthy of further investigation. While the method suggested was simply to ascribe a numerical value (between 0 and 10) to each of the nominated characteristics on each axis and then to use the average of these scores to locate the churches on each axis, the nominated characteristics may not warrant equal weighting in considering the overall position of a church on each axis.

For example, further research may reveal that a clearly articulated mission and vision does not carry as much weight as the value of shared missional priorities within the life of the church. If this were the case, a low score on shared missional priorities may have a far more deleterious impact on the value of the clearly articulated mission and vision statement of the church. In a similar way it could be discovered that a reluctance to accept change may carry a disproportionate weight when compared with the value of visionary leadership. In a similar way, further research may establish the fact that the weighting apportioned to a church's position on the organisational axis may in fact be more significant than the weighting ascribed to the missional conviction axis. None of these suggestions undermines the validity of the posited conceptual framework, but are merely suggestions for further research which may help to refine the instrument.

In regard to the specific categories of characteristics developed in this study it is noted that the responses of the various focus-group interviews regularly reflected on the importance of missional prayer. However, most of these responses were focused around the church's dependence upon

God to work in the lives of the people in the surrounding community and the empowerment necessary for the conduct of the missional activities in which the church was currently engaged in much the same way as Paul urged the Colossians to pray.[11] The literature review, on the other hand, drew attention to the priority that some scholars have placed upon the importance of prayer in the discerning and establishment of the church's mission and vision. Because of the nature of the comments received in the focus-group interviews, the issue of missional prayer was included in the evaluation of the church's missional conviction. However, further investigation may establish an important link between missional prayer and a range of other characteristics which have been identified on the organisational culture axis, such as the church's commitment to the future and its willingness to accept change.

Conclusion

It is anticipated that the application of the analytical framework provided may prove helpful in assisting churches not only to identify their current position in terms of their missional engagement with their local community, but also to help in determining those characteristics which need strengthening if they are to become increasingly effective in their missional engagement.

In an era when many historic inner-city churches in Australia have become increasingly disengaged from the residential communities which surround them and are experiencing a significant decline in attendance, a new era of opportunity is developing on their doorsteps. This opportunity is coming in the form of a significant, and in many cases rapid, growth in the inner-city residential populations of many of our major cities. However, for this opportunity to be realised, serious consideration needs to be given again to the essential nature and mission of the church. Whereas many of these churches were begun by people who embraced a clear sense of the missional mandate of the church, they have, over the years, become increasingly bound by their sense of history and tradition. This sense of history and tradition has often been accentuated by the very nature of the physical artefacts which have served their ministry well over many years. However, for the new day of missional opportunity to be fully embraced, it is incumbent upon such churches to review carefully their current position in terms of their level of missional commitment and the kinds of organisational cultures which have been embedded and normalised over the years. Only after such a process has been honestly engaged will the church be able to take the affirmative steps necessary to strengthen its missional conviction and develop a more expansive organisational culture which will engender the willingness and capacity of such churches to missionally engage the residential communities which surround them.

Peter Francis, after a ten-year career as a high school teacher, entered pastoral ministry and over a twenty-two-year period pastored three Baptist churches in Queensland. He also served for two years as a Regional Consultant with Queensland Baptists and in 2011 took up the position of Field Education Director at Malyon College where he currently services as Vice Principal and teaches Pastoral Studies, Missions and Old Testament.

Life in Community
Church as Network

Robert Morsillo

In "The Rise of the Network Society", Manuel Castells forecast that "inside the networks, new possibilities are relentlessly created — outside the networks, survival is increasingly difficult".[1] This chapter explores "new possibilities" being created through the ongoing transformation of Moreland Baptist Church, in inner-urban Melbourne, from a conventional congregational stereotype towards a network-of-communities prototype, where new life emerges out of the connections with and between various internal and external groups, celebrated through visible and virtual engagement. The chapter examines the decisive missional value of open hospitality, which builds new hubs of creativity and pastoral care. It converses critically with scholars such as sociologist-historian Rodney Stark on the importance of maintaining open social networks, and Ann Morisy on the concept of pastors as community chaplains. Church as network is a tentative, courageous journey of exploration for Moreland Baptist involving mindful re-engagement with the land, local communities, and its faith traditions.

Introduction

This chapter presents some aspects of the contemporary faith journey that is Moreland Baptist Church, which is located in Brunswick West, Melbourne, Victoria. It is *contemporary*, in that it focuses on the last five to six years of the 92-year history of the church; it's a *journey*, in that the church is exploring some new things but doesn't really know what the destination may be; and it is in *faith*, in that it is inspired by the Christ story of the Gospels and remains hopelessly optimistic about being able to continue to care for each other and create a greater sense of community in the city of Moreland. Therefore, it also hopes to contribute to the current discussions about emerging missional churches within our Baptist community in Australia.

The chapter proposes a network model as a fundamental way of developing, organising, and conceptualising Moreland Baptist Church.[2] It focuses on the *connections* that the church has with diverse external groups and congregations, rather than on what the church itself is doing or not doing. It concurs with Ann Morisy that "effective mission is something that emerges as a result of looking and journeying outward rather than by means of a self-conscious and self-regarding process".[3]

The chapter argues that life is found in community, that is to say, in the energetic connections between communities which are linked in the common cause of cultivating our ecology and our humanity. Moreland Baptist is moving away from being a singular community or church trying to be or do everything itself, towards being a community of communities, a network, and the prime directive is to facilitate *connections* between the worshipping congregation and everyone else in order to encourage life to emerge. This process is similar to Darren Cronshaw's description of the Solace community: "As such it sees itself as an interactive network more than a Sunday-centred group".[4]

The life and death of small urban churches, such as Moreland Baptist, has been under scrutiny for many years. Athol Gill, in his book *The Fringes of Freedom*, relates a story at the time he was moving from Brisbane to Melbourne in 1974. He came across a copy of the *Baptist Witness*, the denominational paper of Victorian Baptists. Its lead story was: "Inner-City Churches Closing".[5] That was forty years ago, so it has been a very long conversation indeed, but one that Moreland Baptist hopes to continue to contribute to for some time yet.

A sense of time

Moreland Baptist traces its history back to the opening of the West Moreland Baptist Church on 28 January 1922, which *The Argus* newspaper dutifully reported a few days later.[6] The establishment of the church was sponsored by Coburg and Brunswick Baptists and, in turn, sometime later, West Moreland sponsored the West Coburg Baptist a short distance away to the north. In the late 1970s West Moreland and West Coburg re-combined in ministry and worship, and later the West Coburg property was sold, which provided resources to renovate the Moreland Road property in 2008 and supplement ongoing pastoral assistance.

There is much in the history of these churches which provides precedents for the contemporary exploration. For example, around 1960 West Moreland had a sign out the front saying it was "The friendly church" and there was a strong tradition of welcoming and sharing the buildings with other religious and community service groups such as the Spanish Church, Italian Church, Pacific Islander Church, and the Rehabilitation and Family Therapy (RAFT) service.

Another strong tradition was the encouragement of women in ministry, as deacons, preachers, and ordinands, and offering opportunities to Whitley College students in working with young people and in pursuing their ordination goals. Further, the church would host special services to hear international scholars visiting Whitley College from time to time. It took a strong interest in the Urban Baptist Coalition and Baptist Social Justice Group movements. Since at least 1979 hospitality became an integral part of its Sunday ethos with "Friendship Time" or more prosaically, morning tea, included as part of the worship service.

So, while much has changed over the years, the church recognises and celebrates these filaments of continuity, these foundation traditions that underpin and guide the church as it seeks to offer new forms of hospitality and make new relationships. This is an appreciative approach to renewal and transformation, which values connection and coherence, and a sense of ongoing community.

A sense of locality

Moreland Baptist has a keen sense of place and neighbourhood. It is located some eight kilometres north-west from the centre of Melbourne, or about 15 minutes by car. It is an inner-urban church, if not inner-city. The church relates particularly to the area between the two waterways that form the east-west boundaries of Moreland City: the Moonee Ponds Creek and the Merri Creek. It celebrates this sense of locality in worship each week through an Acknowledgment of Country, recognising the Wurundjeri people as the traditional owners of the land and the continuing work for reconciliation and recognition.

In today's highly mobile, motor-vehicle dominated society, a sense of locality might be downplayed in relation to being church. Instead of locality society has the concept of "brand" that evokes sentiment and experience, which is the way of modern sales and marketing, as well as perhaps modern church movements. While sentiment and experience are not to be discounted, for Moreland Baptist taking locality seriously "is seen as a blurring of the edges of church. The church is in the neighbourhood and the neighbourhood is in the church. Common citizenship becomes more important than exclusive membership".[7] And so, for example, the church has chosen to support the national celebration of Neighbour Day each year, which has the motto "The community you want starts at your front door™" (www.neighbourday.org). As Frost and Hirsch put it, "The missional-incarnational church should be living, eating, and working closely with its surrounding community".[8]

Another important aspect of having a sense of locality is taking the surrounding environment and ecology seriously. For example, the church has participated in "Clean up Australia Day" activities. It has also appropriated a local sign and symbol of hope and recreation. The Sacred

Kingfisher bird at one time was common along the Merri Creek but with the destruction of its habitat was no longer to be seen. Now, however, there is each year in Brunswick a "Return of the Sacred Kingfisher Festival", because with environmental improvements it has returned. And so, this small bird has become a hopeful symbol at Moreland Baptist as part of its logo and livery.

A centre for networking

Ann Morisy talks about "Church community centres = A church with many congregations",[9] and this seems relevant when thinking about the particular locality and property. For example, at Moreland Baptist there are currently over twenty separate groups, including the worshipping congregation, which come to the property each week. Many of these are facilitated by Merri Community Health Service; some are facilitated by the church itself.

However, this chapter pushes the model further to incorporate external people and groups who may be non-local and even non-church, or post-church. In the network model, the church does not incorporate other groups within itself or its property, but is conceived of as one node or hub among many, and the important issue is the quality and quantity of connections that it has with others. The church in this model is part of a network of communities, a community of communities. For Moreland Baptist these other connected communities might include the local Secondary College Chaplaincy Committee, or the proprietor of its "local", the Grandview Hotel, or the community of asylum seekers at the Baptcare Sanctuary in Brunswick. Frost and Hirsch come close in their comparison of their "attractional" model versus "incarnational" model: "If the attractional mode sees the world as divided into two zones, the 'in' and the 'out', the incarnational model sees it more as a web, a series of intersecting lines symbolising the networks of relationships, friendships, and acquaintances of which church members are a part".[10]

The following sections describe some of the major connections and groups which form the Moreland Baptist Church network.

The Merri Community Health Service connection

In 2008 Moreland Baptist entered a long-term partnership agreement with Merri Community Health Service (Merri) to use parts of the church property, which were significantly under-utilised at the time, for community programs. Merri runs programmed activities each weekday, fifty weeks of the year, for various elderly groups in the local community. For example, there is the elderly Italian group, which is a type of symbolic successor to the Italian Baptist Church that worshipped in the same space for fifty years prior to this development.

The agreement included the injection of capital funding by Merri to renovate the large back main hall, adding staff offices, disability facilities, and a full commercial kitchen. The church also took the opportunity to renovate its own sanctuary space at the same time, using some of the funds from the West Coburg property sale. A high priority was to install disability facilities at the front of the property for a growing elderly congregation who otherwise had to navigate their way out the back through a number of problematic doorways, steps, and dark paths, as well as labour a long distance to access what effectively were still outhouses.

Interestingly, it was this proposed new disability facility at the front of the church that became a disruptive stumbling block in congregational meetings when seeking consensus to go ahead with the renovations. However, the church did vote to move ahead and sadly, in part, this led to some loss of leadership capacity. Ann Morisy's assertion that, "The right place is when, without power and at risk of being overwhelmed, we are prepared to embrace struggle on behalf of others" was tested as the struggles of elderly people and people with disability were prioritised.[11]

Around 2010 Merri requested an extension to its agreement to also utilise what is called the middle hall for people with dementia and to utilise the reflective church garden as a working garden. This was particularly useful for the Italian group who love to grow herbs and vegetables, and for local people with disability who otherwise do not have the opportunity to enjoy an outdoor garden space. This was a slightly different negotiation than the previous one, which had allowed Merri to have primary use with the church able, on very special occasions such as a funeral, to negotiate use. With the middle hall, other community groups were already using the space and so the concept of a fully shared area was created in the agreement.

This extension agreement has not been easy to implement and again led to some loss of leadership resources in the church. For some members there was an acute sense of Merri taking over more and more of the property. For them the church's goal was more about expanding and revitalising its own ministry, eventually using more of the building space. Severe disagreements over safety-locks in the middle hall and who would make decisions about how the garden would be developed again became disruptive stumbling blocks, but the church voted to move ahead. Ann Morisy's advice seems pertinent: "Journeying out requires the capacity to rise above the anxiety associated with encountering and embracing a potentially overwhelming outside world".[12] For some, Merri was starting to overwhelm and the church leadership was accused of not standing up to their demands. For others, the relationship with Merri was a trusted one and partnership did not just mean tenancy. Further, the benefits far outweighed any specific loss of control. Perhaps the church congregation's domain was growing smaller but it was in exchange for life-giving activities that were growing larger, and in exchange for many more community connections, so that in reality the church was becoming a broader church, a network of communities that have their own sense of self-determination.

The Studio connection

Recently a new hub has been added to the network of groups which inhabit Moreland Baptist. The Studio began operation in September 2013 to support the creative arts within the city of Moreland, for people to explore, design, and fashion in glass and other mediums, whilst having fun and connecting with others. One of the pastors is skilled in mosaic work and is the curator. In a real sense, The Studio arose out of the energies of the existing networks at the church. These included significant interest and support from Merri Community Health Service program managers, family members of the pastor who helped with the renovation of the space, and newer church members, as well as community responses to a free advertisement in the local paper. The initial classes have been very enthusiastically subscribed, with waiting lists or extra class times having to be organised.

Interestingly, The Studio uses the space that was once called the old Choir Vestry: so the tradition of creating harmony and connecting with each other continues anew. Also, the layout of the building means that artists in The Studio traverse the worship sanctuary when going to the kitchen to make a cup of tea or use the facilities. This inevitably raises conversations about spirituality and wellbeing, as does the dynamic of the groups themselves in getting to know each other's lives more closely, celebrating good times, and offering support during not-so-good times. So, there is a strong pastoral care or chaplaincy element to The Studio that arises directly from the lived experience of the participants.

Ann Morisy talks about "the commitment to bridging social capital by the Christian churches, and the capacity of the churches to widen the radius of trust in the neighbourhood".[13] The Studio appears to be building this "bridging social capital" quite quickly by creating common connections between diverse members of the local community. Future plans include a local amateur exhibition based on a spiritual theme, with prizes and publicity, not unlike some other religious art events such as at

Box Hill Baptist, Collins Street Baptist, and Whitley College.

The worship connection

The church continues to invest in its worship life as a weekly space for reflection and refreshment. It follows a regular, lectionary-based liturgy based on Isaiah 6:1–9a that specifically includes an Acknowledgment of Country, call to worship, praise, confession, thanksgiving, children's time, listening to the Scriptures, theological reflection with an open space to question and comment, community prayers with the invitation to light a candle, concluding with the Lord's Prayer together, then community news and benediction, followed by friendship time or morning tea.[14]

Worship is intended to be as accessible as possible, searching for modern symbols that people can relate to such as Leunig cartoons, pictures of current events, local street art, good humour, unloading burdens in the form of symbolic stones during confession, taking a flower to signify new life and hope, placing pieces on a mosaic to create beauty from broken pieces, and of course, freshly brewed coffee and homemade cornflake cookies.

Participation is encouraged each worship service, for example, anyone may light the Christ candle at the beginning of the service, particularly young people and children; anyone is invited to read the Scriptures on the day; everyone is invited to ask questions or offer comments after the reflection; everyone is invited to bring their everyday celebrations and concerns, to pray and light a candle. Christ as light is an evident emphasis. The church lights lots of candles every week, mainly in prayer and intercession for others' needs in the midst of the darkness of war, oppression, seeking asylum, illness, poverty, and so on.

At least three times a year the church encourages everyone across its networks to celebrate together with a special worship service and garden party. These occasions include national Neighbour Day in March, Spring

Festival in September, and Christmas Celebration in December. Key to these events is formal participation and roles by the various groups in the network, from providing real coffee and cooking on the barbecue, to live music, plants, and craft stalls. On these occasions worship becomes a networking event where local people drop in and the social network friends can actually shake hands and share a coffee.

Another initiative has been instituting a regular lunch after worship on the first and third Sundays down at the "local" Grandview Hotel in Brunswick West. This has extended the church's hospitality emphasis beyond the worship service itself to a number of people who live in supported care, as well as provided an opportunity to catch up with others who do not make it to the worship service.

In summary, worship at Moreland Baptist sounds similar to that of the Solace community, as described by Darren Cronshaw:[15]

- there is an emphasis on "interactive worship" but also on participation by all groups, particularly children;
- there is allowance for "theological questioning" but also with access to contemporary scholarship, and it's a place where "I can think for myself";[16]
- there is encouragement for "everyday spirituality and vocation" breaking down barriers between sacred and secular; and
- there is some "dreaming" but the church is keenly aware of its resource limitations.

Moreland Baptist seeks to appeal in its worship perhaps not so much to the "un-churched" or "over-churched" but to post-church people — those who perhaps for all the wrong reasons have given up on faith and community.

The pastoral connection

Larger churches may be able to dedicate separate resources to pastoral care of the congregation and to working in the community. However, for a small inner-urban church, such as Moreland Baptist, there is often felt to be an ongoing tension between caring for the older people of the congregation and having the opportunity to look outwards and offer pastoral resources to the local community.

Yet, Moreland Baptist has pursued aspects of community chaplaincy at least from the early 1980s, for example, formally getting involved in local community organisations that assist people in poverty or who are homeless. This led to pastoral activities among the non-church community workers themselves, for example, a Baptist minister officiating at a wedding between a Catholic groom and Jewish bride! More recently, one of the pastors led a Cook Island Hair-Cutting Ceremony, which is an interesting take on the standard Baptist child dedication ritual.

In previous years members of the congregation raised funds to support the school chaplain at the local Coburg TAFE Secondary College. More recently, the church is providing resources to the Strathmore Secondary College Chaplaincy Committee at a significant time of adjustment. Also, one of the pastors is formally involved at the Austin Hospital, Heidelberg, in pastoral care and chaplaincy training. Another offers pastoral care as part of The Studio group-work each week which involves people from the various parts of the network and the congregation. The church is open for quiet reflection and pastoral engagement each Wednesday afternoon.

So, today, the pastors at Moreland Baptist have an overt role as community chaplains: as Morisy puts it, "being *priest for the everyday*".[17] Pastoral care is offered and received among the community of communities, it is not restricted to the worshipping congregation. It builds bridges, it brings the care and concerns being experienced elsewhere in the community into the sanctuary for prayer, and breaks down the demarcation between sacred and secular. It does not neglect the care of the congregation, but the "congregation" is now the larger network of communities. Frost and Hirsch counsel that "what is needed is the abandonment of the strict lines of demarcation between the sacred and profane spaces in our world and the recognition that people today are searching for relational communities that offer belonging, empowerment and redemption".[18]

The online connection

Mara Einstein declares that "Religion is increasingly moving from pew to pixel" and so the rise of online communities and virtual social networks has not gone unnoticed by churches.[19] For Moreland Baptist there was the opportunity to be found online by new people seeking a local church. There was also the opportunity of perhaps responding to a long-standing issue, whereby many people who are highly mobile, or have unstable accommodation or work, find the church, like the church, but can only stop for a while until moving onto the next phase of their life. The "wayside church" was once coined as an evocation of so many travellers who stop, refresh, but eventually go on to other places. But this does not have to mean disconnection.

So Moreland Baptist has deliberately sought to build an online presence and online community through a website, Facebook pages, and an email newsletter and invitation list for special events.

- The website, which is fairly static, is a small stake in the Google-verse but remarkably overseas visitors and people moving into the area have found the church, liked what they saw, and come to visit.
- The Facebook page, which now has over 100 followers, is more dynamic and used to promote weekly activities or to record significant events in the life of the church. For example, it was used to promote the *40 ways and 40 days* 2014 Lenten reflections in collaboration with Newmarket Baptist.

- The quarterly e-newsletter, with about 40 addresses, has more significant contributions by members, as well as the rosters. This is also printed and posted to those mainly older people who have connections to the church but who are now in care.

The church seeks to bring the virtual and the physical together from time to time. For example, everyone on the lists is asked to try at least to come to three big garden party celebrations each year. When former attendees say, "we must visit sometime", there is an obvious answer.

Another example is where current members travel and take the time to catch up with past members who have moved for family or work reasons. This ranges from a pleasant train trip to country Victoria all the way to stopping off in Singapore in order to catch up with significant past attendees.

Moreland Baptist is not an online church, nor wishes to be. Its sense of community is primarily local and grounded in good coffee. It has been said that the average online attention span is now down to seven seconds, so online may not be the relevant medium for spirituality and reflection. Yet, Peter Horsfield notes that:

> The changes taking place in religion and social religiosity are intimately connected with the opportunities created by new media formations for revisiting and reworking those previously discounted dimensions of human experience connected with transcendence, metaphysics, mystery and enchantment. Part of this shift in religion … is a shift away from an institutional-dominated, centralised construction of meaning towards a more de-centred, audience-based, autonomously generated meditational matrix.[20]

This shift is driving church as network.

The Whitley connection

Finally, the relationship of Moreland Baptist to Whitley College has been very significant over many decades, at least back to the 1970s if not before, and it cannot be underestimated. It is this connection which has nurtured the church with leading-edge theological scholarship and the church in turn has supported many teachers, students, and pastors-in-training connected with the College. The church's sense of the good news, of discipleship, justice, community, the place of children, hospitality, and so on comes from this ongoing, life-giving engagement.

For example, the church recently held a series of studies on the book of Genesis, which was introduced by the Professor of Old Testament and led by others in the network with connections to Whitley College and up-to-date scholarship. Since the late 1970s, in particular, the church has supported five women training for pastoral ministry through Whitley by providing relevant employment opportunities and institutional support for ordination. The church in various ways has directly supported each of the principals of Whitley College, including providing care and support, opportunities to preach, and a place to call home for the first principal and his partner in the latter years of their lives. Church members have also responded to the request to support theological education and scholarship more generally in Australia and beyond as part of the University of Divinity. This has been one very strong and life-giving connection for Moreland Baptist.

The importance of networks

Sociologist Rodney Stark argues that the early Christian movement grew so rapidly, at least in part, because it fostered and utilised its networks: "Successful movements discern techniques for maintaining open networks".[21] In other words, the edges of the community become the focus for pastoral resources where there are connections to others and other communities. Stark talks up the role of Christian women as spouses who were often the open edge of the early church. It still seems evident today at Moreland Baptist that two partners may have different feelings towards the church, yet count themselves as part of the extended network. For Moreland Baptist, maintaining open networks means having a website, a Facebook page, an open church door during the week, a notice in the local paper, being sensitive to people who appear at the edges seeking support, underpinned of course by a strong theological sense of hospitality, acceptance and respect, diversity, and friendship.

But networks are not just useful, they may be essential. Manuel Castells, also a sociologist, is famous for his three volume *magnum opus* on The Rise of the Network Society, dealing particularly with new technologies and the information age. His assessment is darker: "…inside the networks, new possibilities are relentlessly created — outside the networks, survival is increasingly difficult".[22] This can be applied not just to individuals but to whole cities or even countries that may stagnate if they are not part of the networks, increasingly global, where diversity, vitality, and creativity flow. On this reckoning, "Life" can only be found "in Community".

The energy to connect

When Christians refer to life or energy it is usually in relation to the Spirit. Moreland Baptist probably wouldn't call itself a charismatic or Pentecostal church, yet with enthusiasm it pursues this sense of energy found in the networks and in the connections between the various groups. This is most evident on Sundays like Neighbour Day or Spring Festival when the diverse groups of people come together for a special worship service as celebration and garden party. The inspiration is to make, build, sustain, and celebrate connections, or relationships.

In other words, the sense of the Holy Spirit is the energy for connection, which is articulated by Mary Grey: "The metaphor of connection highlights what Christian theology means by the 'Holy Spirit'".[23] In her lecture series, The Outrageous Pursuit of Hope, Grey affirms that "hope is nurtured ... through the initiative of the Holy Spirit in cracking open culture, creating new transgressive energies for life, for connection across boundaries".[24]

This is very different to traditional concepts of spirituality that are focussed on the individual and their private experience of God. Spirituality becomes a community practice, a sharing in the life that emerges from the networks, the relationships. And where life and wellbeing emerge, then it may be called sacred.

> According to Grey, as the Spirit breaks open the discourse of individualism and replaces it with connection and relationship, a new vision of the church will emerge. Not only will the church view its gathering in terms of an openness to the needs of the world by listening to those on its margins, it will also seek to embody a sense of community.[25]

So, to find the Holy Spirit one must build networks, build relationships, and not just within the community but "across boundaries". It is this sense of the Spirit that helpfully inspires the emerging missional church.

A world of difference

Grey's "transgressive energies" has a hint of danger to it. Stepping outside the usual or comfortable boundaries involves risk, even if it has some attendant excitement. An example of this at Moreland Baptist was the approach by a local KUMON tutoring group looking for a new place to operate since they had to suddenly vacate the previous one. At one level the group's objectives are aligned with the church's values in supporting children in education, particularly those having difficulties. At another level, though, the church was confronted by the fact that many of the regular children and their families come from the Middle-East or Africa and are generally Muslim in faith. So, there may be uncomfortable boundaries to cross for the KUMON group and for the church, which to date are happily negotiated.

Life in community, church as network, then, can have a radical edge to it, which is represented by Gary Bouma in his *Being Faithful in Diversity*:

> In time we may come to understand that cultural and religious diversity is as important for the sustainability of a society as biodiversity is for the sustainability of the biosphere … the question becomes, "Do we have theologies of diversity which enable people to understand religious diversity as God given?" … We live in a community of communities, a world of difference.[26]

This presents a goal that is beyond the end-point of Morisy's "journeying out", where we can live peacefully, respectfully, in a "community of communities".

Conclusion

The contemporary faith journey at Moreland Baptist Church is a work in progress. It has its times of celebration with a full house, and its times of disappointment. The filaments of continuity are thin and may finally break with too few leaders. The struggle is always evident, week to week, but it is not without hope. The church can certainly relate to Ann Morisy's dictum: "It is about being vulnerable, paradoxically creative and yet helpless creatures, with an intimation that we are special".[27]

The struggle is also not without meaning. The church recognises that it is part of a larger campaign in regard to its place in the world. Nobel Prize winning writer Mario Vargas Llosa puts it this way. On the one hand, he says: "I'm convinced that a society cannot achieve a sophisticated democratic culture — in other words, it cannot be free or lawful — if it isn't profoundly suffused with spiritual and moral life, which, for the immense majority of human beings, is indissociable from religion".

On the other hand, he goes on to say: "Churches would negate themselves — they would cease to exist — if they were flexible and tolerant and prepared to accept the basic principles of democratic life, like pluralism, relativism, the coexistence of contradictory truths, the constant mutual concessions required to arrive at a social consensus".[28]

This paradox — between offering spiritual and moral life, but in a way that risks self-negation — poses the question, the quandary, and the quest for life in community at Moreland Baptist Church.

Acknowledgement: This paper was developed in conversation with the people of Moreland Baptist, in particular Luke and Enes Bowen, and Julie Morsillo.

Robert Morsillo has been variously a member, pastor, and leader at Moreland Baptist Church, Melbourne, since 1978. He has a background and interest in computer science, theology, community development, public policy, communications, and consumer affairs. His work focuses on overcoming social and economic exclusion through technologies that create a sense of connectedness for disadvantaged Australians. He is a Senior Advisor with Telstra's Chief Sustainability Office and Adjunct Associate Professor at Swinburne University of Technology.

Encounter Baptist Church's Journey with 3DM Discipleship and Mission

David Wanstall

For the last six years Encounter Baptist Church (and one of its antecedents — Stonnington Baptist Church) has been on a journey of learning how to integrate discipleship and mission into the everyday lives of people in an ordinary Baptist church. We have been learning from 3DM — an organisation that trains churches and Christian leaders to do discipleship and mission in an increasingly post-Christian world. This chapter introduces the language, tools, and processes that 3DM has developed and describes some of our successes and failures as we have sought to implement them in our church.

Introduction

This chapter describes the journey of Encounter Baptist Church (and one of its antecedents — Stonnington Baptist Church) as we have been learning to integrate discipleship and mission into our everyday lives. We have been greatly helped in this journey by the language, tools, processes, and expertise of 3dmovements (3DM) — an organisation that trains churches and Christian leaders to do discipleship and mission in an increasingly post-Christian world.

Our journey has been challenging and rewarding. We haven't finished the journey and we still have lots to learn. There are probably many churches that have implemented 3DM expertise with more success, but we hope that you will see the richness of 3DM material and be encouraged that ordinary small churches can make significant change by partnering with 3DM.

In 2008 our church of 70–80 people engaged in our community and local mission in the following ways.

Some of our mothers ran a Mothers of Pre-schoolers (MOPS) program in the church and approximately once a month turned that into a story time for parents and children at a local coffee shop. The gatherings were made up mostly of church people with the occasional outsider.

We provided our hall for two trivia nights that were run by the tram drivers from the depot next to our building. The drivers ran the trivia nights as fundraisers for the Good Friday Children's Hospital appeal. A handful of our people participated in each night.

The tram company matched the money raised by the tram drivers and so we took up a special offering at church and gave it to the tram drivers to add to their total.

For the national day of thanksgiving we wrote thank-you cards to the teachers at a local primary school and a few of us delivered them to the school and provided the teachers with morning tea. This school was chosen as we had one person coordinating Christian Religious Education (CRE) in that school.

We ran a movie night in the church to which some of our children invited their friends. We ran a marriage course in the church with only one or two couples from outside the church. We ran an exercise where one Sunday we gave all the adults $10 and challenged them to find some needy person outside the church to give that money to in the coming weeks.

Out of all of this activity, there were only a few faith conversations with people who were not Christians and not many ongoing relationships or connections. This was true for me as the minister as much as anyone else in the church.

In 2013 our church of 70–80 people engaged in our community and local mission in the following ways.

In cooperation with a local primary school we ran our third Clean Up Australia day event involving approximately thirty people from our church and thirty from the local community. It was based at the school grounds, advertised in the school newsletter, and finished with a BBQ using the school facilities.

At that same primary school, two of our mothers with children in the school coordinated a thank-you morning tea for staff in conjunction with the school parents association. Later in that year people from our church provided evening meals for the teachers on their parent–teacher interview night. On two other Sundays, people from our church participated in school working bees and provided a BBQ lunch. One of the people from our church ran choirs for students and parents at that school on a voluntary basis. The choirs held a concert during the year as a fundraiser for the school and our church provided the catering for the event.

On December 15 we ran a Community Christmas Service in the school hall with the carols provided by the school students and parents choirs. There were approximately thirty people at the service who don't normally attend church. At the end of the service we invited everyone to help put together Christmas hampers for needy families from the school. The school chaplain then passed them on to the families.

In the area around the school a person we don't know organised a Halloween walk on a weekend near to the actual date of Halloween. Particular streets were designated and if houses were happy to have school children knock on their doors and ask for lollies, they were provided with signs to put on their fences. Two of our church families lived in that area and so for the second year in a row we set up stations at both houses. At one house we provided homemade lemonade to thirsty children and parents, and handed out lollies with Bible verses like "Fear not for God is with you". At the other house we provided a gathering point and had an "after party". There were drinks and pizzas with 30–40 people from our church and the community. Over the afternoon we connected with 150–200 people, many of whom we knew through some of the other activities listed above.

During the year a number of people from our church participated in a leadership network for local community groups. We provided them dinner on two occasions (including a Christmas dinner). At the end of the year we invited those groups to apply for grants of up to $1000 each that we funded from our church tithing. Through the relationships established at that network, we were able to launch an emergency food program with a local neighbourhood house. We partnered with the food bank from a large church to order the food and then we provided it to the neighbourhood house to distribute as they were open five days a week and had deep knowledge of and connection to needy people in the area. Through these connections there have been faith conversations and we have had the opportunity to pray with people.

A monthly book club ran during the year. The group was made up of Christians and people who were not Christians. Contact wasn't confined to book club meetings: people had meals together and went to movies and other events together. During the year both in the book club and at other times there were faith conversations. On various occasions people offered to pray with non-Christian members of the group about issues. One of the non-Christian members who was moving away donated various items to the church. Another came to a Christmas service and has planned to come to our church camp in 2014.

An international students group was launched and ran weekly on a Friday night. It involved a mixture of nights. Some were purely social with food and games. Others involved helping people with English for IELTS (International English Language Testing System) tests, and short Bible studies that helped introduce elements of Christianity to those who weren't Christians.

In addition, our group of 70+ year olds organised a community lunch, inviting people from the local community; there were at least two Christmas-in-Winter Dinner parties with a deliberate mix of people who are Christians and those who were not; our families with teenagers participated in the Red Shield appeal; a couple organised a street party in their street; and we continued to hear stories of people sharing their faith with their friends and offering to pray for them.

Observations on the comparison between 2008 and 2013:

- The quantity and quality of community engagement and local mission had at least doubled or maybe even tripled.
- Most of the community engagement and local mission activities were now located outside our church building.
- There was a great increase in the number of connections with non-Christians. Most of those connections were ongoing.
- Many more people from our church were having faith conversations with their friends outside the church.
- Many were offering to pray for people's needs right then — on the telephone, across the fence, or in the garden and so on — and not just in private prayer times later on.
- There was discernible movement in numbers of people towards Jesus.
- While community engagement and mission activities increased, people in the church were less busy and tired with "running church".

In addition, the engagement in 2013 occurred in a year where the church integrated people from different church communities into a new partnership, sold a building, relocated to different buildings, chose a new name, employed a youth minister, and helped organise a four-day 3DM conference for 110 church leaders from around Australia and New Zealand.

Key elements of the journey

The journey described above looks like a journey into mission, but first and foremost it is actually a journey into discipleship. It wasn't just a journey for me as a pastor in gaining some new skills, learning a new system, or reorganising church but it was also a personal journey into discipleship.

In 2008 I had skills and experience in "running church". I knew how to plan services, preach, lead worship, organise rosters, and provide pastoral care etc. People from our church were capable of planning services, playing music, leading worship, running kids church, organising interactive services, running small groups, providing leadership, and running various events. But we needed to get better at both discipleship and mission.

At the end of 2007 our church council made a strategic decision for our church to go on a 3–5 year journey to change the DNA of our church by learning from 3DM — an organisation that trains churches and Christian leaders to do discipleship and mission in an increasingly post-Christian world. 3DM emerged out of St Thomas Church in Sheffield UK and now helps churches around the globe with the tools and expertise they learned doing discipleship and mission in a western, post-Christian English city where less than one percent of people went to church.

First key discipleship lesson: To be better at discipleship we needed to understand process as well as content.

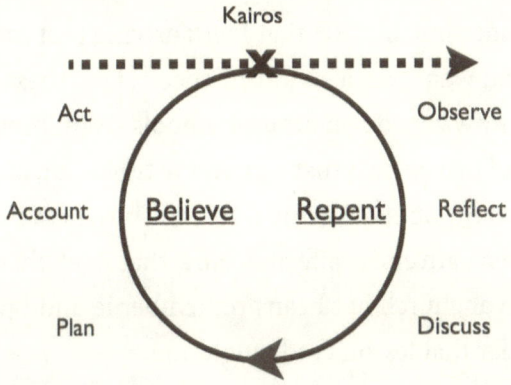

The most significant insight about the discipleship process that we learnt from 3DM was that Jesus' primary discipleship tool was to teach his disciples in the moments of life. The Gospels record a few sermons but most of the space is devoted to recording various moments: the transfiguration; disciples being unable to cast out a demon; Jesus telling Peter to let down his net on the other side; the disciples forgetting their lunch; and the disciples arguing about who was the greatest. In each of these moments Jesus taught them some truth, and changed their thinking and their acting.

This is an extension of Jesus' initial proclamation in Mark 1:15: "'The time [Greek *kairos* = event/moment] has come,' he said. 'The kingdom of God has come near. Repent [change your thinking] and believe the good news [act as if it is true]!'" Changing your thinking and then changing your acting is a reflective learning process.

3DM developed a simple visual tool — the learning circle — that helps people to learn, remember, and pass on this process. (3DM calls the learning circle and other visual tools "Lifeshapes".) Changing your thinking involves observing what has happened, reflecting on it, and discussing it with others. Changing your acting involves making a plan, deciding on a process of accountability for that plan, and then acting on it.

Learning from the moments of life doesn't replace the need for sermons and teaching. However, it is usually in the moments of our lives where these truths are applied and integrated in a lasting way.

It was probably sometime in 2008 that I was driving past my children's primary school and went past a 40 km/hr speed sign. These speed signs are positioned to slow cars down around schools so children are less likely to be injured. I had driven past that sign many times but, at that particular time, God spoke to me about slowing down the busyness of my life so my own children weren't adversely affected. Now that week there was probably a fantastic sermon at church but I can't remember it, and I preached it! But I can still remember that lesson God taught me.

It is not that I hadn't had these God moments (kairos) in my life beforehand. However, as I became aware of the way God was discipling me I was able to cooperate with God and gain full benefit from them.

The learning circle tool didn't just equip me as the pastor; it also empowered people in our church. As we all got better at identifying the God moments (kairos) in our lives and processing them through the learning circle, we found it greatly improved our discipleship. In addition it made our faith-sharing easier. This was because individuals had fresh stories of their walk with God that they could share with their friends.

The second key discipleship lesson: We needed to regularly apply the triangle tool to our lives on a personal, family, and church basis.

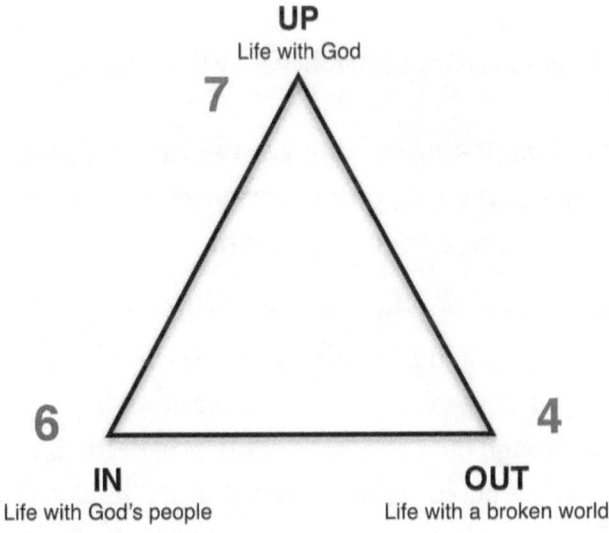

Like the circle, the triangle is a simple visual tool that reminds us that Jesus led a three dimensional life — UP, IN, and OUT. This is seen clearly in Luke 6:12–19 where Jesus spent a night in prayer (the UP dimension of life with God), called his disciples to him (the IN dimension of life with God's people), and then went with them to the crowd on the plain (the OUT dimension of life with a lost and broken world).

We learnt that a simple but deeply powerful way to use this tool was to rate ourselves from 1–10 on each of the dimensions UP, IN, and OUT (using 5 is not allowed). It is surprising how doing this in a small group of people quickly leads to significant reflection on where we are in our Christian lives and what God might be calling us to focus on.

When we started using this tool individually and in groups, we regularly gave the OUT dimension the lowest score. A number of the activities that we engaged with in 2008 were responses to using this tool.

The triangle tool can be explained in a few minutes, remembered for a lifetime, and easily passed on to others. As we have continued to apply this tool, thinking about the three dimensions of our Christian lives has started to become embedded in our thinking and is shaping our church culture. One of the signs of this has been evident in conversations with people. Without being asked a question, people have talked about how the triangle has prompted them to change what they have been doing.

The third key discipleship lesson: We needed to learn to live a rhythm of rest and work, and to embrace pruning as a vital process to make space for new growth.

Many of us live our lives in a rhythm of resting from work. However, a close observation of Scripture reveals the opposite pattern of work from rest. This can be seen in Psalm 23 where you lie down in green pastures before walking through the valley of the shadow of death. It is seen in the life of Jesus where his public ministry started with a 40-day retreat. It is seen in the life of Paul where he spent a long time in the desert before being launched into mission. And it is taught clearly in John 15 where abiding in Christ leads to bearing fruit.

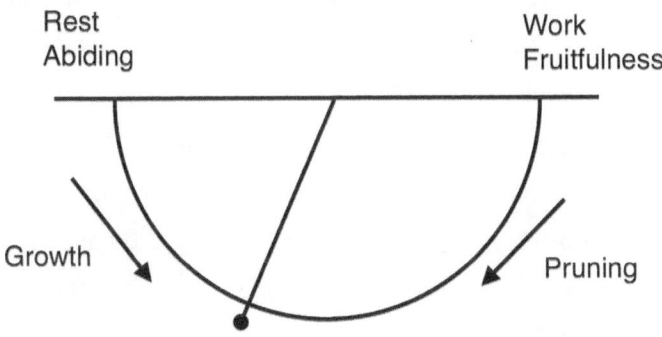

The visual tool (Lifeshape) for this process is a semicircle which is the shape of a pendulum that swings between rest and work, abiding and bearing fruit. In 2008 we were quite busy and tired with running church, and also with many people's stage of life (young children, busy work etc.). The semi circle challenged us to build more rest and abiding time into our lives.

As we were encouraging people to live a rhythm of rest and work in their personal lives we also needed to model this in the overall church life. In order to do that we had to do some pruning; we worked hard to make running church simpler and less demanding. We reduced leaders meetings, we reduced the preparation load for kid's church leaders, we had simple music rehearsals, and we used technology to simplify communications and rosters. We made sure our kid's church had breaks during school holidays to give leaders, who were also the parents, breaks from this ministry.

Over the years, we have continued pruning to make space for rest and to make space for mission. We have gone from having services in January to having combined services with another church in January to having no services in the first few weeks of January. This was in response to the reality that many people were away in January and the recognition that we had a high level of involvement from people in our church during the year. We wanted to give people a chance to rest before another year of involvement.

It is important to note that this pruning was contextual. If we had been a coastal church with large numbers of holiday makers in the area, we would have needed to choose another time of year to cut back.

We haven't always got the pruning right. For example, over a number of years we have deliberately not emphasised small groups because we wanted to make space for other things. In retrospect, we should have found ways to have at least one or two small groups running for those who really needed that sort of community.

In our busy culture, we have found that individuals, and not just churches, need to keep reviewing their rhythm of rest and work. The semicircle enables individuals to do that by giving them a simple but profound way to remember, reflect on, and adjust the rhythms of their lives. Not only that, it can be simply passed on to someone else — even by being drawn on a paper serviette in a cafe over coffee.

The fourth key discipleship lesson: We needed to learn Jesus' mission strategy of looking for and engaging with people of peace.

Jesus' mission strategy is described in Matthew 10, Luke 9, and Luke 10. A key part of that strategy is finding people of peace. These are people who welcome you, listen to you, serve you, and often connect you with their relational networks. In terms of Luke 10, they were those who would invite the disciples into their homes and offer them food and connect them with members of their households. In response the disciples were to stay with them, eat their food, heal the sick, and proclaim the kingdom to them.

We began to learn about the importance of people of peace during 2008. The MOPS group began a story time in a local coffee shop through the owner who turned out to be a person of peace. One of our mums dropped in advertising flyers and the owner invited them to have a gathering at the coffee shop — providing the space for free, good coffees (at the normal price), and free baby-chinos.

The trivia nights with the tram drivers happened because there was a person in the tram depot who was a person of peace. She facilitated the trivia nights and we even began having discussions about the possibility of my becoming a chaplain to the depot. However, at the end of the year, she was transferred and in 2009 the trivia nights and the possibility of chaplaincy came to an end.

I knew I had to learn to do mission by finding people of peace and not just teach the principles. I tried to make contact with international student ministries at a nearby university campus but nothing eventuated. In an effort to get out of my Christian ghetto (where my work environment and all my friends were Christians) I tried to find a local basketball team to join, again with no success.

I was then prompted to ask a Chinese student in our church whether he had any contacts with international students. He had just come across a group of eight to ten students from China who were on a six-month exchange. So he invited them to one of our homes for an Australian meal. We gave them some practical assistance and offered to help them with their English using the Gospel of Mark as a textbook.

One member of the group was a person of peace. He facilitated weekly gatherings at the apartment where they were staying. A few of us met with them weekly to help them with their English, using the Gospel of Mark. Near the end of their exchange, one of the students became a Christian. The following year, as part of a holiday, I was fortunate to be able to visit the students in China. The person of peace coordinated the Shanghai part of my trip. Partly as a result of that visit, he became a Christian and he linked us with the next group that would be coming to Melbourne on exchange. Subsequently at least two others from these two groups have become Christians.

By a process of trial and error, we have discovered that when we led with a program, like a marriage course, we didn't gain much traction. But when we looked for people of peace and listened to them without predetermining what we would do, we found that the things we then decided to do were much more effective. This has put mission back into the hands of everyone in our church.

The fifth key discipleship lesson: We needed to learn how to operate in mid-sized groups of 15–30 people gathered around a particular missional vision (these groups are often called Missional Communities).

3DM have discovered that large groups, like Sunday celebrations, are great for worship, teaching, and inspiration; and small groups are great for caring, encouragement, and challenge. However, it is mid-sized groups — which are often missing in church life — which are great for mission. They are large enough to dare but small enough to care. If a small group engages in a regular mission activity but two people are sick and one person is away on business, it can quickly get to the point where the activity can't go ahead. But if you have 15–30 people, 5–10 people can be absent and there would still be enough of a group for an activity to proceed.

There is an unwritten social rule that makes it easier to include new people (including non-Christians) in mid-sized groups. In large groups people may engage with what is happening at the front and never talk to the person beside them. In small groups, the expectation is that everyone will share and that sharing will often be personal — there is no place to hide. But in mid-sized groups the unwritten rule is that you share a snapshot of what it is like to be your friend. This happens when you meet people at a BBQ. You may talk with one person about work or sport or something else. If you don't feel like you have much in common with them you may move on to talk with someone else. If you are an extrovert you may talk with lots of people, but if you are more of an introvert, it is possible to hang back.

Like most Australians we could have 15–30 people over for a BBQ, but we needed to learn how we could meet in mid-sized groups that had a balance of UP (life with God), IN (life with God's people), and OUT (life with a lost and broken world). So we experimented with doing OUT-focused activities that were based around service. One example was participating in Clean Up Australia Day. We experimented with OUT-focused activities that were social but had a mixture of people from different faith or no faith backgrounds. An example was holding Christmas-in-Winter dinner parties. These had a mixture of friends where we enjoyed good food and good company but it was easy to have conversations about people's experiences of Christmas. We also experimented with IN-focused gatherings based around meals. We included simple accessible spiritual content that would be accessible to non-Christians. For example, we would have three or four people share highlights and lowlights from their week — with the expectation that not everyone had to share. We would ask for prayer points and again get only three or four people to pray for them in short simple prayers.

Following advice from 3DM we formed groups around people who had a clear vision to reach people in a network or neighbourhood. One was focused on connecting with families associated with a primary school and another was focused around people in a geographic area where some of our church people lived.

A non-Christian lady was invited to some of the mid-sized gatherings of the group focused on reaching people in a local primary school. She was a long-time friend of a couple in the group but didn't actually have a strong connection with the primary school. She found a welcoming and loving community, and formed connections with a few people who were able to help her through some significant difficulties. In a smaller group setting they were able to share Scripture and life, and through that her faith came alive. She now regularly comes to Sunday services, meets with people for spiritual encouragement, participates in various OUT activities and invites others to come along.

Cancelling some Sunday services

In the last two years, to help make it possible for people to participate regularly in these mid-sized, mission-focused groups, we have actually cancelled some Sunday services. People only have a certain amount of time to give to "church" activities, and if mission is a key priority, we thought that we had to commit some of that time to mission. This is another outworking of the semicircle: we needed to prune some Sunday celebrations in order to make room for mission activities to grow.

Now this was also driven by our small size. St Thomas Church in Sheffield UK is a church of thousands and they encourage their Missional Communities to come to a minimum of one and a maximum of three Sunday services during a month. Because we are small, if we encouraged half our church not to be there for some Sundays during the month, it would make it hard to run our Sunday services. So we decided to make space for our Missional Communities by giving them the time they would normally be involved in the service on the fourth Sunday of the month. They were encouraged to gather at some time over the fourth weekend — it didn't have to be Sunday morning. This is one of the key reasons that we could achieve the wide range of the community engagement and local mission activities in 2013, and also be less tired running church.

Since we were familiar with Sunday services and small groups, we deliberately worked to avoid making these groups just large "small groups" with too many people or smaller "Sunday services" shoehorned into a home with an out-of-tune guitar. We learned by trying, making mistakes, reflecting, modifying, and trying again.

We were a small church attempting to transition and we took an incremental approach to developing Missional Communities. In order just to get started we made some compromises, such as not always starting with large enough groups of people, not always having leadership adequately defined, and not establishing balanced rhythms of Missional Community life from the beginning. We have proved in our own experience that these are weaknesses to avoid. However, we have also gained a lot of practical experience that we probably couldn't have gained any other way.

Note: Mid-sized groups aren't a modern idea; they are present in the New Testament as households. These households weren't just nuclear families but extended families that often included servants and business partners. The early church met from house to house (Acts 2,4); the church in Rome was made up of various households (Romans 16); and 1 Corinthians 11–14 is probably best understood as giving guidance for household gatherings.

The sixth key discipleship lesson: Huddles are the best place to learn the previous five discipleship lessons and I wish I had been in a 3DM huddle at the beginning of the journey.

3DM have refined a group discipleship/leadership development process called "huddles". These are high commitment small groups that meet regularly for discipleship and leadership development. They are based on the observation that Jesus mentored his disciples in groups and gave them access to his life. The person leading the huddle prayerfully invites people to join them in a huddle and offers access to their lives. They are essentially saying, "come close", and "whatever you see in me that is like Jesus — copy that".

The organised/structured part of that access is a weekly/fortnightly huddle meeting that goes for approximately one hour. The organic/spontaneous part of that access includes unplanned conversations, various invitations to meals, and joint participation in activities like going to the movies, shopping, and gardening etc. that the leader is already engaging in.

In each huddle gathering, the leader helps the members of the group answer two questions:

1. What is God saying to me?
2. What am I doing about it?

Sometimes the focus will be on character, and other times the focus will be on skills and ministry competency. The flow and content of each gathering provide a dynamic interplay between the knowledge and experience of the leader, the sharing by each participant, and the prompting of the Holy Spirit. A vital part of each meeting is checking how people have gone with their responses to question two from the previous meeting.

3DM advises that huddles are the best place to introduce their visual tools (Lifeshapes). They strongly advise against introducing them in sermons or small group studies. This is because we often mistake knowing about something for knowing something. For example, having a small group discussion about bicycle riding is entirely different to going on a bicycle ride in a small group. When a God moment (kairos) is identified, the huddle leader can introduce the appropriate tool, e.g., the learning circle, and the person can apply it immediately. It is not just an interesting bit of information to be filed away, it is a tool that is used straight away to gain insight, understand a scriptural principle, and develop a plan.

I wish I had been a participant in a 3DM huddle at the beginning because:

- I needed to learn these discipleship lessons and apply them in my own life before I could lead others into them. I could read a book and even go to a conference, but there is a difference between learning a principle and knowing how and when to apply it. Books can contain principles but only an experienced person can say "you need to focus on this bit now", or "this is what I found in a similar situation in my life", or in response to a suggested plan they can say, "I don't think that will work because of …. and have you considered … ?" I have been learning these lessons by the grace of God, but it would have been a faster process if I had been in a huddle from the beginning.

- I needed an extended exposure to an experienced person leading a huddle. Over the years I have run huddles or my own modified version of them. However, it has only been over the last few years as I have been in a regular 3DM huddle that the quality of my huddle leading has significantly improved. People have been growing in discipleship and are applying the 3DM tools much more effectively. They are beginning to be equipped to run their own huddles — a process of reproduction that is key to growing a discipling culture.

Engaging with 3DM

People interested in 3DM usually find a wealth of information in the posts in the websites:

www.3DMeurope.com
www.3DMeublog.com
www.missionalcommunitiesblog.com
www.missionalcommunities.org.au
www.3DMovements.com

The 3DM books that introduce their concepts are another helpful source of information.

Building a Discipling Culture by Mike Breen and Steve Cockram captures over 25 years of experience in how to go about making missional disciples. It introduces and explains the "Lifeshapes" referred to above — learning circle, triangle, semi-circle, and others. It also explains the discipleship vehicle called huddles.[1]

Leading Kingdom Movements by Mike Breen looks at the teaching of Jesus and the example of the Apostle Paul in leading a kingdom movement. It also includes many stories from Breen's ministry and his experience at St Thomas Church in Sheffield UK. This is really helpful as it supplies the context in which the 3DM tools and expertise were developed.[2]

Other formational books for the movement include *Multiplying Missional Leaders* and *Leading Missional Communities,* both by Mike Breen; and *Launching Missional Communities: A Field Guide* by Mike Breen and Alex Absalom.[3]

3DM have learned that growing in discipleship and mission requires relational connections and not just reading books. So another helpful step is to connect with people who already have connections to 3DM. This gives you the opportunity to hear their stories and a chance to ask questions. This can take the form of talking to people from churches in Australia, attending an introductory 3DM workshop, or signing up to be part of an online coaching huddle led by a trained 3DM coach. These connections can be made through the above websites.

If through all of this contact and information, you think your church would like to go on a journey of learning from 3DM, the next step is to join a Learning Community. A Learning Community takes groups of leaders from a number of churches on a two-year journey. This is made up of four-day intensives every six months and fortnightly coaching huddles for the leaders. It is a robust process that gives people direct access to experienced practitioners. There is plenty of time to ask questions, make plans, get consulting advice, and reflect on progress against those plans.

Over the last few years a number of churches in Australia have cooperated together to bring 3DM expertise to Australia. There have been regular introductory workshops, people have been linked into online coaching huddles, and in November 2013 the first Australian-based Learning Community was launched. The hope is that more Learning Communities will follow.

Conclusion

We are still on the journey to more effective discipleship and mission. We are not experts and we need to see more people come to Christ and more lives changed. But we have found that the process is not complex and easy, it is actually simple but hard. It is simple because the key processes and principles can be easily grasped. It is hard because they need to be internalised. This involves significant change and the forming of new habits. And this involves acting differently over an extended period of time.

It can be challenging because people have to let go of the familiar and risk something new. It can be challenging because not everyone goes with you on the journey. Over the years a number of people have said, "we think what you are doing is great, but we are going to another church".

Yet the journey has been deeply rewarding. We are a small church which has seen people come to faith and, although we haven't seen enough of this, we have seen more than we used to. We are slowly gaining experiential learning of how this happens.

We have seen people internalise discipleship processes and mission focus. Many of the community engagement and local mission activities have been suggested and led by people from the congregation rather than the pastor. Most of these activities haven't been part of formal plans and most have been resourced by the people participating in them and haven't required support from the church budget.

"If your church disappeared, would anyone notice the absence?" is a question that is sometimes asked. Comparing 2008 with 2013, I think a much larger number of people from the community would notice if our church disappeared. However, I like to hope that they might not notice the absence. Not because we have no impact, but because the people from our church would continue to live out a life of discipleship and mission in their everyday lives whether or not our particular congregation continued to exist.

David Wanstall worked as a chemical engineer for nine years. In the second half of that time he became honorary associate pastor in an independent church and enrolled in theological education. After appointments in small and medium-sized Churches of Christ, he was appointed as the pastor at Stonnington Baptist Church that is now Encounter Baptist Church. As part of the journey with 3DM, he has been involved in establishing Missional Communities Australia that has recently launched a 3DM Learning Community in Melbourne involving 110 pastors and leaders from eighteen churches around Australia and New Zealand.

A Joining of the Ways
Reflections on the Successful Merger of Two Baptist Churches

Ian Hussey

In late 1998 the Nundah Baptist Church and Wavell Heights Baptist Church merged to form the North-East Baptist Church. Subsequent to the merger the church discovered new vitality and grew from around 80 to 500 over the next ten years. The merger also enabled the revitalisation of the church facilities. This chapter reflects on the theology of mergers and the process of this particular merger. It postulates the factors which contributed towards its "success" and those which may have led to its failure. It is identified that, in this case, a sense of God's blessing, desperation, early success, good use of symbol and structure, and fairly similar cultures were contributors to success. A tendency to polarisation, conflict between leaders, and subtle but important differences in church cultures were the major threats. The paper concludes that mergers are a viable option for rejuvenation of Australian Baptist churches.

Introduction

National surveys in the United States indicate that since the 1990s there are a greater number of church mergers.[1] This is happening among churches of all sizes with the typical example being in the attendance range of 100 to 200 after the merger. In their recent book Tomberlin and Bird[2] identify a variety of scenarios and outcomes of church mergers:

- As long-established churches merge, many enter the growth cycle marked by fresh vitality, new spiritual energy, intensified community engagement, and joyful momentum.

- Other long-established churches, facing dim prospects about the future, discover that a merger can translate their considerable heritage into a terrific foundation for a new generation.

- New churches that are growing and are in need of facilities are finding them through a merger with a congregation that has facilities.

- Churches that had formerly separated are being reunified through mergers, having decided they can do more together than apart.

- There is a growing desire among church leaders to become more racially and ethnically diverse. Some are seeing mergers as a way of diversifying their church and becoming more multiethnic.

- Multisite churches report that one out of three of their new campuses are church mergers.

- Mainline and denominational churches are using a merger approach to assist nearby struggling congregations in their faith family, nurturing them back to health and vitality, some as long-term relationships and some as only temporary adoptions.

- An increasing number of churches of all sizes are seeing mergers as a way of ensuring a smooth succession transition as the pastor retires.

It is apparent from this summary that there are a number of church mergers occurring in the United States for a number of different reasons. This is probably the case in Australia as well. Queensland Baptists, for example, have witnessed three church mergers in the last five years. However, the question can be asked: "Don't we need more churches, not fewer? Shouldn't we be opening new churches not closing them?" There is a well developed theology of church planting.

But what is the theology of church merging?

Theological underpinnings

The Bible does not say anything explicit about church mergers. However, a number of doctrines can be brought to bear on the question of whether a church should consider merging with another church.

First, an understanding of the *missio Dei* would suggest that a church should consider merging if doing so means it will better fulfil its mission. Not every church should merge. However, for some churches it may be a way of dramatically increasing their missional effectiveness.

Related to this would be the doctrine of stewardship. Churches should recognise that God has entrusted them with certain human and material resources in order to complete his mission. A church underutilising its material resources should consider whether it is being a good steward of those resources. A merger may result in the release and greater utilisation of scarce resources.

Recently, a number of theologians have argued persuasively for the intentional diversity of the local church. Whether emerging from a study of the doctrine of the Trinity,[3] or a theology of ethnicity and ecclesiology emerging from the Scriptures,[4] many have concluded that churches should be heterogeneous, not homogeneous. Churches should consider, if they are largely homogeneous, whether merging with a church of a different character might introduce more of the mandated diversity.

The unity of the family of God is a key theme of New Testament ecclesiology. In John 17:20–21 Jesus says: "My prayer is not for them alone. I pray also for those who will believe in me through their message, that all of them may be one, Father, just as you are in me and I am in you." Paul says:

> Make every effort to keep the unity of the Spirit through the bond of peace. There is one body and one Spirit, just as you

were called to one hope when you were called; one Lord, one faith, one baptism; one God and Father of all, who is over all and through all and in all (Ephesians 4:3-6).

Although Paul was talking about the dividing wall of the Temple which separated Jews and Gentiles, effective church mergers echo the spirit of Ephesians 2:14: "For he himself is our peace, who has made the two groups one and has destroyed the barrier, the dividing wall of hostility".

Hence, churches merging can be a manifestation of the unity prayed for by Jesus and exhorted by Paul. Indeed, church mergers can represent a "plausibility structure".[5] A plausibility structure provides a concrete illustration of an abstract idea. A merged church is a plausibility structure for the gospel. It demonstrates that the gospel really does have the power to achieve what would appear, humanly speaking, to be impossible. It is an apologetic to the nonbeliever and assurance to the believer.

So, even though the Bible does not make any explicit reference to church mergers, they are not incompatible with Scripture. Indeed, a case can even be made that they are biblical in that they reflect a commitment to mission, good stewardship, and heterogeneity in the Godhead and of the unity of the church. Two independent churches coming into interdependence through self-sacrifice is a powerful witness to the gospel.

The theory of successful mergers

What makes for a successful church merger? Schaller highlights the importance of creating a new worshipping community with a new congregational culture, strong sense of future orientation, a new set of operating goals, and a new sense of unity.[6] In addition, mergers are more likely to be successful when one of the merging churches is healthy and vibrant already.[7]

Rieland identifies the following factors:

- Seek a mission-driven merger, not a survival-driven merger.

- Establish clarity in pursuit of common values, vision, theology, and culture before you start the merger.
- Make sure you have a profound sense that "God is in it".
- Choose your leadership wisely.
- Don't operate by "the biggest will rule" principle.
- Expectations must be clearly defined.
- The result of the merger is one new church.[8]

In hindsight, the insights of Schaller and Rieland would have been very helpful to know before the merger took place! At the time there was little written on the topic and little previous experience of church mergers amongst Queensland Baptists. Still, the merger of Nundah Baptist Church and Wavell Heights Baptist Church can be considered a "successful" merger.

The historical context

Nundah (originally known as "German Station") is an inner suburb in the city of Brisbane, Australia, approximately eight kilometres from the Brisbane central business district. Prior to European settlement, Nundah was inhabited by the Turrbul people. It was first settled by Europeans in 1838 when German Lutheran missionaries arrived to evangelise the local indigenous community.

In the early twentieth century, Nundah became a major suburban centre, due to its location on Sandgate Road, one of Brisbane's busiest arterial roads, and the construction of the Nundah railway station. Sandgate Road and nearby streets were lined with shops, pubs, cinemas, and other commercial premises. However, Nundah's commercial precinct suffered a severe decline from the 1970s with the construction of the nearby Toombul Shopping Town. Increasing motor traffic along Sandgate Road also reduced Nundah's appeal as a shopping precinct. Gradually many shops closed, and those that opened in their place were often pawn brokers, charity stores, and the like.

Although a working-class suburb for most of its history, Nundah has become gentrified in recent years. Today it features a mix of traditional workers' cottages and modern high-density apartment blocks, and the shopping strip is marked by a number of cafes and restaurants. It has the highest percentage of single resident dwellings in Queensland.

Figure 1: The "New" Nundah Baptist Building, 1923

Wavell Heights, the suburb immediately west of Nundah, was established as a residential precinct in the 1940s. Located nine kilometres north of the Brisbane central business district, it is named after Field Marshal Lord Wavell who was the Commander-in-Chief of the Allied Forces in the Middle East during the Second World War. Though lacking a shopping precinct, a number of schools and churches, and a community centre, all provide a sense of community identity for the Wavell Heights residents. Although the suburb has undergone some rejuvenation, it still has a high percentage of retirees living in the houses they built in the post-war period.

Nundah Baptist Church was established as an "outpost" of Jireh Baptist Church in the 1880s. A dispute over who was eligible to participate in the Lord's Table resulted in the Nundah congregation establishing itself as a church in 1888. As Brisbane grew, so did the church. By 1923 a new larger building was required. By the 1950s the church was one of the largest Baptist churches in Brisbane boasting several hundred attendees. Between

1950 and 1969 the church planted three other churches:

- Banyo Baptist Church
- Wavell Heights Baptist Church
- Stafford Heights Baptist Church

However, the rigors of church planting and the demographic changes in the suburb took their toll. By the 1980s the church was in a serious state of decline. In the late 1980s there was discussion among the Nundah, Wavell Heights, and Clayfield Baptist Churches concerning amalgamation. However, when the pastor called to oversee the amalgamation of the three churches resigned for personal reasons, the impetus was lost and each church pursued its own strategy.

On 8 March 1993 the Nundah church inducted Pastor Ian Hussey and his wife Lynette. At that point of time, the church was composed of about 35 retirees and three young couples. One of those young couples left within the first six months. At the induction one of the deacons was overheard to say, "This is the last roll of the dice for this church. If things don't pick up we will close". Over the next six years there was slow but steady growth. By 1999 there were six young families in a congregation of about 60.

The Wavell Heights church had followed a similar life-cycle but on a smaller scale. By the late 1990s it too had dwindled to a largely retired congregation of about 30.

The crisis

In the mid-1990s the pastors of Nundah and Wavell Heights Baptist Churches had again begun tentative discussions about amalgamation. The proposal involved alternating the Sunday morning worship service between the two church properties. However, upon advice from a well respected denominational figure, the Wavell Heights church decided not to proceed with this model.

Figure 2: The Demolition of the Nundah Building

In 1998 approval was given for the construction of the Nundah bypass tunnel. After 35 years of discussion, the final route for the cut-and-cover tunnel construction required the resumption of four properties, including that of the Nundah Baptist Church. The church was given six months to relocate; however, finding a suitable venue for worship proved difficult. Under increasing pressure to find a new worship venue, the possibility of merging was again raised by the pastors of both churches at a men's dinner in mid-1998. From that point the merger process proceeded rapidly. On 1 November 1998, 60 adults from Nundah Baptist Church and 20 from Wavell Heights Baptist Church joined together to form the North-East Baptist Church.

For the first three years of its existence the newly formed church met in the property previously occupied by the Wavell Heights Baptist Church. However, delays in construction and a financial incentive from the property purchaser to settle prompted the church to move into a partnership arrangement with the Wavell Heights Uniting Church for nine months, where the two churches shared the Wavell Heights Uniting Church building.

The compensation from the Department of Main Roads and the sale of the now surplus Wavell Heights and Nundah properties were used to fund the construction of a new multi-million dollar complex on the reinstated church land in Nundah. Although growth was consistent from the time of the merger it accelerated sharply when the church moved into the new building in January 2003:

Figure 3: Average Church Attendance (Adults) 1999–2010

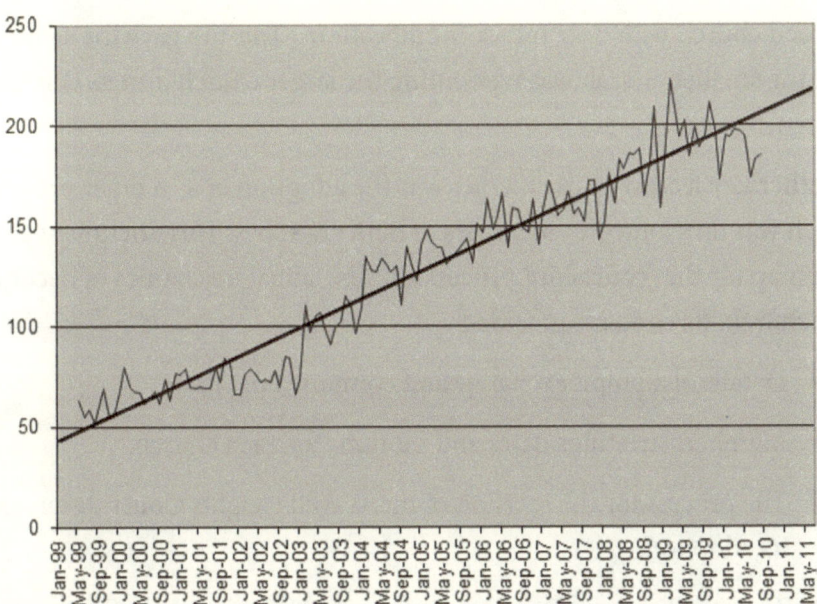

In the period following the merger the average age of the congregation fell sharply as numbers grew. The merger also allowed for the consolidation and rejuvenation of the properties of the church to create a new modern, low maintenance, air-conditioned complex. Although about ten people from the Wavell Heights Baptist Church and one from the Nundah Baptist Church did not join the new combined church for various reasons, there was no widespread sense of dissatisfaction either with the merger process or the new church that emerged. Anecdotally, almost from the time of the merger, the people from both churches believed that it had been a success and were happy with the decision to come together.

Features of this merger

Although Nundah was about three times the size of Wavell Heights Baptist at the time of merger, the effects of this disparity were mitigated to some extent because the smaller church welcomed the larger church into their building. Because the Wavell Heights Baptist Church Constitution had recently been revised it served as the basis for the constitution of the newly merged church with only minor modifications. This too gave the sense that the smaller church was welcoming the larger church into its corporate existence.

Another key feature of the merger was the adoption of a "merger program" which was distributed to members of both churches. This document gave a roadmap for the "courtship" process and the actual mechanics of becoming one church. Its contents included:

- Details of a pulpit exchange and combined picnic.
- Members meetings dates and motions for each church.
- The process for the revision of the Wavell Heights Constitution and its adoption.
- The establishment and functioning of a "Worship Style Committee" to clearly define the worship style of the new church.
- The details of the pastoral team: the Pastor of the Nundah Baptist Church would become the "Coordinating Pastor" of the new church and the Pastor of the Wavell Heights Baptist Church would become the Associate Pastor.
- The formation of a combined diaconate to lead the church for the first year.

One of the crucial issues resolved in the merger process was the role and function of the two pastors. In the initial discussion the pastor of the Wavell Heights Baptist Church, Rev. Dr Kelvin Cole, indicated that he had been sensing a call to move on from the church after about eight years of ministry. Hence it was resolved that the pastor of the Nundah Baptist Church would become the "Coordinating Pastor" and Rev. Dr Cole would be an Associate Pastor, pending his move to another church.

The final feature of the merger worth noting was a philosophy of allowing the ministries of both churches to run "in parallel" after the merger occurred. Although a small number of ministries needed to "merge" (for example the music teams) other ministries, like the play group ministry from Nundah Baptist and the seniors ministry from Wavell Heights Baptist, just continued normally after the merger.

Figure 4: The First Service of North-East Baptist Church, November 1998

Factors in the success

Rieland suggests that for mergers to be a success there has to be a definite sense that "God is in it".[9] There was a definite supernatural aspect to the merger process at North-East Baptist. The timing and the speed at which the merger process was planned and executed (less than six months) would seem to defy logic. Anecdotally many church mergers have been drawn out and problematic but that was certainly not the experience in this case.

However, in contradiction to Rieland's advice, this merger was marked by a sense of desperation on both sides. The Nundah Baptist Church had not been able to find a suitable building in which to operate once the building was resumed by the Department of Main Roads. Similarly, at the time of the re-conception of the merger idea, the deacons of Wavell Heights Baptist Church were considering the option of closing down the church. This sense of desperation in both parties was the driver for the merger negotiations and settlement. If this sense of desperation did not prevail it is doubtful whether the merger would have gone ahead.

Writers on the subject of change management often highlight the importance of "dissatisfaction" or crisis in driving a major change process (e.g., Kotter[10]). Although Rieland's warning about desperation is noted, it should be acknowledged that desperation can also be a powerful motivator for change as people set aside minor concerns in the face of a major crisis.

Once the merger had occurred its success became a driver for more success. At the very first combined church service after the merger, a new family visited and committed themselves to join the church. This young family became a symbol of the "rightness" of the decision to merge. As each new family joined the church the decision was affirmed again. This success became a source of enthusiasm, energy, and excitement in the congregation, which in turn made the congregation more attractive for newcomers. Hence a "cycle of growth" developed.

In order for nuclear fission to occur, a "critical mass" of fissionable material must be brought forcefully together. In a sense this is what happened at North-East Baptist Church. Both constituent churches lacked the "critical mass" to be attractive to church shoppers and non-Christian seekers. However, the combination of the two churches created a church of sufficient size to begin to attract and hold new people.

Figure 5: The Wavell Heights Church Building

The wise and powerful use of symbol was also an important factor in the success of the merger. On the Sunday prior to the merger, Nundah Baptist Church had a public final service. Hundreds of previous members attended a time of remembrance in celebration of the ministry of Nundah Baptist Church. This symbolic act brought a sense of closure and heightened the sense of new beginning in the merged church. A new North-East Baptist Church roll book, which every constituted member of the Nundah and Wavell Heights Baptist Churches signed, was also a powerful symbol of new beginning. The relocation of the sound system and drum kit from the Nundah Baptist Church to the Wavell Heights building for the first service was also symbolic of Nundah Baptist Church finding a new "home" in Wavell Heights.

The combined leadership of the church was a further symbol of unity. Both churches were equally represented on the diaconate and both churches had a member on staff. Even when the pastor from Wavell Heights left (eight months after the beginning of the merger), he was replaced on staff by a church administrator from the Wavell Heights church. This not only meant that both churches felt they had a conduit for communication, but served at a symbolic level as well.

Symbols can be very powerful influences on human emotions and behaviour. This is especially the case in times of trauma, for example at a funeral. Similarly, in the emotionally charged process of transition involved in a church merger, symbols can be extremely significant contributors to a sense of order and peace in the midst of liminality.

Another anxiety-reducing factor during the early stages of the merger was the development of structures. Structures bring security to human beings because they clarify expectations and create predictability. The Coordinating Pastor was naturally gifted in organisation and processes. This particular gift mix was extremely valuable in the midst of change. The carefully designed structures brought a sense of predictability and calmness to the church because each person knew what to expect. Similarly, an emphasis on communication also removed unpredictability in the early days of the church.

The contribution of the rejuvenated church facilities in Nundah to the growth of the church cannot be underestimated. Having a new air-conditioned, integrated and purpose-built facility was a key factor in attracting and holding new people to the church. However, this would not have been possible if the church merger had not occurred and the capital of the Wavell Heights church been released to be used for the development of the new building.

The final factor in the success of the merger was the similarity of the cultures of the two churches. Although there were some significant cultural differences (see below) the churches were largely compatible. This was not surprising given that Wavell Heights was a plant of Nundah Baptist Church. Although it had developed its own culture, on most issues the people from Nundah Baptist and Wavell Heights Baptist felt very much at home with one another.

Why it almost didn't work

Although the church cultures were largely compatible, there were a number of significant differences. The one difference that caused the greatest amount of tension was to do with church membership. At that time both churches practised closed membership — only people who were baptised by immersion as believers were eligible for church membership. However, a significant portion of the active members of Nundah Baptist Church were not formal members. Indeed, a number of non-members were leading ministries in the church.

The issue emerged during the work of the Constitutional Committee. The Wavell Heights Constitution prescribed that ministry team leaders would be church members. Given that a number of ministry team leaders from Nundah were not members this was an obvious cause of concern. Both sides were initially committed to their position. However, the phrase "normally be members" was a mutually acceptable compromise which saved the situation. It may be that the meaning of the wonderful word "normally" saved the entire merger process.

In the early stages of the merger small problems quickly polarised the congregation. The most significant polarisation reached its climax at a members meeting. A member from the Wavell Heights church announced there were serious issues which were threatening the ongoing viability of the merger. These matters were immediately deferred to the diaconate for resolution. Three or four issues were raised at the subsequent deacons meeting. Each was material, but not of major consequence. One issue was that pot plants had been placed in front of the speakers by someone from the Nundah church. The husband of the deacon who raised the concern had always told her that plants should never be placed in front of speakers. At the next members meeting the deacons were able to report to the members that the issues had been resolved.

Figure 6: The New Building

However, by far the most serious threat to the merger was a conflict between the two pastors. During the eight months when both pastors were still employed at North-East Baptist Church their relationship soured and eventually became dysfunctional. The underlying cause of the problem was the difficulties involved in two people who had previously been operating independently in solo leadership functions trying to both operate in the same organisation. In hindsight it was an incredibly difficult thing to do for the pastor of the Wavell Heights church to fulfil the role of an associate. This was aggravated by the fact that he knew that he was not going to be staying in the church long-term. The problem manifested by the Associate Pastor sensing that the Coordinating Pastor was trying to "force him out".

Had news of the conflict between the pastors become known in the congregation it no doubt would have polarised the congregation and may have destroyed the church. However, confidentiality was maintained and the Associate Pastor was able to move on to another church interstate. The Associate Pastor subsequently attended the opening of the new building and the relationship between the two pastors has been restored.

Conclusion

This chapter is a case study of one particular successful church merger. Its findings cannot be thoughtlessly generalised. Indeed, every merger will be unique and so it will never be possible to make generalisations about them. However, it is possible to at least identify some principles from this case which should inform those considering church mergers, without in any way being prescriptive.

First, church mergers are a viable option for church rejuvenation. Certainly the experience of North-East Baptist Church is that the merger dramatically rejuvenated the congregations and enabled them to do more together than they could have done individually. The merger was synergistic — the effectiveness of the whole was greater than the sum of the parts. The merged church was better equipped to fulfil its role in the mission of God, better reflected the heterogeneity of the Godhead and the body of Christ, and exercised improved stewardship of their God-given resources than was possible in the two previously independent churches.

A significant factor in the growth and rejuvenation of the church was the development of new facilities. Many asset rich/cash poor churches struggle to maintain their property, let alone develop them into the contemporary facilities expected by most twenty-first-century Australians. The North-East experience demonstrates the value of liquefying assets in order to develop new facilities.

In a sense mergers are inevitable for most declining Baptist churches in Australia. Unless something miraculous happens most small and declining churches will face the same fate as the dozens of others that have closed in recent decades. Generally when churches close, their remaining members dissolve into other churches and their assets are absorbed into the denominational body. These assets are obviously of great value and often find their way into new church plants. However, the tragedy of this scenario is that the human resources from the church that closes are lost.

If the declining church can find a way to merge with another church before it closes, these human resources can make a tremendous contribution to a dynamic new church. Older congregations can bring significant wisdom and cash-flow contributions to other churches. Further, a pre-emptive move to merger can bring a new vitality to a church member's life which will never occur if the church slips into closure.

It is probably inevitable that in most mergers one congregation will feel "overwhelmed" by the larger congregation. However, it is important to minimise this experience as much as possible. In seeking to understand the success of the North-East merger process, a sense of God's blessing, desperation, early success, good use of symbol and structure, and fairly similar cultures can be identified. All of these contributed in some way to protecting the members of the small congregation.

However, taking steps to foster a sense of peace and control in the midst of torrential change is a crucial factor for both congregations involved in a merger. Good structures and communication are ways of doing this, but there may be other methods that churches can utilise. However it is done, such a sense of peace and control can be a significant contributor to the success of church mergers.

This chapter has attempted to bring a theological perspective to a case study of a successful church merger. However, theologically justified or not, church mergers make practical sense. In an ideal world, and as it is in many parts of the world, churches are multiplying and growing constantly. Yet in the Australian context, both social and economic changes mean that small churches struggle to be viable. Merging is a better option than closing. Such church mergers require three factors: careful planning, sensitive wisdom, and divine intervention. However, these should not be an inhibitor of church mergers — all three of these factors are already strongly present in many Baptist churches.

Ian Hussey moved into pastoral ministry after working as a high school teacher for three years. Between 1993 and 2010 he was solo pastor of Nundah Baptist Church and then Senior Pastor of North-East Baptist Church, the merger of Nundah Baptist Church and Wavell Heights Baptist Church. Ian teaches at Malyon College in leadership, preaching, and New Testament. He also oversees postgraduate research and e-learning.

The Swan Island Peace Convergence
Embodied Mission, Inspired Community, and Costly Discipleship

Simon Moyle

For the last seven years a group of Christians has been engaged in embodied antiwar action at various sites around Australia. Since 2010 this has culminated in the Swan Island Peace Convergence, an annual five-day event in Victoria that focuses on interventional, nonviolent, direct action against Australian and US warmaking. It has grown from just eight people in 2010 to more than eighty in 2013, and includes a diverse range of people from many different walks of life taking prophetic action together that is both faithful to the gospel and politically effective. This chapter argues that the Swan Island Peace Convergence provides a potent and significant model not only for bearing witness to the gospel through activism, but also for community and discipleship formation. It also outlines the model that has been developed which brings together inclusive and engaged community, dynamic and embodied mission, and faithful and effective discipleship training.

The Swan Island Peace Convergence (SIPC) takes place at Queenscliff, Victoria, a sleepy historic military town on the Bellarine Peninsula. Just off Queenscliff is the Swan Island Army Detachment (SIAD), an "ultra secret clandestine warfare centre"[1] that houses the Australian Secret Intelligence Service (ASIS) and SASR-4, a secretive Special Air Service regiment that operates outside of declared war zones.[2] SIAD also functions as a training centre for elite Australian SAS soldiers who have been performing the bulk of Australia's combat and reconnaissance roles in the war in Afghanistan.

The primary purpose of the convergence is to cause measurable disruption to the workings of the Swan Island base, thereby impairing its ability to wage war. We also aim to further develop experience and training in nonviolent direct action to improve capability in future, and increase public awareness of the base and its role in clandestine warfare around the world.

For Christians involved in the SIPC, the aim is primarily to bear witness to the God revealed in Jesus Christ, and God's alternative to war, namely the nonviolent community we call the church. This is done through public ritual, prayer, nonviolent direct action, and the nature of engagement with people including members of the public, police, and the military.

Nonviolent direct action (NVDA) is a way of embodying discipleship by putting ourselves in the way of actions which oppose God's reign. NVDA is distinct from protest in that protest is merely the expression of opinion in an attempt to persuade those we see as being in a position to make change; NVDA, on the other hand, directly and physically intervenes in unjust actions in a way which stops or slows them, thus effecting a change (albeit temporary) without requiring recourse to elites.[3] Sustained intervention can, however, effect lasting change.

Organisation

The organising of the SIPC is done by a small core group. Here roles such as responsibility for meals, accommodation, first aid, running the children's program, police liaison, media spokespersons, etc. are decided. A registration system via the website includes transport options and on-site accommodation.

There is also a concurrent children's peace program, which weaves in and out of the adults' program. The children's program is put together by the children themselves, and run by volunteer parents or others with a valid Working With Children Check. The program includes kite flying (a popular pastime in Afghanistan), lantern-making, cooking, and reading nonviolent children's stories. When the blockade is in place and the space is safe, the children join the adults there for games, music, and other activities.

The program
Sunday

Sunday begins with introductions. This gives participants the opportunity to share why they have come, and hear others' passions and reasoning as well. This sets up a collaborative dynamic where everyone's voice is valued, and the reasons for our gathering reinforced.

We then go on a public peace walk together through the town of Queenscliff, which eases participants into public witness, enables us to announce our presence, and to proclaim the good news of peace. This takes place on the main street with a police escort.

In order for participants to act with integrity and have the ability to speak knowledgeably about the issues, we ensure all participants are well informed. To this end, on Sunday night we have information sessions on the Swan Island facility and its role in the war in Afghanistan, as well as a session on the war in Afghanistan itself. In more recent years we have asked the Afghan Peace Volunteers, a group of mostly young Afghans in Bamiyan and Kabul, to share with us the on-the-ground reality of the war for those most affected. These conversations take place via Skype, and enable interaction and questions on both ends of the conversation. They are able to address some of the complexities that the Western media has left unreported, and share their desires for an end to the wars through nonviolent means. This is always a very emotionally moving time.

Monday

A whole day is dedicated to nonviolence training, in which we cover the theory and practice of nonviolent action, as well as practising the tactic we intend to use (usually blockading). The morning is dedicated to theory, and understanding why nonviolent discipline is essential both tactically and morally. The afternoon includes blockade training, which enables people to practise where and how to sit or stand, and to experience the physical sensations involved before experiencing it in a real situation. As a result, participants can try out different roles, and are then able to make informed choices about their level and mode of participation. We also teach support and accountability for fellow activists. The training session finishes with an arrest workshop which includes a legal briefing by a lawyer, so that people are aware of their rights, the kinds of offences they might be charged with if they participate in certain actions, and what is likely to happen should they be arrested. This enables informed choices about the risks they are willing to take.

It also means that people go into the actions well prepared physically, mentally, and emotionally, and it is this which has made possible the high degree of nonviolent discipline, even in the face of police violence and provocation.

On Monday night the children lead us on a candlelight walk to the gates of the base, where they read statements made by Afghan children, such as, "We wish to live without war", and the Afghan proverb, "Blood cannot wash away blood". These statements are read by the children, and repeated by the adults, before observing a period of silence together.

Tuesday

There is only one way on and off the island by road, via a bridge and causeway. The bridge is guarded by security personnel and its entrance enclosed by a gate. Placing our bodies in front of the gate obstructs traffic from entering the facility.

The focus of the week's activities is attempting to block access to the base by soldiers and ASIS staff in order to disrupt the activities of the military and intelligence services. Blockading is done without mechanical or locking devices, just people's bodies linked to one another by arms, legs, and willpower in front of the gate.

Base workers tend to arrive from 7am onwards. To create and maintain a blockade we arrive an hour or so beforehand. The effectiveness of this tactic has varied according to numbers of both police and activists. As activist numbers have grown and police numbers declined, it has become more effective, such that the blockade has been successful since 2012, and has extended to the wharves as well as the causeway, thus preventing military personnel travelling to the island by boat.

At the end of (and often throughout) the two action days, we take time for debriefing and support.

Wednesday

Blockading continues on Wednesday morning, and depending on whether or not arrests are made, people may travel to Geelong for court or watchhouse support. In 2012 when no arrests were made, we planted a vine and fig tree on the public reserve beside the gate, with a liturgy and ritual involving the children. We then shared the Eucharist together.

In 2013, we changed our strategy and decided to make an attempt at planting the vine and fig tree inside the base. The blockade was maintained, and seventeen people made it through the gates onto the base.

Fifteen of these were arrested, but released immediately.

Thursday

On Thursday, participants have the opportunity to debrief on their experience of the week and share what they have learned. We reflect on what we have done well, as well as ways we can improve next year's event, and celebrate what has been achieved.

We also make plans for ongoing financial and emotional support for arrestees, and give self-care tips for all activists going home.

As mentioned at the outset, these events enable an inclusive and engaged community experience, dynamic and embodied mission, and faithful and effective discipleship training. I will now explain in more detail how these actions meet those goals.

Inclusive and engaged community

One of the features of the convergence is the deliberate inclusiveness of events. Almost the entire program includes children and parents, the elderly, and those with disabilities. The only exception is that children are not allowed to participate in the blockade while there is risk of arrest or injury. The children's program was designed by children to be both educational and engaging, particularly in long stretches where it would otherwise be boring for them. In this way, the convergence becomes a diverse, if temporary, community where all ages and stages are engaged.

Whether in the organising group or the convergence itself, decisions are made using a modified form of the consensus model. Usually one or more decisions are brought to the group when we are all together. The process generally follows this pattern: the facilitator elicits a proposal from the group, at which point there is an indication of agreement or disagreement from the group. If there is any disagreement, someone is invited to speak against the proposal, and make a counterproposal or modification of the original proposal. This continues until there is consensus, or the person with a disagreement steps aside. All voices are welcome to speak and there is usually a high rate of participation due to the high degree of investment in the outcome of decisions. Occasionally where such decisions would be unwieldy to make in the large group, there is a call for volunteers to form a subcommittee, the formation and members of which are ratified by the larger group. Any decisions made by the subcommittee need to be brought back to and confirmed by the larger group. For example, this was done in 2013 when a change in strategy was needed, as floating ideas and making strategy decisions in the larger group would have been too cumbersome. The subcommittee's suggestion was then brought back to the whole group for adoption.

While decisions that affect the whole group are made by consensus, more experienced activists are also at times released and encouraged to take tactical initiative, and support less experienced participants. This has given us much greater flexibility in tactics and the confidence to allow unplanned actions to take place. For example, in 2013, the wharf blockades were enabled through more experienced activists taking charge of small independent volunteer teams. Communication via mobile phones meant that everyone was able to be accounted for at all times, and resources could be deployed with flexibility as the situation changed.

It is therefore worth noting how authority functions in the group. While all ideas are welcomed and considered on their merits, weight is sometimes given to more experienced activists. Authority is therefore earned through experience, not based on position or role but on proven ability and respect.

Less experienced people who are identified as having potential are often given the opportunity and support to try out new roles. For example, we mentored two new people in being media spokespersons in 2013, giving them training and practice before easing them into the role.

Everyone is asked to pitch in with the cooking, dishes, cleaning, etc. with one or two people functioning as overall coordinators.

Much has been written about the alienation of males from church culture and the alleged "feminisation" of the church. One of the aspects of the SIPC that particularly appeals to male Christians is the sense of adventure, and the practical nature of this kind of action. While singing, prayer, and worship all take place, they are situated in a context of practical discipleship action. For example, some churches attempt to keep men involved by having laser tag or high ropes course activities. In contrast at SIPC, the adventure is discipleship rather than being merely tacked on as a form of entertainment to keep men interested in the rest.

Often in the life of a community, particularly temporary ones, a movement is made from being disparate individuals spending time together to a more cohesive community. We have consistently found that this happens in the blockade training. The experience (even in rehearsal mode) of willingly accepting personal risk and the necessity of bonding together for support and safety are key factors in this shift. It is also a great deal of fun, which helps participants to overcome their anxieties.

Dynamic and embodied mission

The SIPC functions as a form of mission to several groups. I will take each in turn.

Police and the law

One of the ways this event is different from other actions is the nature of engagement with police. While we talk through the role of police in protest situations, we also encourage people to engage nonviolently with them. This does not necessarily mean complying with their every direction, particularly where that direction contravenes our moral obligations, but it does mean being respectful and friendly towards them. We have countless examples of the way this engagement transforms the relationship between police and activists — from kicking a football with them to buying each other coffee. Spending whole days in the same place with the same police on multiple occasions enables a depth of relationship with individuals that is otherwise difficult to build or maintain. Some have even suggested their refusal to arrest us in recent years despite our refusal to cooperate with their demands has stemmed from the quality of this relationship.

The amount of time spent, often in close quarters with the police, allows for significant conversations to take place. For example, we have been able to challenge police to consider their role in upholding the unjust status quo. This also extends to theological conversations. In 2013 when I was being held after arrest, one embarrassed policeman took to threatening us.

"We're going to throw you in the cells", he said menacingly.

"Do you think we weren't expecting that?" I asked, somewhat surprised that he would think we'd be surprised. "That's where God is, mate."

"There's 25 people in there already", he said, presumably to intimidate me with the presence of other criminals.

"God is with them too", I responded.

Such exchanges give us the opportunity to challenge dominant ideas of where power lies and what it means to live justly and well.

Having said that, the police are not the primary targets of our actions, and therefore our engagement with them is primarily as witnesses who are opposing our attempts to disrupt the operations of the base. We have needed to repeatedly make this distinction clear to the police who often confuse our friendliness with compliance. They have also at times confessed to having been moved by the actions we have taken and the way we have taken them.

Court appearances also give us an opportunity, often in a more prepared way, to witness to our faith and the reasons for our actions. While we have occasionally taken Jesus' advice in Luke 21: 12–15[4] not to prepare a statement beforehand, most of the time we have prepared one in order to ensure we express ourselves well. Magistrates, who are used to sitting through case after case of selfish or thoughtless behaviour, are often unexpectedly delighted to hear a case of thoughtful actions driven by conscience.

Other activists

Activists, particularly those who identify with the political left, tend to be hostile to Christianity, seeing it as aligned with colonialism, oppression, privilege, hypocrisy, abuse, etc. For many of them, seeing Christians who are antiwar and prepared to put their bodies on the line to demonstrate it proves both unexpected and attractive. The Australian antiwar movement has for many years been led and sustained primarily by Christians, particularly in actions involving civil disobedience. It is primarily as a result of this sustained embodiment that these Christians now have the authority to talk about Jesus amongst secular activists without being dismissed or ridiculed.

"I haven't had much time for Christianity", one activist admitted to me after the peace convergence in 2013, "but watching you all walk over that bridge so calmly, with such peace, was utterly amazing to me. I've never seen anything like it".[5]

The church

Part of our mission is helping the church realise the radical implications of the story into which we have been engrafted. That Jesus is Lord is not just true for me, but for the whole cosmos. The church has been charged with the task of bearing witness to that reality.

Often Christians who become involved in social justice issues assume that liberal theology comes along with it. The tension between the Christian worldview and that of secular activists means that liberalism can be a means of avoiding conflict as we work together. But there are those of us who do this work because of our faith who believe the gospel is such good news we *cannot* remain silent about it. For this reason, a significant proportion of the growth of the SIPC has been from evangelical Christians who want to make a difference in the world, but also want to remain evangelical. It can be a difficult balance to avoid alienating secular activists in the process, but so far that balance has been maintained.

This gives evangelical Christians a means of embodying their faith authentically without having to hide its Christian impetus. We want to encourage the church to see NVDA as not just a legitimate, but also a *desirable* expression of Christian discipleship in a world which does not recognise the lordship of Christ. NVDA gives us the means not only to express Christ's lordship with our words, but embody it with our lives.

Participants are encouraged to share their stories with the church through speaking engagements in our own communities and denominations, writing for online and print publications and other Christian media, and sharing with their Christian friends through social media.

The military

Engagement with the military is very limited due to military personnel avoiding contact. We generally take what little opportunity we get to express our personal concern for them, as people who are at risk of both killing and being killed. It is also an opportunity to remind them that they are moral agents who are able to make choices for themselves despite the military's claim that they must obey orders.

The general public

In recent years we have made engagement with the people of Queenscliff a priority so as to increase understanding on both sides. Particularly given the parochial nature of small towns, and Queenscliff's pride in their military history, our presence was always going to be challenging. We also understand that most people invest a significant degree of their personal and societal security in the functioning of Australia's military, and that our actions challenge that functioning. This is not inconsistent with our mission — Jesus provided significant challenge to the idols of his age, and people were angry enough with that challenge to kill him. It is important though that we take time to listen to the concerns of the people of the Bellarine peninsula, and that we calmly explain our own concerns and the reasons for our actions. While some continue to express their anger, others (particularly as the war in Afghanistan became less popular) have warmed to our presence.

In terms of media, far from being an opportunity to spread our message, we generally have little control over how our actions are interpreted and reported (mostly negatively and superficially); and the few opportunities we have to speak in the media are sometimes devoted to refuting spurious and inaccurate claims. Our actions do, however, speak for themselves to some degree, and there have been occasions when our motives and methods have been accurately communicated, but largely the mainstream media is not our main vehicle for expression.

Faithful and effective discipleship training

As Christians we are engrafted into the ongoing story of God's redemption of the world, and it is through this story that we learn to understand the world. This is why it is essential for us to teach participants in SIPC, particularly those who are Christian, to make sense of the world through the story of the Bible, rather than making sense of the Bible through the world's categories and ideas.

Learning from nonviolent Christian movements in history such as the civil rights movement, we learn to read our world and place ourselves in archetypal biblical stories such as the exodus and exile. For example, in the September 2013 incursion while being pursued by police we had to make our way through knee-deep water to enter the military facility. I encouraged activists to "wade in the water, like the children of the

Israelites", alluding to the Israelite escape from Egypt through the Red Sea. I later learned it was this way of making sense of our current predicament, with police bearing down on us, which gave other activists the resolve and courage to move into and through the water to the other side. In this way the Bible comes alive not as an irrelevant historical document, but as the living word for us today, as we learn to recognise God's faithfulness to his people in every age.

My experience has been that Australian churches, particularly those dominated by the middle classes, often provide a spiritualised gospel which is merely for the inner realm of the individual. Rarely do they provide the kind of challenge to our social, economic, and political systems that Christianity entails. As a result, most Christians lead lives that are not significantly different to their neighbours, despite a claimed difference in worldview.

The church therefore needs practices that continue to recognise, celebrate, and embody the story into which we have been engrafted; the story which makes us peculiar, and therefore different from both secular activists and the mainstream culture. Such practices form the training necessary for us to be faithful Christians. The Swan Island Peace Convergence attempts to provide some such training, including the following practices.

Morning and evening prayer

Each year we attempt to maintain a rhythm of morning and evening prayer. This is most difficult on the mornings where blockading happens, but most other days it is the last thing done before bedtime and the first thing done after rising. This gives stability to each day, encourages the recognition of God's presence with us throughout the day's events, and provides space and time for stillness amidst the action. It also deepens the meaning of phrases and liturgies that have sometimes been prayed ritually for years. For those of us in privileged First World circumstances to pray the psalms with the prospect of arrest looming, or lines from the Daily Office such as,

"In peace we will lie down and sleep
for you alone, O Lord, make us dwell in safety"

carry considerably more meaning than they would when prayed under ordinary circumstances.

Nonviolence training

The training enables people to explore the theory of nonviolence, and practise the kinds of scenarios they will face, and find their centre. This develops confidence, and often makes the difference in being prepared or unprepared to do civil disobedience.

It is difficult to challenge our socialisation into compliance to authority figures. Doing so calmly and in a measured and discerning way is even more challenging. The training enables the practice of calm, centred, nonviolent resistance, even when police are being violent, threatening, or provocative. In 2012, it was those who were doing resistance for the first time who first walked back onto the road after police had dragged them off, and they did so calmly but with great determination. In the 2013 incursion, people remained centred and walked patiently all the way into the military base with police and security present. That kind of peaceful, determined resistance is rare and valuable, but is the embodiment of the kind of nonviolence Jesus demonstrated.

Nonviolent direct action

We encourage people to see our actions as a faithful incarnation of God's story rather than merely ratbag behaviour or even action for social justice. It is out of our experience of God's love and call to be a people of peace and reconciliation that we put ourselves in the way of our country waging war on our brothers and sisters in other countries. Such actions push us out of our comfort zone, teach us reliance on God, and give us an experience of solidarity with our suffering brothers and sisters.

Arrest

The Bible also provides us with stories that make sense of arrest, trial, and jail for acts of principled civil disobedience (or divine obedience). Just as Jesus and the apostles were arrested, tried, and jailed for bearing witness to Christ and his kingdom, so also we should expect a similar fate. Jesus himself says in Matthew 25 that when we visit those in prison it is visiting him. This helps make sense of such choices in a world that teaches us to avoid suffering and obey all authorities without question. This has led to a disproportionately high number of Christians among those taking actions which risk arrest at SIPC.

Jesus repeatedly defines discipleship in terms of the cross, insisting that his way will be costly for us. The cross names not merely any difficulty in the life of a disciple, but was the social and political price of loyalty to God's kingdom rather than the world's. As John Howard Yoder has put it, "The cross of Calvary was not a difficult family situation, not a frustration of visions of personal fulfilment, a crushing debt or a nagging in-law; it was the political, legally to be expected result of a moral clash with the powers ruling his society".[6] We therefore see arrest for civil disobedience as an occupational hazard for Christians.

We see Romans 13 as a call to submit to whatever punishment the State might mete out as a result of remaining faithful to Christ, rather than a blanket call to obey the State unconditionally.

Ritual

Planting a vine and fig tree has become a yearly ritual at the SIPC. In began in 2012 in the park next to the main gate of the base, where all participants joined together in a circle. Here we made the connections between climate change, poverty, and war through the ancient symbols of vines and fig trees, connections made in the prophets Isaiah and Micah of a day when:

"They will beat their swords into ploughshares
and their spears into pruning hooks.

Nations shall not lift up sword against nation,
neither shall they learn war anymore.

But they shall all sit under their own vines
and under their own fig trees

and no one will make them afraid
for the mouth of the Lord of Hosts has spoken." Micah 4:3–4

In planting a vine and fig tree on or beside a military base, we enact this prophesy and give imagination to the alternative world God is calling into being in Christ. We bear witness to an end to war and the preparation for war, to what it looks like to care for God's creation, and to economic self-sufficiency, all of which are under threat as a result of the military.

Eucharist

Along with the vine and fig tree planting, all of us share the Eucharist together as one body in remembrance of bodies broken and blood shed by wars, poverty, and climate change. We maintain an open table for this, which invites others into the significance of this sacrament of remembrance in a way that is meaningful for all of us, contextually appropriate, and faithful to its intention. We remember Jesus' body broken and blood shed in order to make peace, in contrast to the world's peace made through shedding others' blood; we also remember others whose bodies have been broken and blood shed as victims of war.

Singing

Much has been written on the importance of singing for social movements. Songs allow us to remember, internalise, and publicly express narratives that could otherwise be difficult to remember. In particular we have found that spirituals have a simple structure that allows for them to be adapted to the circumstances, while maintaining a deep sense of tradition.

Songs such as *Wade in the Water, Down by the Riverside, We Shall Not Be Moved*, and *Oh Mary Don't You Weep* are all based in biblical imagery which places our baptismal commitments in the context of embodied political struggle and costly discipleship. The words and ideas have a formative effect, even as the process of singing them unites and bonds the group.

For example, at the 2013 SIPC as arrestees were released from custody one by one, we gathered around them and sang the following adapted spiritual, with the arrestee's name filling in the blank:

> As I went down to Swan Island to pray
> Studyin' about that good old way
> And who will stop this ugly war?
> O Lord show me the way
> Oh _____ let's go down,
> Let's go down, come on down
> Oh _____ let's go down,
> Down to Swan Island to pray.

This constituted an expression of solidarity, as well as an honouring of the risks each person had taken by placing themselves in an arrestable position, but most importantly it placed each person's actions in the context of an ongoing struggle for justice (with reference to the history of spirituals) and of their baptismal vows (down to the *river/island* to pray).

When I've been put in the cells, I often find the first thing that emerges from me is singing. Having memorised worship songs helps makes sense of being there, is a source of comfort and strength, and connects us to what Rev. Dr Martin Luther King Jr called the "cosmic companionship of Christ".

Hospitality and sharing meals together

Living and eating together is a prime community-building opportunity to deepen relationships and build connections. As Christ shared meals with rich and poor, and his followers in the early church pooled their resources to do the same, so we gather with diverse people around a common table.

Conclusion

What if churches took direct action to change some of the most egregious injustices of our times?

What if churches got in the way of the coal transports that are fuelling our climate crisis? What if old and young Christians together blocked the coal seam gas drills that are destroying farmers' livelihoods and contaminating our food and water supply? What if a new Christian sanctuary movement nonviolently rescued asylum seekers from appalling detention facilities and took them into our own homes? What if churches blockaded pokies venues until they were no longer financially viable? And what if we were prepared to see the costs of these actions as what it looks like to take up our cross and follow Jesus?

What kind of potent witnesses would we be to the alternative world that has come into being in Christ?

I can't help wondering whether the church might be in a better position to tell of the difference Jesus makes for our lives if we had more proof. The church has the resources to do any or all of these things — it has the people, it has the money, it has the practices to sustain such actions over the long haul, and it has the support structures. Most of all, it has surrounding and undergirding it the God who created the universe, whose Spirit "is able to do immeasurably more than all we ask or imagine, according to his power that is at work within us".[7] Our brothers and sisters around the world face grave dangers, and if we are to demonstrate

God's "complete" love to them, a love that extends not only to us and our neighbours but even our enemies, then that love has to be practical.

Rev. Simon Moyle is an Elder at GraceTree, a Baptist church in Melbourne. He is an antiwar activist who trains churches, schools, and activist groups in nonviolent direct action. Simon is passionate about equipping the church to embody Jesus' alternative politics. He is married to Julie and has four children.

Imagining a Renewed Story at AuburnLife
Utilising Congregational Timelines for Congregational Transformation

Darren Cronshaw

Drawing a congregational timeline and mapping local church history is a useful exercise for congregational transformation. It helps a church understand its story: its origins, narrative highlights, key characters, crises, and values. It can also help a church see its narrative in the context of biblical tradition, church history, and societal and church trends. This chapter evaluates processes for inviting a congregation to map their narrative timeline, develops and trials an exercise with AuburnLife, and evaluates the results. One result is a locally produced storyline of Auburn's history. The appreciative inquiry questions of the exercise revealed distinctive features of the church's history that are also values for current and future mission: especially being a leadership farm and a space for multicultural hospitality. The aim of the exercise, ultimately, is to imagine a renewed story — to utilise congregational narratives for congregational transformation. It aims to help a congregation get in touch with their own congregational narratives (using appreciative inquiry and storylines), in order to practically help the church imagine fresh vision and new mission directions.[1]

Imagination-grabbing stories

In the book and movie *The Fault in our Stars*, Augustus Waters asks, "So what's your story?" Hazel Gray replies, "I was diagnosed when I was 13". Augustus cuts her off: "No, no, not your cancer story. *Your* story. Interests, hobbies, passions, weird fetishes, etcetera". She replies, "Ummm … I am pretty unextraordinairy". "I reject that out of hand," he says.[2] I love that scene. Part of my role as a pastor is to help my church to explore their extra-ordinary story and get a glimpse of God's presence and purposes.

Helping a church get in touch with its story or stories is critical for helping it understand its identity and mission. For anyone who wants to see a declining or plateaued church transition towards revitalisation, a good place to start is to take the church on a journey of discovery about where it has come from and where it has functioned at its best. The idea is not to dwell long in a celebration of the past, but to identify key themes to empower the church for mission today and to prepare for innovations for the future.

Church planter J. R. Woodward suggests that a church's narrative gives clues about where God is calling, asking: "As you consider the congregation you serve, is the narrative of the community shaping people to love Christ more, be more like him and deeply engage the world in order to see God's kingdom become a greater reality?"[3] He counsels asking about the different stories that shape the church, of which there are three groups. Firstly, what Bible stories does the church focus on, and how do those stories help them love God, and their neighbours and enemies? Secondly, what history stories from the church are rehearsed? Thirdly, what missional stories from current experience are retold? These three sets of stories help identify what a church values.[4] Future writing may explore improvising a renewed story at AuburnLife through the biblical narrative and living an alternative story as a witnessing missional community. This initial chapter follows Woodward's second group of questions about a church's narratives and especially its history stories that are rehearsed in order to frame congregational discussions and to structure evaluation of how these stories shape congregational transformation.

AuburnLife's congregational narrative

A central aspect of imagining a renewed story is inviting a church to reflect on its own historical narrative. What is the church's history? What history stories are rehearsed? What does its timeline look like? Drawing a congregational timeline and mapping its history is a useful exercise for congregational transformation. It helps a church understand its story — its origins, narrative highlights, key characters, crises, and the values that continue to shape the church. A timeline can illuminate a congregation's values because it shows how a church is formed through its founding personalities and events, which is what gives it an inheritance for how it functions and who it attracts.[5] It may also help a church see its historical narrative in the context of the biblical story it follows on from, broader church history and societal trends, and even the local neighbourhood and denominational histories.[6] Furthermore, in a post-Christian society, it is important to explore how far we see our story within a foundational Christian metanarrative, and what its relationship is to other competing (counter-)narratives of late/post modernity.[7] It would be helpful to explore what authority different narratives hold for the church community as a group. They are issues for further exploration. But the basic aim in drawing a timeline of a congregational narrative — which is what this chapter does — is to identify a church's vision, values, and identity through its history, and to discuss how to incarnate that for the future — to imagine a renewed story.

As an exercise in congregational transformation at AuburnLife, and to evaluate the process, we conducted a congregational timeline exercise on 11 May 2014, and followed it up with further teaching on "This is My/Our Story". The method of the exercise was twofold. Firstly, I conducted an oral history interview with David and Joanna Hughes, who have been at the church for forty-one years. David was deacon, secretary, and/or treasurer for forty of those years. Secondly, I invited the congregation one Sunday morning to reflect on their experience at Auburn. Both methods used appreciative inquiry (AI). Some consultancy approaches assume weakness and dysfunction in a church rather than looking firstly for strengths and potential. The use of imagination, memories, and stories in AI is a more positive strategy for navigating change.[8] Thus, my questions to David and Jo Hughes were about how the church functioned at its best at different times, what different ministers were most appreciated for, who other significant people were, and where the church was at its best in mission and worship.

The congregational timeline exercise was similarly framed around appreciative questions:

1. When did you first come to church here and what did you notice and appreciate about the church that made you want to join?

2. In your opinion, where and how has the church been at its best over the time you have belonged here?

3. What are the most significant events and people that characterise the history of your church as you know it?

4. What was going on in your community/ culture/ wider church at different times of the church's history, and when has the church been at its best in being relevant to those external factors?[9]

The room was set up with photos of old pastors and deacons, and with communion chairs and their memorial plaques to inspect. Participants were encouraged to gather in small groups with people representing different lengths of time at Auburn, e.g., a visitor or newcomer in the last year, someone who joined the church in the last few years, someone who came four years ago with the change of pastors, and someone who was here for more than four years. The groups were invited to discuss their responses to these questions in small groups.

To transition into the timeline exercise, people were invited to line up along the timeline laid out on tables according to when they came to the church — from the Hughes at one end forty-one years ago, through to a couple who were visiting for the first time (and only time as it turned out) that morning. Everyone explained the year they arrived. I gave an overview of the church's history, underlining the main periods discussed below. Then I invited everyone to ask questions of those who had been around longer, and to write history, draw pictures, or paste photos on the timeline as a group project.

What was most interesting about interviewing David and Joanna Hughes, and reading previous pastor Ross Morgan's historical summary of the church, was noticing ways that earlier patterns and interests were repeated.[10] I mentioned these trends in the service and we discussed them as we worked on the timeline.

Founding era, early glory days, and decline 1887–1949

In July 1887, sixteen people met in the Hawthorn Town Hall and resolved to start a Baptist church. In August they started services. In February 1888 they constituted as a Baptist church, and moved to the current site. In their first three years, Auburn was a hive of church-planting initiatives, helping plant Hawthorn West and Camberwell Baptist Churches. In the first eight years the church grew rapidly, and by 1895 had 237 members and 331 Sunday School scholars. However, numbers declined from that high point of attendance. By 1942 membership was down to 94, then down to 79 in 1953, and 48 in 1957. The church found it difficult to pay a full stipend from then.[11] So the founding era and glory days came early and close on top of one another, followed largely by decline, and a plateaued history since, with a couple of resurging periods of revitalisation. The church is a typical inner-suburban church story, which started strong on the outskirts of the city, but as the city grew it has had to reinvent itself to survive and thrive.

Generosity with buildings

The church has an interesting, informally attached relationship with its buildings. In 1846 the site had been left to the Congregational and Baptist denominations and a church chapel built in 1866 (notably only three years after Collins Street Baptist built their present church which is Australia's oldest Baptist place of worship still used as a church). The place of worship of the Auburn Baptist Church was built in the normal Gothic revival architectural style of the time, used for most churches, e.g., characterised by pointed arches. Moreover, Auburn's place of worship has three stained-glass windows — a feature shared only with Armadale among Victorian Baptist churches. Baptists did not like the Gothic architectural style because of their aversion to and persecution from inherited denominations.[12] But the building was first built and used by the Congregationalists, initially as a place of worship and then as a Sunday School. They had relocated across the road to a larger new building for worship services, making room for the Baptist church in 1888, which later took full possession in 1921. David Hughes said the *basilica* predated the *ecclesia* in that Auburn Baptist inherited an existing church building. Basically the trust deed for the church stated it was to be used for non-conformist worship, and the Baptists negotiated with the Congregationalists that they were better placed to use it for worship since the Congregationalists were only using it for Sunday School.[13] The handover was friendly, reflecting healthy ecumenical cooperation that was part of Auburn's early years. Another generous handover of property was to occur later.

After the Baptist church took over the site in 1888 they extended the auditorium, into the area that is now the kitchen and vestry. The 1890 foundation stone lies at the base of the extended church building. As Baptists, they changed from the Neo-Gothic style of the original chapel to a Neo-Classicist or Greek Revival style; built it in a Spurgeon-like "tabernacle" form of building, including dentils in cornices still there in the Boreham library upstairs. As Ken Edmonds commented, Baptist non-conformist architecture reflected non-conformist political and theological reasons.[14] Auburn's plan was to complete the other two-thirds of a master plan, expanding the current sanctuary first and then stretching the "tabernacle" out to the front.

The church later realised they could not afford nor would likely need the master plan extension. But in 1930 the church was renovated and a front porch added. In the 1960s the sanctuary was remodelled again while Milton Warn was pastor. They turned the "back" of the building, where the choir and pulpit and front of the sanctuary worship space used to be, into a new kitchen and offices. A disabled-access toilet now exists where the old kitchen used to be. In that renovation, they removed the old organ that had been a pedal and then blower organ.[15]

In 1971 Australian Baptist Missionary Society (ABMS, now Global Interaction) leased the offices, renovated, and opened them as "Moore Potter House" in 1972, and then bought the building in 1978.[16] The handover involved ABMS paying the church $2 for the building, but promising reversal usage rights, maintenance, and utilities covered, and a quarterly financial payment back to the church for however long the church existed. This left the church with no significant assets to bank on, but a solid foundation for ministry without having to worry about buildings.

Following the church centenary in 1988, a conversation began with ABMS to explore renovating the church's place of worship. ABMS organised this in 1989 (with the Lyons Brothers as architects from Geelong). They put a bluestone feature wall and cross at the front of the sanctuary, and replaced the old underfloor baptismal with an above-floor fibreglass baptismal which made more room for ABMS in their offices below. ABMS and the church also replaced the front wooden doors with glass doors, and replaced the lawn out the front of the church with a car park.[17] In 1995, having received a donation from the family of Frank R. Boreham (basically royalties from his prolific writings), ABMS filled in the space above the ceiling out the back and turned it into the Boreham library, training and resource centre, and added the existing kitchen and toilets.[18] Architect Ken Edmonds designed this "Boreham training centre". There is still another additional upper floor of space that could be developed.[19] ABMS, now as Global Interaction, has also upgraded the lower ground floor offices and their offices on the first floor, which continue to host their national headquarters staff and operations.

The other building the church has use of, but does not own, is the "Sutton Brae" manse. Hedley Sutton, legendary ABMS missionary to India, built it after returning home to Melbourne to be Vice Principal of Carey Baptist Grammar School from 1929. Hedley became a life-deacon of Auburn in 1939 and died in 1946, and when his wife Elsie died in 1951 she left the house to the Baptist Union of Victoria to be held in trust and for the use as a manse for the pastor of Auburn, or for BUV staff, ABMS missionaries, or Carey teachers, in that priority order. Auburn has been using it since as a manse, and only has to pay for maintenance and utilities.[20]

Leadership farm (student pastor years 1950–1989)

At least 42 pastors have served Auburn over its 126 years, 1888–2014. Thus the average length of service is 3.0 years. In the glory days it was easy for the church to support a full-time pastor. But in the four decades 1950–1990, most of the pastors were student or interim pastors.

There were at least thirteen student pastors who served between six interim pastors and six other "permanent" pastors (though two of those stayed for less than a year). The average pastoral tenure over this period was just under two years. In the late 1950s BUV encouraged a joint pastorate with West Hawthorn, to no effect, but Home Mission subsidised the stipend of Rev. Mills 1957–1959. Then the church sold its tennis courts in 1960, which helped the finances. But Mills was the last full-time pastor, apart from one short exception (again with BUV assistance). ABMS, in conversation with Whitley, looked after pastoral appointments for most of the 1970s and 1980s. They would recommend to the church a student or interim pastor who served while studying at Whitley and living in the manse. Prof. Basil Brown from Whitley and J. D. Williams the ABMS Director were supportive and regular speakers. But it is interesting that for a significant chapter of Auburn's life Auburn saw themselves as an ideal setting for student pastors. Today the church also prides itself on being a "leadership farm" and giving leaders-in-training experience for future service.

Another strength of the church has been faithful lay leaders, albeit at times few and declining in number. When David and Jo Hughes came in 1972, Gavin Collinson was the student pastor. But the more influential figures were the team of deacons: Lola Cameron, Merle Rees, Florence Potter — whose relative, Rev. Ron Potter, was a missionary who drowned and after whom "Moore Potter House" is named[21] — and Doris Wilkin, who had come to the church when a boarder from Kerang at MLC, and is still a member and life deacon (although at 106 years old, she now lives nearby at Karana Nursing Home and no longer attends). Within a year of arriving, David joined this team of women, serving for 40 years as deacon, secretary, and/or treasurer. Another woman, Sue Hammond, joined the team and served as secretary for one period. The team dwindled in numbers, but the survival of the church is a tribute to them.

Hospitality and an increasingly multicultural church (1988–2010)

When David and Jo Hughes first arrived in 1972, they remember the church as a smallish church, with a core of locals, and a few overseas Swinburne students, mainly Malaysian Chinese Christians, and then some Vietnamese and Korean people. For example, Steven Din had been brought to Melbourne by the Air Force to train RAAF pilots at Point Cook, and could not return after the war so married and stayed in Australia and worshipped at Auburn. Apart from some earlier Chinese members, Steven was one of the first of the culturally diverse members of Auburn, and many others have come and gone since. Today the church continues to be a place of multicultural hospitality to students and migrants, focused through the ministry of "AuburnHub" hospitality space and English classes. The shift towards hospitality and an increasingly multicultural church happened during the ministry of the last student pastor.

Ross Morgan served at Auburn February 1987 – June 1990. Although officially a student pastor, he broke the mould of previous students because he had completed his theology degree at Bible College of Victoria before coming to Whitley (and Auburn), and he stayed longer as pastor, including eight months after his ordination. Morgan started with a congregation of eight people. After a year of little change, he collected census data and studied local demographics, noticing a large local student and transient population. He presented the church with what he saw as their options — to change or to close. They were unanimous and determined not to close, and accepted the need for change. They totally refurbished the sanctuary, including replacing the pews with chairs and carpeting the floors, and updated the constitution. More significant than cosmetic changes, however, was an influx of students that the church received with hospitality. A new Korean member, Kim, had come to Melbourne to study English and computing. He was also keen and evangelistic about his faith, and was the main influence in bringing in twenty students from eight nationalities. The church experienced its biggest revitalisation that I know about. When Morgan left in June 1990, there were 38 people from 17 nationalities making the church their home.[22]

Moreover, in 1990 the church changed from mostly student pastors to then calling a series of permanent pastors and a few interims. The longer serving permanent pastors increased the average length of pastoral tenure at the church from what had been an average of two years over 1950–1990 to four years, 1990–2014, or 7+ years if interims and co-pastoring are not factored in. Each of these pastors also helped Auburn grow as a place of hospitality and increasing cultural diversity.

Rev. Keith Pickett (1990–1998) was the first permanently called pastor for at least a decade. He is also the only full-time pastor since 1961, helped for a time by BUV support that was not able to continue. Pickett started Bible studies at the manse and he and his wife Coralie were appreciated for their hospitality and social outings. The church grew and experienced further revitalisation, including a good number of students, especially Indonesians. Cei Cai Yip, a Swinburne student from Malaysia, arrived in 1993, and is still living locally and worshipping with the church. A Romanian congregation came, initially just to use the property, but Keith supported them and preached in their services. One family from the Romanian congregation continues to worship at Auburn, but the church itself has relocated to the outer south-eastern suburbs. Pickett was also chaplain and hosted at Auburn the inter-church "Twenties-plus" young adults group, and introduced an electronic sign on the back wall of the church which thousands of train-line travellers could see every day. Coralie Pickett also befriended some locals while walking their dog, including Eunice (who is still a member though cannot attend services after 2012), and another generous-hearted neighbour. The significant lesson from the Picketts' ministry is the eagerness and life that comes to the church in connecting with students and people of other cultures, and the potential of witness simply living in and sharing life (and dogs) in the neighbourhood.[23]

Rev. Keith Adams (six months in 1998) and his wife Dawn and family emigrated from South Africa, and Auburn was their first appointment for a short-term or interim arrangement, but they helped the church become more multicultural and less prejudiced.

Neil Jayasuria (1999–2000) was an interim pastor for six months, extended to twelve months, and Auburn provided a gracious context to help Jayasuria settle back into ministry after a time out of ministry and out of the country.

Rev. Jillian Stewart (2000–2009) had been a teacher and then chaplain at Carey, and was teaching in India when the church called her for three days per week. She is remembered and appreciated for her entertaining and Bible studies in the manse, preaching and community building, and connecting with students. Jillian initiated weekly volunteer English classes at Swinburne, in partnership with St Columb's Anglican Church and others. She also persevered in leading the church and services with limited lay leaders.

Over 2003–2009 it was only David Hughes who served as a deacon (and combined secretary/treasurer) alongside the pastor. Jillian Stewart encouraged and recruited Jackie Murphy as a deacon in 2009, and so there were two lay-leaders when the church called the Cronshaws.

Replanting a mission-shaped multicultural church (2010–2014+)

Darren and Jenni Cronshaw (2010–) came initially as a team of co-pastors. Jenni resigned her employment in June 2011, staying involved in the church, and Darren continues to lead as a two-day-per-week pastor. Turning to autobiographical reflection here, the highlights of Auburn ministry come in yearly points of celebration.

The highlight of 2010 was forming and building a leadership team, growing from three to seven that year, and at one later stage up to ten leaders, as others came to Auburn to help replant the church.[24] Part of negotiating a call to Auburn included Auburn talking to Kew Baptist about sending some young adults over to help replant Auburn: Mark Payne and Irene Schuringa (who married later in 2010), and Tim Hunter and Beth Rumble (who married later in 2012). Others came from other churches too, initially Rob and Sue Hand from Canterbury. They were attracted by the invitation to come and dream about rediscovering church and mission. We turned the church worship space around to face sideways with a semi-circular interactive format. Those who come and stay often say they appreciate the interactive format of our gatherings, and permission to question and express doubt and struggle as well as faith and hope. The church adopted the BUV model constitution and at the same time changed to be "open-membership" in welcoming people who had been baptised in another church tradition, whether or not immersed as adults. The church felt optimistic with a new team and plans for the future.

In 2011 "Claire" and "Shane" tentatively walked in off the street, were surprised by the welcome and hospitality of the church, did an Alpha course, and were baptised. But it was almost the whole church that was involved as a community in leading them to Jesus.[25] As a couple, they helped redesign the church website and logo as we changed the name to "AuburnLife". Also in 2011 Mark Payne and Robyn Song started as interns. A Swinburne PhD student, Wei, started a Bible study on campus and invited a number of Swinburne international staff and students along to Auburn. Rob Hand led the church in joining in with St Columb's Anglican Church's "SPL Cricket" which connected with international and especially Indian students.[26] The church was pleased it was functioning well as a community in evangelism.

In 2012, Mark Payne and Robyn Song completed their internships. Mark finished by serving as interim pastor for four months while the Cronshaws were on long-service leave, and then went on in early 2013 to serve as a pastor at Northern Community Church of Christ. Robyn finished as she transitioned to AuburnHub coordinator. Mark Payne coordinated "Sunday Stuff" with Julia Rhyder, who had come to the church in 2011 with Tim Rhyder, and who also moved on in early 2013 to study a PhD in biblical studies in Lausanne, Switzerland. It was a proud moment for the church as it saw new leaders grow and go into other ministries, but it was also a reminder to make the most of the time anyone spends at Auburn — to nurture their faith and leadership potential as they will likely only be with us for a period.

In 2013 the church started "AuburnHub" hospitality space and English classes for international students on Tuesdays. With the help of a Baptcare community grant, the church employed Robyn Song to coordinate the

Hub, with a team of volunteers including Tim Hunter, who had been in the church since 2010 but did an internship in 2013 focusing on community ministry, AuburnHub, and SPL cricket. Robyn worked to develop good relationships with campus groups, and led a Friday night Bible study that met sometimes on campus and sometimes at the church. Towards the end of the year, the Hub developed a good relationship with Carey students who volunteered and helped with a new "Homework club" that was trialled Tuesday afternoon after school. The church was pleased with this community ministry program and the way it expressed multicultural hospitality and outreach to Swinburne.

In 2014 the church looked forward to what else God was preparing to do. The highlight of the year was surprisingly to welcome Indonesian and Chinese congregations to share the use of our place of worship. AuburnLife is exploring partnering in mission with both groups and not just sharing space. The Indonesian ministry, "Garam Ministry Melbourne", has two other congregations and started a new congregation at Auburn as their third congregation, meeting on Saturdays to complement their other groups in other parts of Melbourne.[27] The Chinese, Mandarin-speaking congregation is a new church plant which meets on Sunday afternoons. AuburnLife as a church aspires to be "growing as a vibrant multicultural, mission-shaped community". We say if we could do only one thing well, we would want to offer a space of hospitality and witness to international students, and if we can also be a leadership farm as part of that journey, that is ideal. As the church looks at its congregational narrative, it sees that being a leadership farm and a multicultural community are not new and novel ideas, but part of an inherited ethos.

What are your missional stories to celebrate?

The congregational timeline exercise helped identify what people appreciated about their time at Auburn — ranging from lots of discussion to a church camp, from thoughtful Easter services to seeing "Claire" and "Shane" come to faith. At a deeper level, it helped map trends and highlights of our recent and longer histories. As the narrative-based consultants suggest, in our culture we need to do better at remembering. For Auburn, inviting people to share their stories was an insightful and confidence-building exercise.

The congregational timeline exercise and Woodward's framework for that encouraged the church to consider another group of stories which are important for congregational transformation — current missional stories.[28] The stories that a congregation retells about what people are doing in mission reveals what is important to its culture and what heroes it celebrates. But retelling stories is also an important formational process; it encourages people to aspire to particular missional engagement and gives them clues on how to go about it. Says Myers:

> Shared stories may not fit neat and tidy into a chart or on the back of the Sunday bulletin, but we grow to trust them as a powerful way to measure whether what we are hoping for is taking place. Shared stories are the easiest way to ensure what is important is taken into account. Story helps us measure the life of our communities.[29]

At Auburn we wanted to continue to engage with our congregational narrative of local history but also of contemporary cultural and missional engagement, and to build story-sharing into our regular "AuburnWay".

Our desire for hearing one another's stories, especially the missional stories we wanted to celebrate, led to a simple innovation in AuburnWay gatherings. As part of the opening of our gatherings that we labelled in our liturgy as "Invitation", we started asking a simple question to help uncover missional stories that are worth retelling:

> What is happening in your life and what is God doing in your life and neighbourhood that we can celebrate with you?

This question was designed as an open-ended invitation for one or more people to share something and set the scene for our worship. It has the effect of inviting people together and calling people to worship, and focusing us on God and the mission of God for which we are called together.

The purpose of a congregational timeline exercise, and the aim of the refreshed approach to storytelling that the exercise inspired for AuburnLife, ultimately, is to imagine a renewed story — to utilise narratives for congregational transformation. The ongoing renewal of our story and witness comes from exploring what ways AuburnLife can continue to live into our congregational (and biblical and missional) narratives.

Appendix: Auburn Baptist Church Ministers[30]

1	1888–1895	Rev. A. Bird
2	1896–1897	Rev. J. T. Mateer
3	1899–1907	Rev. J. East Harrison
4	1908–1913	Rev. F. E. Harry
5	1914–1916	Rev. W. G. Pope
6	1918–1921	Rev. E. L. Watson
7	1922–1931	Rev. A. D. Shaw
8	1932–1935	Rev. A. W. Bean
9	1935–1938	Rev. E. McIntyre Kippax
10	1939–1942	Rev. J. Warwick Lindsay
11	1942–1944	Rev. A. E. Smith
12	1944–1946	Rev. V. J. Edwards
13	1947–1949	Rev. Raymond Farrer
14	1949–1950	Student pastors D. Shinkfield & K. Wade
15	1950–1951	Student pastors K. Wade & P. Mellor
16	1951–1951	Student pastors P. Mellor & K. Webb
17	Jan–Mar 1952	Student pastors K. Webb & T. Farmilo
18	Mar–Aug 1952	Rev. Neville Kirkwood

19	Aug–Nov 1952	Student pastors
20	Dec 1952–Jan1953	Rev. E. T. Laxton
21	1953–1956	Rev. A. A. Hardenberg
22	1956–1957	Interim pastor Rev. R. Farrer
23	1957–1961	Rev. John Mills
24	1961–196?	Student pastor R. Vinen
25	1964–1970	Rev. Milton Warn
26	1970–1972	Interim pastor Rev. D. O. Mountford
27	Aug 72–Jan 73	Student pastor Gavin Collinson
28	Mar 73–Dec 73	Interim pastor Prof. Basil S. Brown
29	Feb 74–Dec 74	Student pastor Ian Cook
30	Jan 75–Jul 77	Student pastor D. Cosson
31	Oct 77– Feb 78	Interim pastor Rev. A. L. Moore
32	Mar 78–Dec 80	Rev. M. Brewer
33	Feb 81–Dec 83	Student pastor R. Matthews
34	Mar 84–Jan 87	Student pastor Peter Holmes
35	Feb 87–Jun 90	Student pastor M. Ross Morgan
36	1990–1998	Rev. Keith Pickett
37	1998–1998	Interim pastor Rev. Keith Adams
38	1999–2000	Interim pastor Neil Jayasuria
39	2000–2009	Rev. Jillian Stewart
40	Jan 2010–Jun 2011	Co-pastor Jenni Cronshaw
41	2010–ongoing	Rev. A/Prof. Darren Cronshaw
42	Sep2012–Jan2013	Interim pastor (during the Cronshaws' long service leave): Mark Payne
43	2015–	Associate Minister-Mission Catalyst Beth Barnett

Darren Cronshaw is pastor of AuburnLife and Mission Catalyst Researcher with Baptist Union of Victoria. He is Associate Professor in Missiology and Head of Research with Australian College of Ministries (SCD), Honorary Research Fellow with Whitley College (University of Divinity), and Adjunct Professor with Swinburne Leadership Institute. Email: pastor@auburn.org.au

Part B:
Theology and Tools for Congregational Transformation and Consultancy

Four Questions To Ask when Leading a Church into Change

Gary Heard

Leading a church through cultural and missional shifts can be a minefield requiring a blend of pastoral and leadership skills alongside the clarity of vision for the future. Excited by the latest literature on missional church life, a pastoral leader needs to ask some important questions before embarking upon the challenge of leading the people of God through into a new paradigm of ministry. However, the trail of major change in church life is littered with casualties, contributing a not-insignificant number to the fastest growing group of Christians in the Western World — those who no longer belong to a church community, whilst still barely touching the increasing numbers of unchurched people in the community. Change leadership involves consideration of the blend of pastoral, theological, missional, and sociological thinking, and a deep awareness of one's own calling and identity. In this chapter, four key questions are identified which provide a prism through which the challenges of change leadership in a local congregation can be evaluated, giving insights to both the responses of the people and the motivations and intentions of a pastoral leader. By asking questions such as these, a pastoral leader is enabled to reflect upon their focus in a pastoral, missional, and evangelistic perspective.

Since the 1960s we have seen a succession of exciting new movements in the Western church which have sparked significant growth amongst particular congregations and demographics, and ignited hope amongst the wider church that the best is still not behind us. From the emergence of the church growth movement and the charismatic movement, through the worship wars, on to the small groups movement, followed by seeker-sensitive churches, a brief sojourn through the Toronto Blessing, and into purpose-driven and now missional churches, there has been a pathway of creativity and renewal which needs to be affirmed.

And yet, the end result is that the fastest growing group of Christians in the West is those who no longer belong to a local church! Alongside the pathway trod by leaders in these movements lie wounded churches where efforts to introduce the same principles have brought pain and left many broken — and faithful — people in the wake. Statistics tell us that the church in the West continues to go backwards. Even my own Baptist denomination — which surveys show is still indicating small numerical growth — is at best marking time, but in reality in decline, not matching growth with the overall population, and masked by an important and growing ministry amongst new settler communities. We are not effectively reaching the Australian population, and steadily losing those who have long been faithful members of the community.[1]

The reasons for this are more complex than what I am addressing in this chapter, which is focused on the questions leaders should ask of themselves before embarking on the journey of leading a church through change. Leading a church through cultural and missional shifts can be a minefield requiring a blend of pastoral and leadership skills alongside the clarity of vision for the future. Excited by the latest literature on missional church life, a pastoral leader needs to ask some important questions before embarking upon the challenge of leading the people of God through into a new paradigm of ministry. However, the trail of major change in church life is littered with casualties, yet still barely touching the increasing numbers of unchurched people in the community. One of the reasons for this is pastoral leadership which ploughs ahead with grand visions but with poor understanding of how to lead the church into the vision.

I have stumbled into many mistakes in my passion and commitment to lead the church into greater engagement with its context. In the first month in my current church — a small inner-city congregation which had long been in decline — we were visited by a small group of men from a local shelter. Over a four-week period we were visited by a small number (two at a time) until on the fourth Sunday ten men turned up together, overwhelming the long-standing members of the church. These men were in various stages of recovery, and were clearly unaware of the impact of their presence on the church folk — at least that was the way it seemed. In the following week conversations with the church folk echoed a similar theme: *When we prayed for new people to come, we thought they would be just like us!* A refreshing honesty. Wondering how they would follow up the next week never became an issue — the men clearly received the message that they were not welcome, and never returned.

At that point I had two choices: risk alienating the people who were still a part of the church by pointing out perceived failings, or use it as a learning experience in the hope that the next time (should it come) there would be a different response. Coping with change is never easy, even for those who are willing and working for it. Challenges arise which cannot be predicted, and demand more of us than we can predict at the outset.

There are four questions I have learned to ask of myself before seeking to lead a people through change. An honest response to these questions can help me avoid many of the pitfalls which lead to alienation of people on the pathway to a different future.

1. Do I love these people?[2]

This might seem like a superfluous question for a pastor to ask of themselves, but in reading some of the literature around the latest model of church there appears the implicit suggestion that the work of God is taking place exclusively outside of the church, and that the real opposition to the work of God is the church. At this point I know that many readers — particularly those who have borne the scars of an unsuccessful effort to lead a church through change — will be nodding their heads in agreement with that assessment. That very notion has a deep and long historical and theological underpinning. The greatest opposition Jesus received in his ministry came from those who were identified as religious, and his strongest affiliation seemed to be with those who found themselves as outcasts by the same system. But, as leaders of the church, we need to remember that we are not being called to lead some abstract concept of church, but a real people of God grounded in a particular time and place, and who have borne the image of Christ long before we have arrived and will continue to do so long after we have gone.

The call we have received is to pastorally care for these people.

Now I am aware that the ministry of "pastoral care" for ministers is downplayed in some places, often used in a pejorative way as though pastoral care was diametrically opposed to the notion of leadership. But I would argue that any notion of leadership that is not pastorally caring lacks the fundamental which is gospel. To "pastorally care" is to accept responsibility under God for the formation of a people. Pastoral care is not about maintaining the status quo, but about formation of a people, individually, corporately, and missionally.[3] The pastoral role bears some analogies with a parenting role. The focus of a caring parent is not to keep their child as they are, but to help them to understand and fulfil their calling and potential.

Pastoral care includes the ministries of leadership, care, administration, education, mission, ethics — and evangelism. Pastoral care is the exercise of a holistic concern for the people of God — individually and communally. One cannot exercise the ministry of pastoral leadership without a love for this people and a respect for what God has been doing in this place.

The *missio Dei* includes the work of God inside the church as well as in the wider community — a community in which the people of God live and work when they aren't inside the church building. As an evangelist, I carry a primary concern for the people who are not yet enfolded into the grace of Christ. But I recognise that there is a need to care enough about the growth of the people of God in Christ also, to discover the good news of Jesus in their own contexts as those inside the church.

One of the ways to express our love for the church is to honour its history.[4] Ignoring the history of the church we are called to pastor is to risk conveying the message to the people that we do not believe that God has been at work in that place. On the other hand, the call forward is often strengthened by the call of the local history — reminding the people of the pioneering spirit which drove the congregation from its outset. Our preaching is based on the premise that the past enlivens us for what lies ahead, as we draw on the stories of Scripture. There are stories of grace in any church community which provide a platform and a catalyst for future ministry. Exploring the history of the church, and appropriately honouring it, opens up a shared journey into the new work of the present. And it may well bring to the surface issues in the church community which need to be dealt before being able to open up the future.

The church is not simply an abstract theological concept, but the people whom God has called the pastor to lead. The church is the people in front of you when you arrive — a people who have borne the image of God's grace in that place in ways which need to be affirmed.

2. Do I understand my context?

Church and other people organisations are good at adopting metaphors from the spirit of the age in framing our understanding of organisation.[5] In the industrial era we talked about economies of scale, of streamlining, and refining processes. We still hear this language of efficiency and "bang for buck" which are primarily grounded in the modernist mechanistic worldview of the industrial era. In more recent days, with our mindset framed by the computer technology era, we talk much more in terms of codings, with particular reference to DNA. However, these approaches are once again top-down approaches, seeking to drive change by imposing structures or refining them from above.

Instead of thinking in terms of DNA, it might be more helpful to think in terms of RNA. Both DNA and RNA carry genetic information. DNA is the long-term storage of genetic information. RNA is responsible for the transfer of genetic information into a particular context within the body. RNA is continually made, broken down, and reused. It is much more resilient. The difference between the two, put simplistically, is that RNA engages with particular elements in a local context to create proteins and life, and only appears when needed. DNA is a much more blunt instrument, self-replicating whether needed or not.

Or to use an old metaphor: straight transplants are doomed to fail. There needs to be some tissue match in order for the transplant to take. An oft-overlooked aspect of the analysis of some very successful models of church has been the way in which they reflect and were a strategic response to their particular context. We could well ask whether purpose-driven life would have emerged outside of its Orange County environment. Alpha exhibits a strong response to local English context. Willow Creek grew in a way reflective of its circumstances, as well as an expression of a particular theology. These ministry responses represent a critique and response in context. There is no doubt that there have been translatable aspects of the experience in those settings, but there is a danger of doing so without doing a similar critique of our own contexts.

In considering the leadership of change, sensitivity to context becomes even more important. Or in the words of missional church thinkers, an awareness of the *missio Dei* is central — an understanding of what God is doing in the local context, both inside and outside the church.

In my time as a professional sports chaplain I have often pondered the very question posed by the *missio Dei*: sitting courtside during a training session, I would contemplate where the ministry of the church might engage in the lives of athletes who work closely together seeking to maximise their potential and who live with the highs and lows of crowd reactions and journalistic interpretation. As a local church pastor I ask a similar question in a different context. I look across the street from the church at the homes of people I know and of others I don't, and I ask myself the questions, "What keeps them up at night?" "What gets them out of bed in the morning?" "Where does the gospel intersect with their lives?"[6]

People outside of the church do speak of theological themes, but not in the language commonly used inside the church. They exhibit, express, and live out a faith, hope, and love. If we are to be effective at leading the church into engagement with the local context, it is incumbent upon us as leaders to understand the theological implications.

God-images exist in every context. Beliefs in the ultimate are present in the here and now. These are very different in my present pastoral context than it was in the two previous churches I have pastored. They are obviously reflected in the widely divergent political preferences across those three areas, but not exclusively confined to that. This is a part of what God is doing locally. We need to do a good exegesis, not only of Scripture but of the context in which we are seeking to incarnate the gospel.

Knowing what drives the people in the wider community, and those already inside the church, will help to understand where bridges of ministry and growth might be found.[7] Understanding the theological imagery and language used by the non-Christian community may help build bridges of understanding and communication for the church.

3. What theology guides me?

The leadership of change requires a love of the church, a knowledge of context, and a range of management skills, but we are not required to abandon theology any more than we need to abandon our pastoral responsibilities. Pastoral care and theology are essential to the ministry of change leadership in our churches, and theology not only provides a constructive framework for change, it gives us a language and a connection to the story of God in doing so. The danger is using theology to manipulate, rather than to educate and connect.

The most common theology I have heard expressed about leading change in the local church in recent times is that of *Death and Resurrection*. This is clearly a powerful theological theme within the Christian church — it is central to our faith, and the core of all that we believe: *"For whoever wants to save their life will lose it, but whoever loses their life for my sake and for the gospel will save it."* (Mark 8:35) However, there are some significant concerns with the use of this theology on its own in the context of transformational leadership. At the core, it appears that it is employed in the justification of one particular alternative for change, rather than to underpin an openness to *any* future, and in that sense is in danger of being used in a power struggle between the pastor on the one hand and the church on the other. Implicit in this theology is the suggestion that what the church is currently doing is wrong, that the day of the current practice is over, and those present must stand aside.

While there may well be times when this theology needs to be front and centre, it is important to recognise that this is inherently a theology of conflict, one which forces those who are being asked to change to defend their ground. The end result is often a circling of the wagons to protect what is left, which in the end only embeds people deeper in the status quo rather than in opening the church up to change. That isn't to say that there may be a time in the leadership of change where the challenge to let go is issued, but as a first step it is often counterproductive, breeding mistrust and breaking down the core element required for a pastoral leader to lead a church through change — trust! It is important that this wasn't the note on which Jesus began his ministry; rather an invitation to experience the kingdom of God which had drawn near.

Theologies connect us with the deep history of the Christian tradition, and can engage communities and open up dialogue about the future. In the following, I offer only some starting thoughts for pastoral exploration:[8]

The Pilgrim People[9]

God's people on a journey to the promised land is a strong theme in the Hebrew Bible. Setting out (and liberated) from the known to embark upon a journey towards a promise yet to be revealed is an important theme. The notion that we are the pilgrim people of God opens us up to a continued sense of change and discovery, without necessarily defining what the "promised land" might look like from the beginning. A community which has rested on its laurels, or stuck in a particular pattern, could well be asked to explore this theme.

Faithful remnant

This is one of the forgotten and overlooked aspects of Israel: the people who remained in the land and maintained a presence and a sense of community during the exilic period. These people held on to a tradition that was almost destroyed, but essentially bookmarked the land until the time of restoration. There is something to be honoured about this faithfulness: those who by their perseverance hang in there when everyone else has moved on to a new place, awaiting a day of return which they may never end up witnessing themselves. They do hang on in the belief that a new day is coming. And yet, when the exiles returned, the faithful remnant had real difficulty accepting the new breaking in. An opportunity for constructive reflection exists within this imagery.

Exiles

The other side of the faithful remnant imagery is the challenges faced by those taken into exile. This imagery is both rich and diverse in the biblical literature, most poignantly expressed in the psalm, "How do we sing the Lord's song in a strange land?" This lament represents a sense of despair and loss over against the more optimistic response of Ezekiel in the first chapter. Where one group of people laments the remoteness of God (and the temple), Ezekiel sees a new and dynamic vision of God. The exilic theme both recognises and articulates a lived experience and opens the door for discovery together about the circumstances and what it asks of God's people.[10]

New community

The entire book of Acts could well be regarded as an articulation of a church community struggling with what it means to be faithful in a difficult context: new people, new traditions, new contexts, new questions all being confronted. Inside the documented record in Acts there is a demonstrated struggle on the part of the church to understand what it is that God is asking of them as they face challenges they had never anticipated.

This theology is reflected in the name change which the West Melbourne Baptist Church adopted some years ago. Faced with a jaundiced response to the church's identity, the community reflected on the image which it sought to present first to its context and settled on the name *The Eighth Day* as the reflection of its mission. After the seventh day of creation, the humans had to work out how to live in the world God had created. The eighth day of Holy Week is Resurrection Sunday, which meant that the disciples had to work out what it meant to live in the light of the death and resurrection of Jesus. The symbolism represents a continuing journey of discovery, one which also touches on the challenges of our present 24/7 world in which many people wish for more time to pursue their real passion. The imagery of *The Eighth Day* invites them to step out of the 24/7 mindset and ask what it is doing to them, and whether this is their preferred lifestyle.

Good pastoral care for a community helps the community understand its own story, and in so doing opens pathways to a new future. The pastoral leader functions partially as an exegete or interpretive guide[11] and partly as a storyteller who helps the community edit and retell its own story in ways which make sense of the present and which open up a new future.[12] To undertake this important task requires a healthy self-understanding on the part of the pastoral leader, who should be able to articulate their own assumptions, values, and biases.[13] The process of developing understanding is an interplay between community and individual, including the pastor themself.

We do not need to abandon theology or Scripture in the leadership of change. On the contrary, theology and Scripture provide a rich resource for conversation for communities to articulate what is happening in their context and in identifying opportunities and challenges alongside the understanding of the community context.

4. What things "need" to be changed?

The leadership of change can easily degenerate into a power struggle between a leader and the congregation.[14] Every congregation has its own sacred cows, whether they be stories, spaces, or special traditions which are vigorously defended by individuals, families, or wider sections of the community. Balancing the challenges of the longer-term goal with the demands of individual aspects within the community presents unique pastoral challenges. A key question a pastoral leader needs to ask themself relates to the matter of timing: *How patient am I? Am I looking for overnight change — is it to come about by evolution or revolution?* One of Martin Luther's key struggles in the context of the reformation revolved around this very issue, framed for him as, *Do I tarry for the magistrate?* The answer to the question of how long one has to wait to take the people with you is a very personal one, both for you as a pastor and for the congregation gathered. The negotiation of timing is something which occurs in the pastoral relationship.[15] The next question is around what aspects can be lived with and/or adapted to the new future which is hoped for. With some flexibility and creativity, old traditions can be reshaped or embraced into a new future. Forging a partnership with the congregation allows healthy reshaping of existing traditions, including a decent burial for those that have outlived their usefulness.

An important pastoral consideration in leading change lies in identifying what is negotiable towards the longer-term objective, which needs to remain clear in your thinking and communication. Remember that no particular outcome can be guaranteed. Although our intention might be to reach people for Christ who have no background in church, for example, the changes to be implemented cannot guarantee that this will happen. Though they might improve the likelihood by removing barriers or creating new pathways, we do well to remember that the results are in God's hands.

Conclusion

In leading a church through change, it may seem odd to state, but taking the church WITH you is much more effective. Pastoral ministry is focused towards empowering[16] the people to undertake the ministry of the gospel, something which I am convinced that most Christians want to do, yet are deeply intimidated by. A strong pastoral leadership encourages God's people in fulfilling this mission. Change is not merely about what the church as an organisation does, but about empowering God's people in their own settings: where they are the neighbours, the workmates, the members of the clubs of the same people you are seeking to reach.

The transformation of the church in its mission is a church task, not just that of the minister. This means that the translation of the vision into action is a dialogue among pastor, church, and community. Many successful models of ministry have been developed within and in response to particular contexts, and there are any number of models available for leading organisations through change. However, these models are insufficient on their own. No model can be successfully implemented without strong relationships built on a common understanding. In these four questions I have found a beginning of wisdom and guidance for leadership of change: ways which strengthen community cohesion and commitment towards the future which God is inviting us all to share in.

Gary Heard has learned the lessons of change leadership in local congregations over 25 years in ministry. He is currently pastoring an inner-city church which is undergoing a fundamental change in its approach to church life and ministry in the community, with a strong focus on ministering in and to its local community. Gary is also Dean of Theological Studies at Whitley College (University of Divinity).

When the Wineskins Burst
Intentional Interim Ministries Enter the Teens (2013-2019)

Alan Gordon

A new era has come. The five Development Tasks of Intentional Interim Ministries (IIM) need updating. New models have been developed in social and individual sciences that resolve IIM-related issues which have long proved difficult to solve using older methods. One of these models, developed by a Harvard Business School professor, has been very successful in "turnaround" companies that had been struggling for existence. Other highly researched, parallel approaches had also proved successful in "turnaround" companies. The secular approaches were blended with Christian "turnaround" material. When I trialled this orientation in two IIMs in Australia, I observed that they readily crossed-over with surprising effectiveness into the five Developmental Tasks that constitute IIMs. The resultant development is a paradigm shift for IIMs, which brings them into the "teens" of this century (2013-2019).

The New Wineskins Symposium derived its name from Jesus' familiar metaphor: "And no one puts new wine into old wineskins. For the old skins would burst from the pressure, spilling the wine and ruining the skins. New wine is stored in new wineskins so that both are preserved" (Matthew 9:17, NLT). Before the age of glass bottles, wine was stored in leather containers.[1] Old leather became brittle and hard, and therefore would be burst by the fermentation and expansion of new wine. Jesus was clearly implying that the hard, rigid legalism of Judaism could not cope with the power of his teaching and, as understood after Pentecost, the inner power of the Holy Spirit. A new "container", the church, was required.

Today, the church itself must continue to learn this lesson. An old generation that is bound by a tired, hard, unpliable status quo cannot cope with the vigour of fresh, dynamic expressions of biblical faith in a new generation. New wine must be put into new wineskins: new understandings of truth require new, external expressions in which they operate.

Sometimes, old-wine Christians induct a new-wine pastor into their church. Some church members respond positively to the new-wine message; some others resist vehemently. Jesus' metaphor comes into effect: the ferment causes the church to split and the red wine spills like blood on the floor. Intentional Interim ministers are called in to reconstitute the church, which is seeking, with the assistance of their opinion leaders, to relocate the remaining wine into new wineskins.[2] This process is one of congregational transformation. Thankfully the transformation is easiest with an organisation in this precarious situation: "everyone recognizes that change is necessary",[3] because without it, they will not continue as a church.

Intentional Interim Ministries began when the now old-status-quo-generation was the younger generation. Over thirty years ago, Loren B. Mead developed Intentional Interim Ministries (IIMs). The excellence of his wisdom, training, and experience is best comprehended when you're in the pressure of IIMs.[4] He spoke as a highly trained modernist leader to modernist trainees who ministered to a modernist world.

However, major changes have occurred in the Western world. The milieu has largely changed to postmodernism, although strong elements of modernism have remained, e.g., in science and technology departments in universities.[5] Many new problems have developed since Mead created the IIM training course: for example, the Carver model of management.[6] Excellent new approaches have emerged in the social sciences that directly impact upon the IIM process. Social commentator, Hugh Mackay, describes how the young adults of the generation that Mead trained differ radically from the young adults of today.[7] Therefore, new approaches are needed to respond to current realities. I believe that Mead's Five Developmental Tasks of Intentional Interim Ministry need updating.

The process begins with the reminder of the words of Jesus Christ, "I will build my church" (Matthew 16:18). It is an invitation for us to join him on this venture. The concepts and skills that will be described are our part of the joint venture.

The goals of this update of IIMs:

The goals of this update of IIMs are to facilitate skills in a variety of tasks: to develop a leadership style that is appropriate for a contemporary IIM; to obtain early buy-in from the church members; to obtain the most appropriate people on the Transition Team; to achieve greater healing of the church's troubled past; to encourage a church in its present situation; to create an appropriate leadership structure for the church; to develop a new identity that is healthy and growing; to initiate missional ministry; to obtain recognition among community leaders that the church makes a difference; to develop a network of religious, community, and political groups; to raise the church's profile in the community so that many more people will consider the church as an option; to turn the church's eyes outward toward the community; to understand the psychological dynamics of the change process involved in an IIM; and to facilitate the process of calling a quality new pastor to follow the IIM.

How to obtain early buy-in from the church members

Michael Watkins recommends that interviewing key people within the first few days helps to achieve quick results in an IIM.[8]

Member Interview when first entering an IIM church:

When interviewing the members, Michael Watkins' questions proved very effective: What are the biggest challenges our church is facing? Why is our church facing these challenges? What are the most promising opportunities for growth that we are not fully using? How can we seize these opportunities? What do the members of the community want that they are getting from our alternative organisations and not getting from us? If you were me, what would you focus attention on?[9]

Watkins' approach proved to be beneficial in IIMs. Members felt understood early with the IIM. This led to quick approval. A-item priorities (desired goals in core problem areas) were achieved early. It was time to select the members of the Transition Team (TT).

How to obtain the most appropriate people on the Transition Team (TT)

Patterson, Grenny, McMillan, and Switzler advise the use of opinion leaders on teams whose goal is radical change. Opinion leaders are the members whom you have to convince to ensure your future policies are accepted by the church. If they are part of a TT, they formulate the policies and therefore support them at Members Meetings. They serve the added advantage of commending TT policies in their regular contacts with church members.[10]

But how can opinion leaders be identified? Firstly, they resemble the group for whom they act; which means that they dress and speak just like those whom they will represent. Secondly, they also can represent the group for whom they act; which means that they generally have above average intelligence and are articulate.

I divided churches into broad age groups and requested that each group vote for one man and one woman from their age group who follow the above criteria for the TT. The results of the selection process resulted in TTs consisting of opinion leaders.

Having opinion leaders on the TT resulted in slower decision making, but the quality of the decisions improved considerably. After the election, I stated to the Members Meeting that each age group had its own representatives on the TT. I requested that the church members constantly ask their representatives what decisions were being made during the IIM process. If members wanted to make a contribution on any decision, their representatives would take the contribution directly to the TT. The members could participate in the decision process. Because of this, excellent buy-in resulted from the members. The scene was set for Developmental Task One.

Developmental Task One: Coming to terms with history

The history of a church can significantly impact the characteristics of the present. The original vision of the church may need revisiting. Mapping the history of a church by a Transition Team can help find the recurring themes that need investigation. However, much in the church's present need must receive immediate attention.

How to achieve deep healing of the church's troubled past

The first priority is to stop the bleeding. By visiting people from both sides of the conflict, not only is a balanced perspective gained, but healing is also regularly obtained as people feel heard. Some departed members returned to the church. Most people from both sides of the conflict gravitated toward the centre, which enabled the development of a map of the conflict.

Mapping the conflict

Visualising the conflict clarifies its dynamics, as proved true in a complex conflict in one of my IIMs that I conducted.

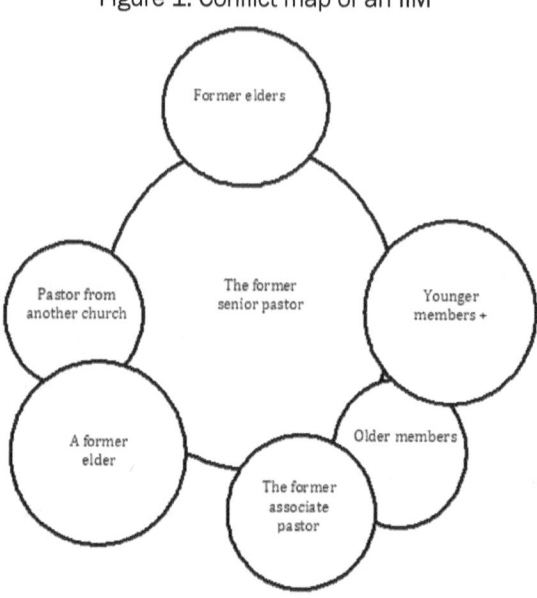

Figure 1: Conflict map of an IIM

Negotiating delicately

Deep healing was needed but was difficult to achieve. My wife, Rosemary, who is also IIM trained, commented, "We need to build a South American bridge. They begin with a slender thread". The South American Indians shoot an arrow attached to a slender thread across a deep ravine. The slender thread pulls a thicker thread across the gap. The threads become bigger until the whole rope bridge is built — which permits regular commuting between the two sides.

God himself provided the slender thread that led to the desired bridge. Warm but firm pastoral care persuaded a former elder who had been strongly involved in the conflict to apologise during the upcoming Reconciliation Service.

Reconciliation Service: Coming to terms with the negative sides of history

Successful Reconciliation Services require much work and much prayer.

Preparing thoroughly

Hours are spent inviting people to a Reconciliation Service. Their names were obtained from every possible source. Thankfully, an office secretary prepared the publicity and sent out the invitations. Many people received one-on-one invitations.

Preaching graciously

Preaching focused on forgiveness and reconciliation. Stories of Christian forgiveness of war atrocities came from movies and books. When these atrocities were compared with the presumed wrong done by fellow Christians in our church, our church members felt shame if they could not forgive others.

Leading the Reconciliation Service

During the Reconciliation Service, four leaders who had been involved in the complex conflict came forward and made a public apology to the packed building. Members were invited to come forward to pray for them. When the former elder described above made his apology, almost the entire church moved forward to pray for him. The power of this reconciliation was deeply felt as it prepared for the sermon.

The sermon used was John Bevere's DVD title, *Bait of Satan*,[11] which urged the members not to take offence. This very relevant sermon made a powerful impact on all of the congregation as it spoke to division within a church.

Both sides spoke of their side as "us" and the other side as "them". This needed to change. We prepared dark clouds with "them" written on the clouds. These clouds were placed around the cross on the church's wall. Each member was to be invited to remove a cloud and replace it with a flame (symbol of the Holy Spirit) with the word, "us", written on it. This committed them never to use an "us-and-them" division of people again in the church. In future, *all* of God's people were to be "us".

Well before the prepared time, one man spontaneously came out; flung a cloud into the bin with disgust; replaced it firmly with a flame — and the whole church followed! While the people were coming out to pull down the clouds and put up the fires, I looked over my program for the day, threw the sheets of paper into the air and said, "That's the end of my program: the Holy Spirit has taken over!" A huge cheer erupted in the church.

The Reconciliation Service provided permanent healing of almost every person in the congregation. However, sometimes a Reconciliation Service is not the most relevant service to conduct.

A Restoration Service

Leaders struggle to make decisions during a conflict and this can cause long delays in beginning an IIM. By this time, most of the original anger has dissipated. In that situation, I have witnessed two different disorders, the first being Attachment Disorder.

Attachment Disorder

In one of my IIMs, there had been repeated pastoral resignations, and the departure of 70 percent of the church. This created deep grief through the congregation. The grief helped to create an Attachment Disorder church.

Attachment Disorder was the experience of Russian orphans who were regularly changed from one "parent" to another in Russia. At each home, they would want love but they were continually moved on. A mission group brought many of them to America and placed them into fine Christian homes. The orphans craved for love and the Christian house-parents sought to give it. However, the orphans rejected their love, creating deep grief.[12] Such grief is also evident in the Gallipoli Syndrome.

Gallipoli Syndrome

At Canberra's National Archives display, "*After the war, came the battle*", parallels were most evident between the aftermath of World War I and the conflict in my IIM church. The Archives described the large numbers of Australians who were lost through the war. Their bodies were never brought home, which exacerbated the grief. Many key workers who had gone to the war could never return to their former jobs. Finances were critically low. Grief was a dark cloud hovering over the hearts of the nation. As I read the display at the National Archives and compared it with the situation in my IIM, I put a tick beside most descriptions — other than the numbers of people involved.

In order to deal with the two disorders, we conducted a Restoration Service. The preparatory preaching was about healing from emotional pain. In the sermon itself, both syndromes were directly addressed with a biblical response. Many people commented on the deep healing that came to them during the service. Some members who experienced considerable pain were commended to free Christian counselling outside of our denomination.

Throughout the preparation and conduct of these three services, especially in the Reconciliation Service, the people were urged to respond to the negatives that had occurred in the church's past. This was the opposite of the Celebratory Weekend.

Celebratory Weekend: Coming to terms with the positive sides of history

During the second half of an IIM, I used a Celebratory Weekend to rejoice in the successes of the past. Such a weekend is easier to prepare if there is a special event to celebrate, such as a centennial celebration. The event required considerable preparation as it was over an entire weekend.

The churches held a picnic on Saturday afternoon and a concert at night. On the Sunday morning, the churches' positive past was celebrated with gusto. These Celebrations were very important to the successes of both IIMs. The focus was on the good that had occurred. Each of these celebratory services was very uplifting and memorable. What assisted the celebration was a publication of the churches' histories.

A history of the church

I sought to have a book written about the church's history and released on the Celebration Sunday. It needed to be well researched and presented. It can bring a tangible reminder of the many ways God has blessed the church. Ensure that you have read it carefully before it goes to publication. This book represented the final act of Developmental Task One.

Developmental Task One was concurrent in its later stages with other Developmental Tasks, such as Leadership and Decision Making.

Developmental Task Two: Leadership and decision making

I chose to begin Developmental Task Two with developing a leadership structure.

How to develop a leadership structure for the teens (2013–2019)

One of the most difficult aspects of this Developmental Task is leadership structure. The following model for leadership structure was shared at a board meeting by its chairman, John Woodley, a professional leadership trainer, when I was a pastor of North-East Baptist Church.

Figure 2: Leadership structure designed for development[13]

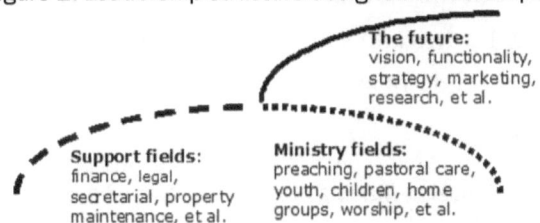

Each of the three fields is important. When developing a church, keep the future line on the board's agenda. When the structure of the church was in place, it was important that the leadership style match the situation.

How to develop a leadership style appropriate for an IIM church

Dr Michael Watkins[14] proposed five distinctive situations in organisations in his book, *The First Ninety Days*. One of these, the Turnaround, constantly equated with the IIMs that I had been conducting, and therefore I applied his approach to my IIMs.

Watkins' process for Turnarounds is specific. Rapid diagnosis is needed. There is a need to act quickly with incomplete information. A little success goes a long way. Tough calls are needed early in the IIM. The selection of future leaders needs to occur. Demoralised workers need to be energised; the church needs to feel hope for the future. Existing ministries need strengthening. Early wins are essential.[15]

Such a process fitted well with the decision-making model that we used, which was designed for a "teams-sized church".

How to develop a decision-making model for a church that is "team-sized"

The second Developmental Task also considers decision making. Very small churches largely make decisions as an entire body. Small churches leave the decisions to be made by the board and ratified by the Members Meeting.

The teams-sized church model that we used at North-East Baptist Church empowered both lay leaders and staff members. At the same time, the Board of Management did not appear inferior to the Board of Leadership: the difference is role.

Figure 3: The Decision-Making Model for a teams-based church[16]

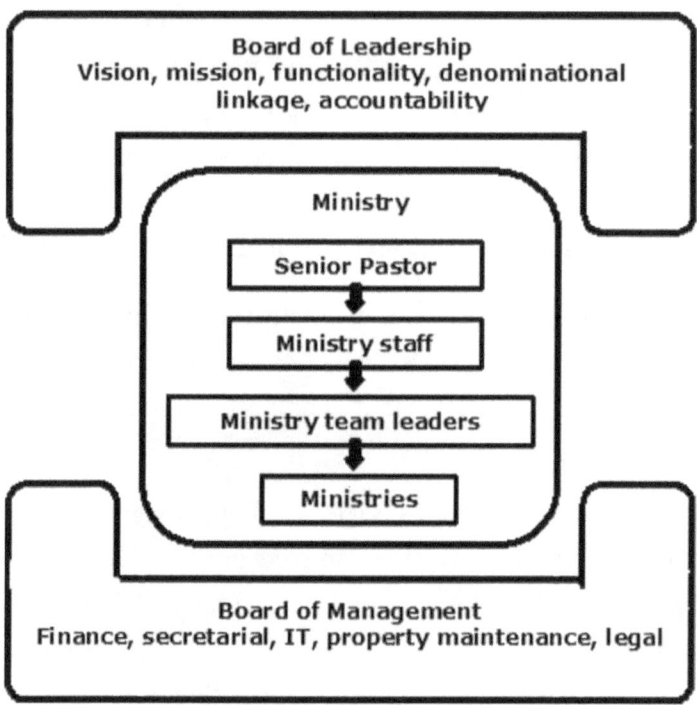

The leadership model adopted by North-East Baptist Church had been developed by Wynnum Baptist Church during the pastorate of Peter Van Donge.

Once the church is healing (DT One) and has resolved leadership and decision making (DT Two), it is time to develop a new identity.

Development Task Three: Discovering a new identity

How to develop a new identity that is healthy and growing

Based on extensive research on qualities that result in organisational effectiveness, Cameron and Quinn have produced an adaptable tool for developing a new identity.[17]

Figure 4: Organisational Culture Assessment Instrument (OCAI)[18]

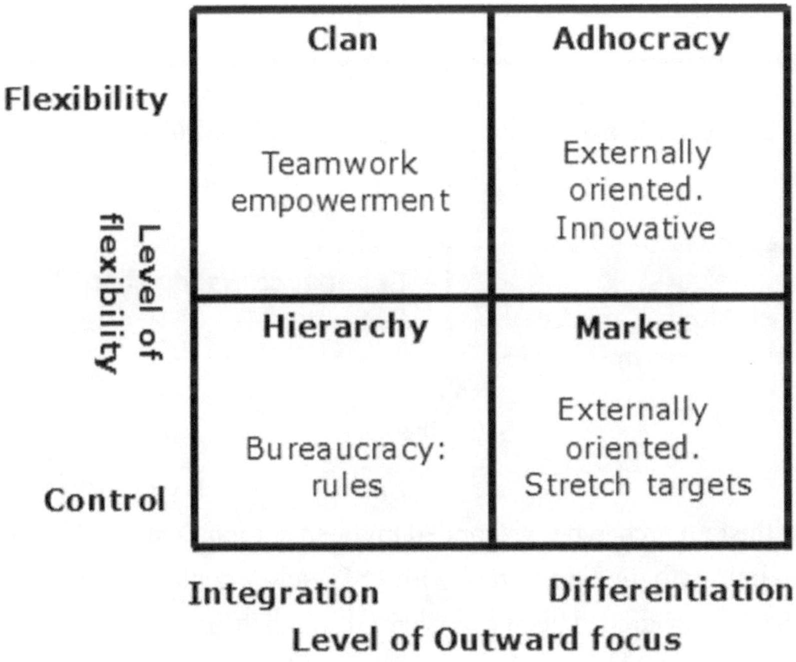

	Clan	Adhocracy
Flexibility	Teamwork empowerment	Externally oriented. Innovative
Control	**Hierarchy** Bureaucracy: rules	**Market** Externally oriented. Stretch targets

Level of flexibility (vertical axis)

Integration — Differentiation
Level of Outward focus

By using OCAI in my IIMs and maintaining the two axes, I observed the quadrants had gravitated in ministry emphases: empowerment, mission, attraction, and coordination.

Figure 5: Organisational culture for churches[19]

Each of the four archetypes responded to the major issues of the churches. Mission links into the community, with an IT-style orientation. Attraction seeks to win unchurched people to Christ through its ministries. Empowerment builds up the body of Christ for the work of ministry (Eph 4:12). Coordination focuses ministries on achieving the church's vision.

OCAI measures church culture with a diagnostic tool.[20] The TT members ascertained the level at which the church was currently working in each segment. This level was placed on the diagonal lines in each segment. An unbroken line joins the four levels, as shown in the example.

When the Wineskins Burst

Figure 6: OCAI as a diagnostic tool[21]

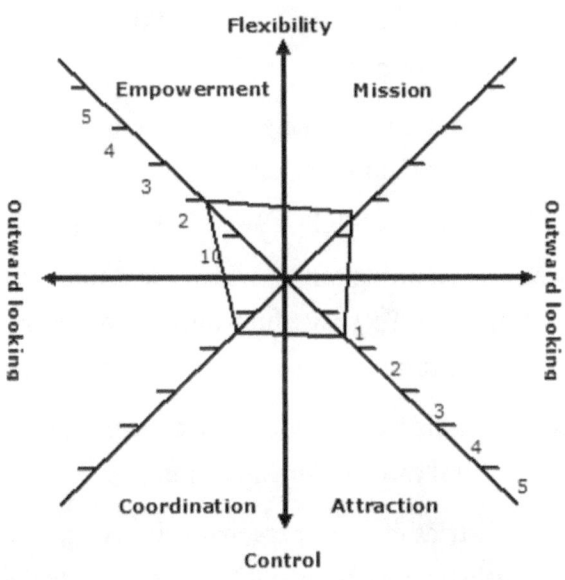

Prayerfully, the TT members write down where they believe, under Christ, the level should be in each segment if the church's vision is to be achieved. The mean of each segment's score is marked on the scale. These scores are joined by broken lines.

Figure 7: Church planning using the OCAI model[22]

Because all known qualities that lead to effectiveness were incorporated into the model, its balance facilitates church health. Because half of the quadrants are directly evangelistic, it assists church growth.

The Empowerment quadrant can easily slip into a maintenance approach, which is self-focused. The empowerment emphasis concentrates on discipleship and leadership training, which then strengthens all quarters.

OCAI is also used as a planning tool in which each ministry/activity is related to its quadrant. The TT prayerfully decides the level at which each ministry/activity should functioning so that the church vision is attained.

- *Empowerment* ministries include: biblical instruction, worship, fellowship, pastoral care, leadership training.
- *Attraction* ministries include: personal witnessing, evangelistic home groups, evangelistic preaching, publicity, appearance of property, welcoming program, and assimilation program.
- *Coordination* ministries include: internal communication, and promoting the vision and mission statements.
- *Mission* ministries need more extensive consideration as they operate in the community.

How to initiate missional ministry

Community ministry begins by researching the community with three forms of research: quantitative, qualitative, and literature review.

Quantitative research

Quantitative research is conducted using Australian Bureau of Statistics (ABS) data. After the results are graphed, they are interpreted in relationship with your church.

Seek comparisons: e.g., compare age groups with each other; compare ethnic groups with the mean of your suburb/town; compare your suburb/town with the state or national mean; compare groups over two or three censuses.

Look for such results as: significant differences in the comparisons, significant changes that occur over time, and anomalies. Some of the questions that emerged from my ABS research included: Why was there a spike at age twenty-seven in the age graph that was missing in this old suburb's last census? What are the implications when the percentage of children under 15 greatly exceed the Australian median and the mortgage levels greatly exceed the Australian median in a quickly growing outer suburb? What factors caused a small city to be very high in relative deprivation?

Data provides significant information that can shape a successful ministry, especially when given flesh by supportive qualitative research.

Qualitative research

Community leaders are interviewed: politicians, school principals, school chaplains, social workers, real estate agents, and so on. Social workers provide details of unmet needs and generate important contacts with whom you can network. Social workers invite you to join their network so that they can refer people to you and you to them. Real estate agents can give you data on the dominant people-groups entering your suburb/town and where each group can be located. The agents can pass on a range of current data about your suburb/town.

The following interview questions proved effective for community leader interviews. How long have you lived/worked in this region? What are the greatest advantages that the region possesses? What are the defining characteristics of the region? What are the community trends in the region? What are the most critical unmet needs of the community in the region? What are the dominant aspirations of the community in the region? What question should have been asked on this survey, and why? Whom else would you suggest that we contact?[23] The final question enables you to penetrate more deeply into the community.

In the latest research project with which I have been involved, every leader who was interviewed wanted a copy of the report; they were aware that it would be the most thorough ever made of their community. These interviews place you and your church into the community, and into a relationship with these leaders. The quantitative and qualitative research is then enhanced by professional reports.

The literature review/Meta-analysis

Reports are obtainable from government departments on all three levels, from university research, welfare reports, and so on. Literature reviews are more effective in small or medium-sized cities rather than in most city suburbs, because they are units that are more readily defined for statistics. Reports may be obtained on issues such as: tourism, suicide, Aboriginal issues, the city plan, poverty, aged care, business report, in-migration, NCOSS Consultation, and health. The three forms of research then combine to create the Community Research Report.

The Community Research Report

To write a Community Research Report, combine all aspects of your research: quantitative, qualitative, and literature reports; discover the critical issues; and create a list of recommendations for the Transition Team. Present your statistics in graph form where possible.

The cover and format of this report should match BHP-Billiton's Annual Report in quality. A hard copy is given to interviewees in influential positions and a .pdf file on a CD to all interviewees. A PowerPoint presentation of the Community Report is presented to the board and the church members, and included on the CD for interviewees. The report promotes the work of the church through the community, but it also becomes a very useful tool for the church.

The Community Report enables you to develop vision and mission statements that are relevant to your community. Through the report, you can write a strategic plan which is based on the specific needs and aspirations of the community. If your church has been inward looking, its eyes turn outward. Yes, it takes considerable time and effort to create a Community Report, but it is invaluable. It opens the door for you to enjoy very profitable networking.

Developmental Task Four: Networking

The absence of adequate networking was identified by Loren B. Mead to be a serious weakness of churches that were prone to division. Churches need to recognise that they are not matches in a box but branches of a vine.[24] This is particularly important in the new millennium.

On the first day of the new millennium, Rupert Murdoch was in Australia being interviewed on ABC radio. Murdoch was at the peak of his career.

"Mr Murdoch, what do you consider to be the most important trend in the new century?"
"Networking!" Murdoch flashed back.[25]

He has proved correct.

Training for IIM pastors has traditionally focused on denominational networking. However, in the new era, there are four areas of networking that are important for IIMs. *Denominational networking* is facilitated when denominational leaders speak on Sunday mornings about how a local church and its state denominational office can work together. *Inter-denominational networking* is usually achieved through your local Ministers' Fraternal. *Community networking* is facilitated by your Community Research. *Social media* is the place where most external networking occurs today.

In 2004, Murdoch was more specific: he saw that the present and future are digital in orientation.[26] Ministry must enter the digital age more fully that it has done.

David Meerman Scott describes how Mark Batterson, the lead pastor of The National Community Church in Washington, uses the online media as a vehicle for ministry. The pastor [Batterson] uses video technology, blogs, podcasts, and the web to tell stories and build a spiritual community both online and off.

The TheaterChurch.com site includes a content-rich website, podcasts of the weekly services, a motivational webcast series, video, an email newsletter, Batterson's extremely popular Evotional blog (tagline: "Spirit Fuel"), and Twitter feed (@MarkBatterson) with more than sixty thousand followers…. "The greatest message deserves the greatest marketing", Batterson says:

> Our website and my blog are our front door to National Community Church. The site is a virtual location in a sense. We have a lot more people who listen to the podcast and watch the webcast than who go to the services, so it is a great test drive for people. They can get a sense of the church before they arrive physically.

His blog is followed by tens of thousands of readers all over the world, and the podcast is one of the fastest growing church podcasts in America. "The two most powerful forms of marketing are word of mouth and what I call word of mouse. The message has not changed, but the medium has changed. We need to continually find new vehicles to get the message out."[27]

So the main fundamental aspects of ministry are being covered adequately in the new media ministry, although approached in a very different way. Effectively, the first four Developmental Tasks have concluded. Now comes the crucial matter of succession.

Developmental Task Five: Commitment to the future

Unless the incoming pastor is appropriate for a congregation, the church is in danger of repeating its past mistakes.

How to facilitate the calling of a quality pastor to follow you

Mead, in his wisdom, recognised the need to pass the baton. How can a quality pastor be obtained as the next spiritual leader of the church? One initial observation reaches back through the first four Development Tasks. If God has used IIM pastors to turnaround a church, quality pastors will consider the former IIM church as an option.

How can this happen? When asked for advice, I commend that the Pastoral Selection Committee consider two methods to their search for a new pastor. Firstly, profiles of both church and pastor are important. It is essential to discover a "fit" between the church and the pastor.[28] Secondly, case studies in the fields of decision making, problem solving, and conflict resolution helped during an interview of potential pastors. I have been asked to write the case studies and I did so based on recent issues that occurred in the church. The answers to the case studies identify who has the wisdom and training to take the church into the future, under the leadership of Jesus Christ, with a much lower possibility of another church split occurring. One of the reasons why my IIM churches had difficulty was that their pastors, in whose ministry church splits occurred, had been selected largely because of their preaching ability. Nevertheless, this is not universal.

How to understand the psychological dynamics of an IIM change process

Prof. Rosabeth Moss Kanter developed a model for an organisation that has been in crisis, which is based on experiments in the field of organisational psychology in turnaround situations.[29]

When the organisation goes down, it takes the mind with it. There are feelings of disappointment, discouragement, frustration, disenchantment, and sometimes, pessimism.

When the mind rises, it takes the organisation with it! It moves on the upward Success Pathway. Success and failure relate to the mind. However, the mind has to rise above these negatives if it is to create positives in our churches.

Figure 8: Rosabeth Moss Kanter, "The Psychology of a Turnaround"[30]

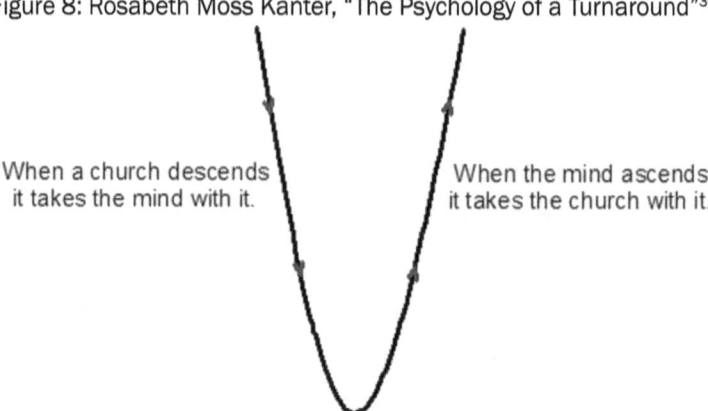

When a church descends it takes the mind with it.

When the mind ascends it takes the church with it.

Strong, inspirational leadership raises people to act out the strategies of the new vision and new mission.

Alan Gordon is a Graduate of Vose College, has doctoral degrees from Denver Seminary and Australian College of Theology, has completed Intentional Interim Ministry training, and is an accredited Baptist pastor. Currently he is trialling recent developments in the human sciences in preparation for a book on how these developments impact the use of the culture model in churches as they enter an emerging new milieu.

From Stuck to Growing
Examining the Place of Church Consultancy in Revitalising Churches

Ian Duncum

This chapter explores the nature of church consultancy and its place within a wider framework of consultancy. Research compares ten churches who had invited a church consultancy with those that had not had a consultancy, and analysis is focused around "weaker" churches from both groups. This is done using interviews, pre-consultancy and post-consultancy "snapshots", five years apart, of church health (using National Church Life Survey {NCLS} data) and congregational attendance. Two of these consultancy churches are reviewed in more depth. Results revealed significant increases in health and numerical growth for the consultancy group of churches, and indicate this model's effectiveness for transformation of churches. Some implications for pastors and church consultants are then outlined.

> "Congregations need to see themselves as the source of their own healing... An effective outside source of help will not support dependency. Rather it will help the congregation to build the inner resources that can stabilize life together and produce a more adequate organization for the future."[1]

There are many ways in which congregations are transformed. While some churches have themselves instigated the process of church transformation well, others turn to one or more of the many external intervention options available. Three assertions frame or provide a foundation for the ensuing discussion about church consultancy's place in church revitalisation. Firstly, there is no "silver bullet" — the work of restoring or enhancing church health is a long-term venture. Secondly, there are many elements that together make up or support church health. Thirdly, "new wine" or new life in churches is ultimately something that God releases — sometimes in partnership with our efforts, and sometimes despite them.

Church consultancy is a process whereby trained consultants work alongside a church and its leadership to serve and support that church, with a view to improving the health of the congregation so that it may have a greater impact for the kingdom of God.[2] Church consultancy seeks to build the capacity of a church to clarify and fulfil its mission and goals in a way that releases that church towards sustainable transformation.

Approaches to church consultancy

Maula and Poulfelt differentiate between two generally opposed styles of consulting: "content-based" where knowledge flows "from the consultant to the client", and "process-based" consulting characterised by "interaction and feedback between the consultant and the client".[3] Adding a middle perspective, Schein differentiates between three broad types of consultancy in any context, according to the level of client involvement: the purchase of expertise, where the client identifies the problem and the consultant fixes it; the doctor–patient relationship, where the consultant identifies the problem and offers a remedy for the client to act on; and the process facilitator–participant/learner, where the client takes responsibility for the problem and engages the consultant in a process of helping and training them in assessing the difficulty and implementing organisational change.[4] This is the approach taken in Baptist churches in NSW/ACT.

A process-based approach offers the greatest potential for client ownership of the problem, buy-in, action, and lasting organisational transformation in a church context.

Church consultancy that is process-based respects church independence, and places the responsibility for a church's life, health, and mission back on the church. Such an approach is contextualised: that is, rather than a standard "off the shelf" consultancy program, it will use different approaches for different types of church consultancies.[5] That contextualisation extends to affirming and analysing the demographic context of the local community in which a church does mission. It also emphasises partnership, since the local church invites the consultants and sets the objectives for the consultancy. While trained consultants bring their skills they also seek to uncover and utilise skills in the church, and together seek to discern God's call for the church.[6]

Provided that the church actually carries out the recommendations of the consultants for "sustainable transformation",[7] process-based church consultancy is one of the more efficient uses of outside resources, as churches are walked through a process whereby their capacity is built to increasingly solve their own problems and further develop their health and growth.[8]

There are some similarities between church consultancy and organisational development.[9] However, church consultancy has some unique characteristics in that its goal is the effective ministry and mission of a local church in its community context. So theology, such as ecclesiology and missiology, informs the work of church consultancy. Identifying what is happening between the church and God is a crucial component of church consultancy. Therefore prayer is a key component alongside any methodological consultancy processes, and clearly sets church consultancy apart from organisational development.

Church consultancy research project

Many churches, at some point or points in their history, go through periods of crisis, difficulty, or are plateaued in their growth. The leadership of some churches may deny that a problem exists or attempt to solve it on their own. However, increasingly, churches are inviting outside assistance.[10] For some, it is to deal with a specific issue, for others to envision the future, or perhaps to get some insights about breaking through a growth barrier.[11] The ten churches used in this study were selected for having completed both NCLS–2001 and NCLS–2006, and having commenced a church consultancy in 2001 or 2002. This yielded a long-range study of the impact of the church consultancy on the health and growth of the church over a four- to five-year time span. They are a broad mixture of churches, large and small, multi-pastor and sole pastor, rural and urban. They have also entered into consultancies for a variety of reasons.

Analysis of interviews

Interviews with those who were the pastors of five of the consultancy churches at the time of the church consultancy were undertaken. This was done to provide a method of confirming (or not) and interpreting the quantitative data that had been collected through each church's participation in NCLS–2001 and NCLS–2006. The questions asked reflect the NCLS core quality indicators and NCLS quantitative measures.[12] Indications as to whether these had grown, declined, or remained about the same, subsequent to the consultancy, were sought and coded.

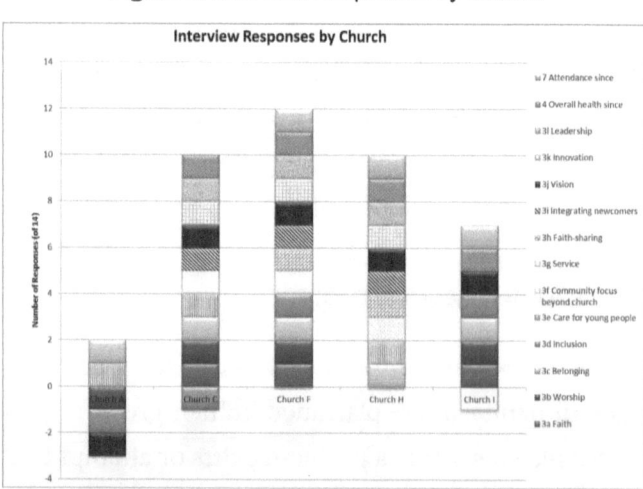

Figure 1: Interview Responses by Church

The number of responses was then graphed as stacked columns by church.

This was done to give some indication of each pastor's perception of what changes, if any, had occurred in the church they pastored subsequent to the consultancy. It is evident from the interview responses by health and growth indicators that pastors observed an increase across *almost all* health and growth indicators. Additionally, 80 percent of interviewees indicated growth in the *overall* health of the church since the consultancy.[13] And four of the five pastors interviewed indicated a growth in attendance subsequent to the church consultancy.

What are the mechanisms identified by the pastors interviewed for the church consultancy to foster health and growth in their church?

First that, in conjunction with the leadership of the church, the consultants identify and address the issues facing the church.[14]

Second, that church consultancy provides a pathway and suggests next steps for a church to follow.

Third, that church consultancy "encouraged people in their ministries in the church and the community" so that "worth is engendered in what they were doing and could do".[15]

Fourth, church consultancy puts a church in touch with people or program resources to assist them in addressing their objectives.

Fifth, church consultancy brings an objective, realistic assessment of a church's health and assists a church in facing their situation and being "held accountable for what we are doing".[16]

Sixth, church consultancy brings hidden blockages to health, such as "systemic patterns of communicating and relating", out into the open, where they can be addressed.[17]

For some of the pastors interviewed, the consultancy was perceived as effective in dealing with a range of specific issues such as: dealing with conflict, prompting inclusion of the Aboriginal community in the church's ministry, or in instigating a strategic plan for growth. Others identified areas for improvement in church consultancy such as "could bring stronger recommendations" and "further follow-up from consultants".[18]

Analysis of core vitality indicators

From their research of churches over many years, NCLS Research has isolated nine core qualities of healthy and vital churches: an alive and growing *faith*, vital and nurturing *worship*, strong and growing *belonging*, a clear and owned vision, inspiring and empowering leadership, open and flexible *innovation*, practical and diverse service, willing and effective *faith-sharing*, and intentional and welcoming inclusion.[19]

To make a more reasonable comparison between the consultancy and non-consultancy groups of churches, an analysis was performed where only churches with lower core quality indicators in NCLS–2001 were included. This was done because the churches requiring a consultancy would most probably be of lower health, whereas the "no consultancy" group would be mixed; some with strong health and higher NCLS core quality indicators, and others with weaker health and lower NCLS core quality indicators. This process clearly confirmed that the consultancy group of churches were less healthy. The methodology used was that churches with stronger health (five or more {out of the nine core quality indicators} scores over six {out of a maximum ten}) were removed from both groups, leaving nine churches (from ten) remaining in the consultancy group and 74 churches (from 88) in the non-consultancy group.

Results of this analysis are represented graphically at Figure 2.

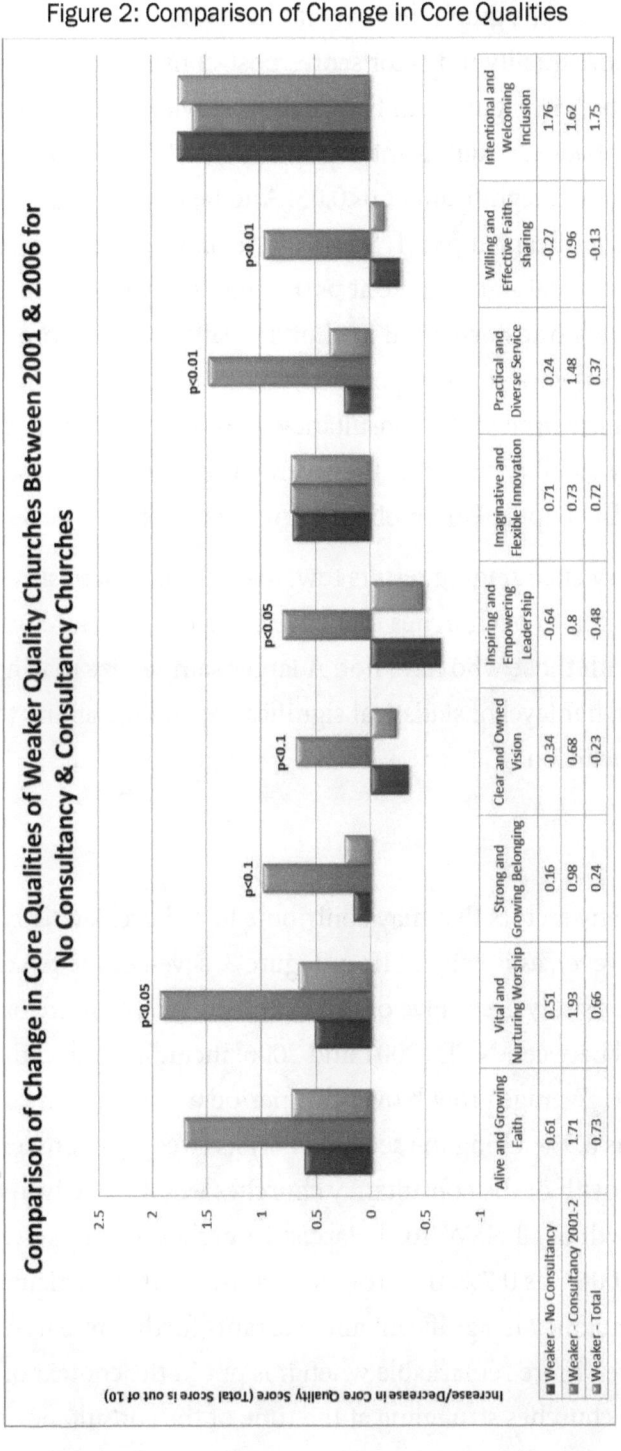

Figure 2: Comparison of Change in Core Qualities

It is evident from the graph that overall there was an increase in eight of the nine core quality indicator scores post-consultancy. As shown by the labelled bars in Figure 2, in this analysis service and faith-sharing are extremely statistically significant at $p<0.01$. Worship and leadership are highly statistically significant at $p<0.05$. And belonging and vision are statistically significant at $p<0.1$. So six of the nine core quality indicators had some statistical significance at $p<0.1$, with one more, faith, just outside this range. Such transformation in church health is even more remarkable when put in the context of 50 percent of the consultancy churches struggling at the time of the consultancy with their numerical, financial, and ministry viability such that they were in receipt of a ministry subsidy, either from the Baptist Union of NSW/ACT or another source.

These are very encouraging results towards indicating a positive correlation between the health of churches that have engaged in a church consultancy, compared with those who have not. A larger sample size may have helped towards a higher level of statistical significance and the ability to draw a stronger conclusion.

Growth

There are many factors that may contribute to a church's vitality and growth. However, as is evident from Figure 3, seven of the ten churches that form this study grew. Five of these grew by 20% or more over the five-year interval between NCLS 2001 and 2006, including one church that grew by 65%. Average growth over this period across the ten consultancy churches was 8.9%. Using the second analysis (weaker churches, n=9) aggregate growth of the consultancy churches was 9.7%. Given that average growth of all NSW/ACT Baptist Churches over this five-year interval to 2006 was 0.7%, the growth of churches that participated in a church consultancy is significant and warrants further research.[20] Such growth is even more remarkable when it is put in the context of 50% of the consultancy churches struggling at the time of the consultancy with their viability such that their ministry was subsidised.

What follows is background regarding two of the ten churches, consultancy objectives set by each church's leadership, and indications towards the impact of the church consultancy over the period to 2006 on each church's health and growth.[21]

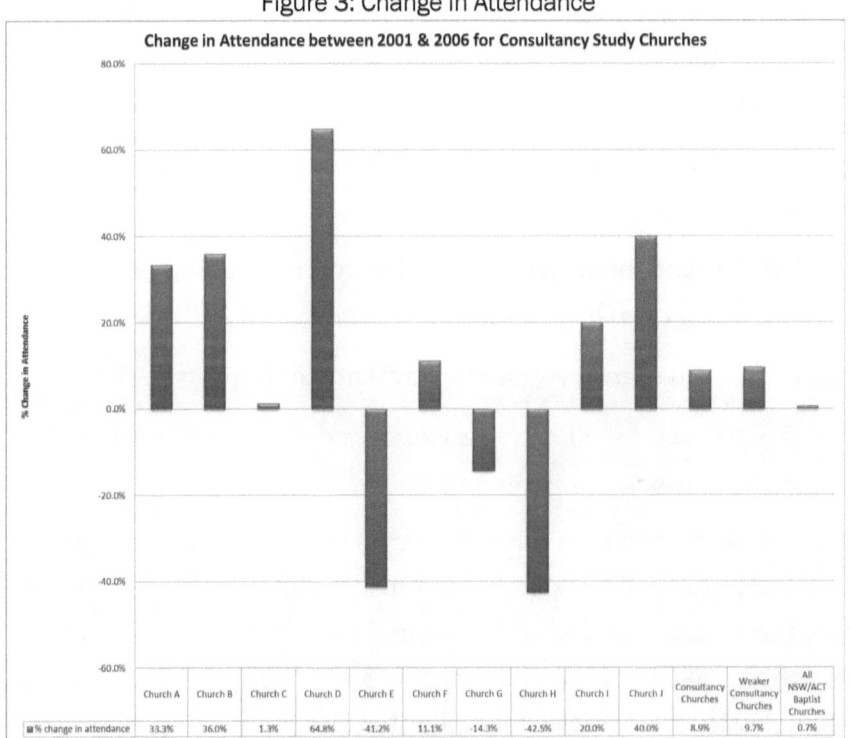

Figure 3: Change in Attendance

Church consultancy case study: Church D

Church D is located in the developing suburban ring in Western Sydney and had an attendance of 91 at the time of the church consultancy.[22]

In this suburb, the country of origin is Australian-born for 68% of residents (Sydney 61%). The largest age group is those aged 20 to 39 (34%; Sydney 33%), with a correspondingly high proportion of those aged five to nineteen (25%; Sydney 14%) indicating that this is an area where young families settle, with many purchasing homes (46%; Sydney 23%).[23]

Rather than seeking to address a serious problem, this proactive consultancy was mainly focused around growth issues; how to inculcate vision to those who are joining the church, structures that will be effective for this stage of the church's growth, and enhancing communication in the context of the church's development.[24] While there will always be issues to address in any church, inviting outside assistance early to assist with navigating expansion issues is perhaps a more effective use of the church consultancy process, enabling such churches to take the step to the next level of growth.

The following objectives were established by the church leadership for the consultancy:

1. Develop and implement appropriate communication processes within the church.

2. Define and share a vision in a way that the church owns it.

3. Design the most effective structures and strategies to achieve the church's vision.

The leadership team and the church accepted the consultancy report. The church had already taken "significant steps…to address communication, vision, and structure issues" addressed in the consultancy report at the time of its writing.[25] NCLS–2006 indicated that a clear and owned vision was the church's strongest core quality indicator, and this had increased 67% from NCLS–2001. The core quality indicator of inspiring and empowering leadership increased 121% over this time, reflecting that effective structures and strategies (along with strong empowerment of attenders for ministry) to achieve the church's vision had progressed. Considerable increases were recorded for each of the nine core quality indicators, leading to an overall increase of 63%.[26] The Senior Pastor serving the church in 2001 has continued to lead it to the present. Attendance grew to 150, an increase of 65% over the period to 2006.[27]

The benefits of using church consultancy proactively to address structures and strategies surrounding growth — rather than reacting to problems — are underscored in this case. This would be a worthwhile area for further research.

Church consultancy case study: Church F

Church F is located in an isolated mining city in the far west of NSW, and had an attendance of 45 at the time of the church consultancy.[28] The average age of those attending the church in 2001 was 57 years, 5 months.[29] This is well above the average age of attenders in all NSW/ACT Baptist churches who completed NCLS–2006 (n=150) of 46 years eight months.[30]

In this city, a high 95% of residents were born in Australia. The community has a higher than average 22% of residents whose stated religion is "no religion" (NSW 13%). Occupational groupings indicate a lower socio-economic profile.[31]

This church was, at the time of the consultancy, in receipt of a subsidy from the Baptist Churches of NSW/ACT, and as such was encouraged to consider a church consultancy to seek to address any issues of health and growth.

The following objectives were then established by the church leadership for this consultancy:

1. To explore ways of encouraging non-members to take the step into membership.
2. To encourage and support the Aboriginal leadership in the growth and development of their fellowship within the life of the church.
3. To develop the corporate prayer life of the church.
4. To develop mission strategies that will lead to effective church growth.
5. To enhance the overall music ministry of the church.

6. To become a financially [self] sufficient church under the guidance of God.[32]

The leadership team and the church accepted the consultancy report. Many of the recommendations from the report have been implemented. There is a sense of energy, encouragement, and anticipation among the congregation, since "the consultancy in some way provided some hope; that it didn't necessarily mean that when the money ceased, life would cease".[33] The number of children from outside the church attending the Oasis ministry continues to grow. The growth of the Aboriginal Fellowship continues, with involvement of Aboriginal young people in the music ministry of the church. This alleviated some of the concerns raised in Objective 5 of the 2001 Consultancy Report regarding the ongoing viability of worship music in the church, as health concerns raised questions surrounding the future availability of the organist. Finances continue to be an area of concern for the church. The lack of clarity regarding the church's vision, mission, and values did not appear to have been addressed when a review consultancy was conducted in 2003. However, the focus beyond the church into the community grew over this timeframe, and the church gained encouragement as they felt "maybe we're achieving something here…being more effective".[34]

NCLS–2006 reveals an increase in the proportion of church attenders who are employed (22% in 2001, to 36%), and a decrease in the proportion of church attenders who are retired (52% in 2001, to 36%). Clear advancement in Objective 6 is demonstrated in those not giving to the church declining from 14% (2001) of the congregation to zero, and those who regularly give 10% or more of their net income increasing from 36% (2001) to 41%.[35] The work the church has put in to enhancing its life and outreach is reflected in the overall increase of core quality indicators of 52%. The only core quality indicator to decrease is vision. The effort put into an intentional welcoming strategy for newcomers is reflected in the core quality indicator for inclusion increasing by 150%. During the five years to 2006, the attendance increased by 11% to 50, and the proportion of 30 to 49 year olds attending the church increased.[36] It is encouraging that despite the church's smaller size, operating in an isolated community environment, and having some significant viability concerns in 2001, an intentional engagement by the church in the consultancy process has resulted in encouraging outcomes in both attendance and health indicators over this five-year period.

Evaluation and interpretation of results

Many of the churches that form our study were struggling numerically and financially prior to inviting a church consultancy, evidenced by 80% of these churches having an attendance of less than 100. This numerical and financial stress is also indicated by 50% of consultancy churches being in receipt of a ministry subsidy at the time of the consultancy, either from the Baptist Union of NSW/ACT or another source.

Broadly speaking, the above results are encouraging in terms of the impact of church consultancy on a church's health or core qualities, and on a church's growth. This study is limited by both the number of churches that submitted reliable data for both the 2001 and 2006 NCLS and the number of churches that undertake a church consultancy each year. These factors impacted the significance levels that were able to be obtained in statistical analysis, particularly for the three attendance measures (attendance, newcomers, and young adult retention); therefore the value of a study expanded to include a higher number of churches is indicated.

Marked improvements in church attendance were evident from the consultancy cohort, but these were not statistically significant. The increase in eight of the nine core quality indicators, along with a statistically significant increase in six of the quality characteristics (service, faith-sharing, worship, leadership, belonging, and vision) between 2001 and 2006, gives scope for asserting that church consultancy has been an important factor in restoring or improving church vitality in the group of consultancy churches. In other words, that there is a link between churches that have undertaken a church consultancy and churches that have improved their health through deliberately addressing deficiencies in various areas of their church life.

The interviews confirmed the positive impact of a church consultancy on a church's growth and health. There was slight variation between the interview responses and the NCLS data for each church regarding health and growth. The interviews validated the role of church consultancies in identifying and addressing areas that were blocking health and growth in the life of each church, resulting in such outcomes as: merging congregations and seeing a resultant growth spurt, gaining a clearer vision and specific strategies for moving forward, addressing relational conflicts that were holding the church back, or identifying strategic opportunities to launch out into new ministries that impact the surrounding community.[37]

Implications for pastors and church consultants

Church vitality can be impacted

While external factors such as local community context, national context and trends, and national denominational characteristics have an influence, local church internal characteristics are the most significant determinant of a church's health and growth.[38] This is good news for churches, church leaders, pastors, and church consultants, because it means that they can exert some influence over church vitality. Of course, this is not straightforward, and requires a deepening dependence on God alongside any technical skills. Responsiveness to local demographic characteristics and national trends will still be important if a church is to be missionally relevant. Indeed, some of the churches included in this study had challenging local contexts but were empowered through the church consultancy process to respond to those settings.

There is hope for existing churches

The positive energy generated by exploring new models of doing and being church, and of advancing frontiers through church planting cannot be underestimated. But sometimes the implicit message heard (though perhaps not intended) is that church revitalisation is of lower importance. Of course, having a church consultancy is no golden pathway to revitalisation, but at its best consultancy embeds into the ongoing life of a church: good process, the church as participant/learner, a team approach as a consultancy oversight group works with the leadership team and pastor, and big picture vision and strategies. Additionally, this research underlines that revitalisation, while not undemanding, is a possibility for churches that have plateaued or are declining.

There is hope for small churches struggling with viability

Of the churches that underwent a consultancy, 50% were struggling at that time with their numerical, financial, and ministry viability such that they were in receipt of a ministry subsidy, either from the Baptist Union of NSW/ACT (four) or another source (one). Over the succeeding five years, four out of five of these churches grew: Church B and Church J recording growth of 36% and 40% respectively, albeit off a low base. The interview with the pastor of Church F indicated that, for them, the removal of the subsidy was a spur to lift their ministry to the community and their giving levels: "the consultancy in some way provided some hope; that it didn't necessarily mean that when the money ceased, life would cease".[39]

For churches in situations of struggling ministry viability, pastors, churches, consultants, and denominational leaders can often give up hope. However, while possibilities for struggling churches can be precarious, to abandon hope is not an appropriate response in the light of this research (nor theologically). For a church to acknowledge that something is wrong, even not knowing exactly what that is or how to move forward, and then to invite outside assistance, can be the first step to new life as a church and a renewed mission in their community.

There may be opportunities for good churches to become great

Often church consultancy has been used as a last resort for broken churches, and denominations inadvertently carry the message that their resources are focused on islands of sickness rather than to enhance health.[40] While no problem is insurmountable, the difficulty of using consultancy in situations where a problem has existed for one, two, or ten years is clear. Rather, what would happen if, instead, external intervention resources, whether coaching/mentoring or consultancy, were focused proactively on the middle third of churches (either in size or health indicators)?

Churches of any size can benefit from an outside perspective and external facilitation. While it is only one example, the situation of church D may be instructive. Many of the issues facing the church were growth-related: communication, vision, and leadership structure. When some of the bottlenecks were released, rapid growth of 65% over five years ensued. Some already healthy churches regularly access outside interventions, say every three years. What could happen in church health and growth if *all* churches did this?

Ownership enhances buy-in and partnership

The opportunity for the appointed leadership of each church to set consultancy objectives — and therefore give shape and direction to the consultancy process — is important. Because it is in this partnership between the consultants and the church leadership/pastor that new possibilities for the church are forged. Ownership of the process and an ongoing commitment to see it through are key ingredients in sustaining greater levels of church health.

In a similar vein, the focus of the process facilitator–participant/

learner type of consultancy is on building the capacity of the church through adding to the strengths of existing and new leaders. The use of a consultancy oversight group to lead and facilitate the process with the church and other leaders is one key part of this capacity-building. An issue or problem can generate a lot of energy and, with that energy, people who are motivated to learn, serve, and lead to be part of the solution.

The place of church consultancy in revitalising churches

Church consultancy is one significant catalyst emerging for the revitalisation and transformation of churches. Drawing from disciplines such as organisational development and theology, church consultancy can be a process-oriented ministry tool for a local church to listen to God and fashion a response to their circumstances. Church consultancy is not the only health strategy that is available to churches, and there may be situations when other approaches such as mediation, an intentional interim pastor, or coaching, are more appropriate. However, church consultancy can make a substantial contribution in either proactively addressing a specific problem, managing a specialised response to difficult situations of transition, recovery from crisis, or conflict, or unlocking bottlenecks to church health and growth. This research highlights that even for churches that are stuck, plateaued, declining, or on the edge of viability, God can still produce new life and transform inflexible wineskins so they may hold the "new wine" he releases.

Ian Duncum has worked in many Baptist churches as a pastor, Intentional Interim Pastor and church consultant. He has also trained church consultants and is an Associate Researcher with NCLS Research. This chapter is drawn from Duncum's DMin research: "Explore the Impact of One Model of Church Consultancy on Church Health and Church Growth in NSW/ACT Baptist Churches" (Morling College/ Australian College of Theology, 2012).

The Work of Transformation
A Psychodynamic and Trinitarian Synthesis

Jeff Pugh

Many pastors have had the noble ambition to transform a conventional member-centric church into a "salt and light" missional variety. For years I too assumed that if I taught and modelled the concepts and the faithful voted for them that the change to a missional focus would be automatic. Like many of my peers I underestimated the pervasive power of church culture to subvert the purest of intentions. This chapter seeks to do two things. One is to describe the nature of congregational rigidity from an organisational cultural perspective and to posit a possible way that we can evaluate the congregational culture change in theological categories; then to address the question of how the influence of the Spirit might be discerned within those moments in church life when positive culture shift actually occurs against all expectation.

Church cultures are unique, multi-level patterns of relating, feeling, valuing, and thinking. This framework includes the patterns of deference and submission that operate both at conscious and unconscious levels of group life. To discern the divine influence within such a complexity is to sift through the meanings, moods, and emotion-laden narratives of church life for evidence of divine influence. We argue here that if our triune God has been involved in a culture shift then there would be some features of the culture that mirror the attributes revealed to us about the essentials of the triune society. This is not to assume that parallels make the divine- and mundane-relating identical, or that one would be able to discern such transforming work with certainty. Discernment is always probabilistic. To sharpen our discernment we bring into dialogue two complementary frameworks; trinitarian theology and organisational psychodynamic lenses.

The politics of the Godhead

Reflection upon the relationship between trinitarian and ecclesial life became important in the latter parts of the twentieth century. A wide body of writers explored the connection between social trinitarian aspects and the design implications for a church made "in God's Image".[1] The two writers who have drawn the strongest parallels between the divine society and human community culture are Moltmann and Volf. They both note that churches which espouse subordinationist Trinities tend to have correspondingly formalised or disempowering church cultures that exhibit a high power distance between leaders and subordinates. Those who operate out of a more adequate trinitarian perspective develop mutual and reciprocal power distributions.

> The periochoretic unity of the divine Persons who exist with one another, for one another and in one another, finds its correspondence in the true human communities which we can experience — experience in love, in friendship in the community of Christ's people who are filled by the Spirit and in the just society ... the Spirit who is glorified "together with" the Father and the Son is also the wellspring of the energy which draws people to one another, so that they come together, rejoice in one another and praise the God who is himself a God in community.[2]

Moltmann's protégé Volf, who displays an indebtedness to early Baptist radical thought, maintains that the interrelating of local churches should visibly parallel the relating of the persons of the Godhead specifically, as this was Christ's high priestly prayer *"... that they may be one, even as you*

Father are in me and I in you, that they also may be in us, so that the world may believe that you have sent me" (John 17:20–26). Both theologians give weight to the notion of perichoretic interrelating of the triune persons as setting the pattern or ideal for ecclesial community if not the agenda As within the Godhead, so also within the new covenant church; genuine freedom is given for differentiated yet coordinated centres of action, united in love with a passionate concern for the same mission. Any distinctions within the Godhead on substantial grounds, or linear subordinationist processions are inconceivable. So also the church in the image of God should exhibit a *"polycentric and symmetrical reciprocity of the many"*.[3] The interpenetration of divine Persons is equated to interdependence and mutuality of members in service of God and his world.

Volf is particularly critical of "monist" models of the Trinity which can serve as a basis for hierarchical or mystical notions of church. For Volf this comes about when thinking about the issue begins at an inappropriate theological starting point. If we conceive of the Oneness of the Godhead as ontologically prior to the three-in-relationship, history shows we are liable to downplay the importance of the local manifestation of the church in favour of the church catholic. If the Father is viewed as more essentially divine and conditions the divinity of the other persons, the local church then has only a derivative legitimacy. Consequently, the church is present in its pure form in the bishop or council rather than the local ministries. Hierarchy itself is viewed as essential. However, if reflection upon the divine Nature commences with the plurality of equal yet distinct divine persons, rather than upon the unity of substance, a more mutual and polycentric view of ecclesial authority results.

The critical upshot of this oversimplified summary is that Volf and Moltmann also intuited that this mis-imaging of the triune society would produce a prevailing psyche in the local church adopting these categories. If ministry is the privilege of an alien leadership that is qualitatively distinct from the membership, the result is either passivity or an escapist enthusiasm that seeks to draw down the *eschaton* into present mundane life as a compensation for real ministry.[4] We should not think that congregationally governed churches are automatically inoculated against a monistic view of the Godhead and its paternalistic correlates. The notion of the pastor as "anointed" in ways that the church is not, or that the pastor has more "know-how" as the resident expert or CEO, can be just as disempowering for the member. Such linguistic symbolism can affect their self-evaluation of their own contribution to the mission of the church as being of a secondary significance in God's political economy.

Volf therefore discriminates local churches in terms of their political culture along two axes as shown below. The first domain is the distribution of power as either a monocentric/asymmetrical distribution vs. a symmetrical and polycentric. The second dimension relates to the principle of cohesion; either one that is externally coerced or one that is a volitional collaboration. He really is only concerned to contrast the extremes of monistic 1 and 4.[5]

	Monocentric (Asymmetrical) Power distribution	Polycentric (Symmetrical) Power distribution
Coercive external power sources and restraints	1	2
Volitional internal power sources	3	4

The ways persons are socialised into an institution also reflects or contradicts a trinitarian ecclesial parallel. A trinitarian-shaped culture should exhibit minimal formalisation in terms of community rules and restraints as externally applied to the average believer. The proliferation of regulations simply signifies the distance the church is from its eschatological goal and the less likely it is to reflect the mutuality of friendship that should typify kingdom siblings. The tendency for centralising of political structures and their associated "monist" Trinities, manifests throughout the history of the church whenever it perceives itself to be under threat in the form of challenges from within or without. The new covenant vision of a church growing into the fullness of Christ "as each one does its work" (Ephesians 4.14) gives way to a qualitatively distinct leadership while members see themselves primarily as a recipient of pastoral care rather than as Christ's co-workers.

This deficient trinitarian perspective indeed is also the primary mental hurdle with which any change agent has to contend in any attempt to turn the culture of the church outwards toward the central value of mission as integral to Christian discipleship. Consequently, churches formed in such an image are liable to also develop the dynamics of mutual frustration. Apathetic memberships viewing the church as their carer reward the sorts of leaders who will relieve their fragmented inner states with unconditional love. This results in a de-skilling of the membership, shrinking the aggregate capacity that the leadership can exploit. Leaders sense this apathy but ironically equate random member initiative as subverting their own capacity to "make things happen". They close this reinforcing cycle by employing political strategies to garner more power to their coterie thus extending the distinctions between themselves "the essential actors" and the receiving and compliant membership. Every time leadership demands subordination for the sake of the mission as a trade-off for their sponsorship by the needy, the triune image of God in the church further evaporates. This dynamic goes unquestioned as it feels like orthodoxy itself. Members who subscribe to this transaction sense they are honouring some divine arrangement. Consequently, this dynamic is simply replicated wherever more of these co-dependencies are franchised out as new church plants. No amount of spiritual gift discovery programs or calls for sacrificial giving overcome these inherently disempowering centrifugal forces that suck these churches down the vortex of subordination.

The necessary contribution of the psychodynamic dimension

It is critical to note for this discussion though, that the two theologians noted associate forms of power distribution with the subjective psychological states of people within churches. This talk of passivity and utopian enthusiasm calls for a shifting of discussion of organisational politics through a psychodynamics lens. Volf and Moltmann speak as if poorly conceived models of the Godhead which justify these asymmetrical forms happen via a consciously deliberate thinking process. But human cultures are not primarily rational deductive outcomes of logical design. If most cultural energy has preconscious origins,[6] how much more effectively will the regressive and collusive aspects that pervade the deep levels of all group culture generate the very power distributions that foster passivity, immaturity, and missional disinterest. Inadequate views of the Godhead that buttress these sorts of neurotic dependency will be espoused as orthodoxy at the conscious level of group culture.[7]

Those who struggle to attempt transformational change typically fixate upon the surface symptoms and symbols of rigidity such as the weight of constitutional dogmas and past policies, the glacial pace of church meeting processes, and the seeming inability to construct a forum for the imaginative exploration of possibilities. But these surface events have a deeper psychological origin in the shared preconscious experiences of a congregation. And until this deeper level of analysis is employed any agent of change is liable to "tilt at the wrong windmills".

Discourse about regressive behaviour and the emotionality that paralyses normal functioning is the stock-in-trade of organisational psychologists.

The benefit of their psychodynamic view for church culture is that the work of culture forming is occurring both at the surface and the preconscious level of culture, prior to rational confessional conceptualising. It cannot be consciously constructed or manipulated. Under anxiety-producing conditions churches are just as prone to irrationality as secular groups; regressing to infantile positions together without notice.[8] The power of such cultures comes from the fact that we all share the same imperfect primal developmental histories. At the same time though, as we shall see below, this pre-rational perspective can contribute to insights regarding how a group may be transformed in positive ways conducive to the rational collaboration in a shared mission.

Since the early days of their discipline, organisational psychologists attribute the power of group dysfunctions and irrational reactions to their shared "phantasies",[9] or their "basic assumptions" that particularly revolve around the purpose of the group and the expected role of the leader. Wilf Bion observed in his post-World War II therapy groups the same sorts of disempowered responses to group work that Moltmann and Volf anticipated theologically.[10] A group under stress can trigger three sorts of neurotic "basic assumptions" that are entirely unconscious but subvert the espoused reason for the group coming together. "Basic assumptions" exist at the level of the emotional ground of organisational culture and are triggered particularly in times of heightened anxiety, such as occurs in times of change. Being the community of the Spirit does not inoculate the church from these human realities. Any transformation work that neglects these potentials is liable to be frustrating and confusing.

By their fruits you shall know them

Firstly, a "dependency group", signified by *baD*, will project idealisations upon their leader as one who has omnipotent powers. They are the ideal with whom the group desires to merge. When the leader takes up the suggested role or "valency" the prevalent emotion within such a group will be *euphoria*. The unwitting leader may drink deeply from such wells of appreciation but the shadow side of this *baD* projection is always lurking. Other emotions such as resentment at one's personal impotence as a follower and guilt for feeling such things can complicate this seemingly useful position. Such a basic assumption works against any espoused or mature missional purpose as the group is immersed in infantile relating in search of the narcissistic world of the womb. When a leader moves on, *baD* groups become pathetic or dependent on the group manual or rulebook. The *baD* group is pretty unforgiving of pastors who throw responsibility back to the group. Evidence of *baD* sabotage of transformational leadership can be heard underneath charges that the disgruntled spokespersons cast at the pastor, such as "being uncaring", "social gospel", "pushing out the oldies", or "never visiting like...(insert name of idealised former pastor)".

In contrast the "flight-fight" group, *baF*, exhibits paranoid tendencies and under conditions of stress resort to splitting their world, their denomination, or even their church into good and evil coalitions. Those people who affirm their particular coalition are by definition "good" and those with a contrary agenda are by definition "evil". A high blame quotient in church life that attaches to change-oriented pastors can absolve the *baF* church from examining their own poor performance or taking responsibility for the present. Such groups minister suspicion rather than hope and have a simmering hostility toward any transformation that would disturb this paranoid agenda. Pastors may be praised by *baF* groups if they can identify external enemies of orthodoxy. The group can avoid real mission in the real world by focussing their shared projections in depersonalised hostility upon the opposition or any new change-oriented pastor who has the audacity to suggest they are capable of real work! If none exist, a pastor who has a few internal demons of their own can be a welcome substitute. Being the pastoral appointment following a pastor who has cultivated a *baF* is a fool's errand.[11]

Finally, Bion also noted the *baP* which is called the "utopian" or "pairing group". Such groups exhibit the semblance that there is a qualitatively new era, new idea, age, or person still unborn who will magically deliver the group from their present anxiety-producing predicaments whatever they may be. Such a group may deceive the unwary leader that they are actually filled with faith and hope, and even a narrative of sensuality and sexually charged charisma. But it is only the *unfulfilled* vision that motivates them and any leader who takes on this messianic mantle is in a double bind of making sure such a hope never materialises in real group work while fuelling the devotee with future visions that stimulate *the feeling* of hopefulness. Such enthusiasms vanish in the light of rational auditing and can also turn hostile with the transformational leader being charged variously with being either a "false prophet" for their lack of magical impact or "an unbelieving liberal" for failing to stoke the opiate of baseless optimism. Fixation with revival rather than the actual ministry achieved within present time and space holds the group anxieties in check.

These phantasies are impervious to rational confrontation and simply do not respond to theological education. They consume the oxygen of those who would fan the flame of missional ministry. Moreover, such groups in ecclesial settings will come wrapped in their own preferred theological metaphors, proof texts, and pet God Images. While these can illuminate the keen observer to the particular *ba* beneath the conscious surface[12] they justify and reinforce neurotic positions with reforming zeal. Not surprisingly many churches can therefore espouse the missional mantras of the coming kingdom, while in real time work out the dictates of their primal underworld.

Bion has done transformational leaders the service of stripping away any naïveté regarding the simplicity of the process for inducing transformational change. Only a minority of groups constitute what Bion termed "*W*" or "working groups" where leaders were able to facilitate group work rationally and "scientifically" investigate the espoused group task.[13] The bad news is that psychodynamic theorists are far from optimistic about the potential of inducing change in an organisational culture defined by a basic assumption or shared phantasy.[14]

The way back is the way forward

The good news is that primal development processes also indicate a way forward to overcome the phantasies that bedevil missional refit work. Another breed of organisational theorists operates from an "object relations" framework.[15] These analysts see parallels with the world of organisational life and the healthy maturational process through which infants individuate and mature rather than the positions through which we all pass. They posit that in adult life the world of work can be remarkably reparative, making up for less-than-perfect parenting environments and less-than-complete negotiation of the developmental tasks of infancy.[16] Remarkably the two preconditions for the workplace to have this reparative impact are determined by whether the organisation performs in a way analogous to a predictable parenting in the infant–mother relationship. Firstly, organisational life needs to supply an "adequate holding environment" or a relatively responsive level of attending to the legitimate needs of persons "held within the arms" of organisational culture. As the mother's arms are the first culture the infant learns to negotiate so the organisational culture is like a second mother who can compensate for the deficits of the first infancy. As the infant struggles to differentiate from the mother in tantrums yet at the same time grieving over hurting the one who loves them, so a secure robust organisational culture provides the security for individuation by consistent socialising without threat of rejection. A member can learn to accept a less-than-perfect church life just as the infant can accept that their mother is neither an extension of themselves nor the perfect carer.

Secondly, the provision of "transitional objects" such as the comforting rugs, thumbs, and toys of the infant enable the child to handle the stresses associated with maternal absences. They are of great symbolic value to the child as in fact surrogates of motherly care that enable the child to develop a non-anxious identity. In organisational life these objects are the assigned tasks of the workplace. Just as the symbolic substitute which can be both manipulated, even attacked, and used as a source of comfort, so also the role supplied by meaningful ministry into which they can "sink their teeth". By the same token, the removal of responsibility or destruction of one's investment in one's career can be as emotionally threatening as the removal of the pacifier or destruction of the infant's teddy-bear. These objects of infancy and adulthood both share an illusory role, the latter being both useful objective artefacts and at the same time meaningful subjective symbols of self-worth.

> Such organizations create developmental cultures because people are free to focus on the work they do, can achieve a greater sense of wholeness, and therefore restructure their relationship to their own internal objects. Because the focus is on the work itself, people are less afraid to scrutinize their working relationships and are therefore less likely to distort them with projections and introjections that limit their capacity to observe and learn.[17]

The ecclesial equivalent developmental culture happens when members participate in symbolically meaningful ministries that matter to significant others too. Conscious acceptance of one's distinct function within a bounded reliable body of believers (Rom 12.4–8) is enormously reparative psychologically since there can be no more reparative integrating group therapy than understanding and finding one's place within the inviolable *missio Dei*!

Here then is the crux of the matter. While primal phantasies provide the most delicious escape routes from spiritual maturity in mission, it is the partnership with God's redemptive work that is the ultimate panacea for phantasy and the road to rational adulthood. The parallels with the Pauline manifesto are obvious.[18] It is no accident that the core function of the church leader is to "reset the dislocated"[19] member of the body for the sake of the maturation of the whole (Eph 4:14–16). There is a strong argument here that the work of the new-creation-order effectively utilises the creation order developmental processes for more ultimate ends; the process of rejuvenation of the image of God within and among his saints.

Synthesising trinitarian and psychodynamic insights for culture change

So, what then determines whether a particular church culture will ever take up its missional option when human nature, in the form of our propensity toward phantasy, works against real work? And how do we discern grace within the chancy natural processes in the church? If grace and nature converge so neatly, a pragmatist may be tempted to synthetically induce the effects of spiritual regeneration through their own managerial smarts. We would surely prefer to work synergistically with God's Spirit rather than proceed on a single track under our own steam. Therefore it is critical to discern where our church culture is situated relative to the designs of God's Spirit. Here sacred and secular change agents follow parallel processes.

1. Firstly, we need to take stock of the sorts of attributes of the triune interrelating that God desires to form in the cultures of churches that carry his image.

2. Secondly, change agents then need to diagnose where or how the church is functioning relative to those ideals by objectively reading the symptoms of these on the narrative surface level of their church life over time.

3. Thirdly, utilising what we now know about the parallels between an object relations role in individual maturation and organisational change, we need to cultivate the habits and mindsets that match those processes. This involves far more than formal levels of structuring which is no match for the informal power of shared

phantasy. It requires the vigilant reinforcing by leaders, modelling and rewarding any actions which move in the direction of a trinitarian culture form. Transformational leaders have the responsibility of creating a dependable "holding environment" through a consistently just ethos and a cultivation of persons through ensuring all members' own "transitional objects" find space for expression.

Although the very notion of the image of God within human politics has been criticised recently,[20] the internal politics and imperatives of the apostolic writers reveal many striking parallels to the triune relating. Some that come to mind include the following.

1. *Polycentricity*: decision making is participatory, consensual, uncoerced, and respectful of individual dignity (Acts 15:2, 22) and aspirations to lead are encouraged (Romans 12:8; 1 Timothy 3:1).

2. *Unity of Will*: A godly church is devoted to the wellbeing of all, not just the prominent members, and receives the contribution of many charisms for the sake of the one body (1 Corinthians 12:7, 13:8–13; Eph. 4:3–6).

3. *Flexibility*: The contextual variation of the church reflects the sovereign decision of the Spirit (1 Corinthians 12:11) who distributes the charisms as he wills situationally rather than prescriptively.

4. *Reciprocity*: While leaders are respected for their gift, their role is to foster the giftedness of others into services (Eph. 4:11–16). It is such wisdom that commends the leader in the first place (1 Timothy 3:4, 5:17, 18).

5. *Interpenetration*: While not ontologically possible, the parallel here is that the work of the Spirit brings with it the endorsement of Son and Father (1 Corinthians 12:4–6, Ephesians 4:4–6). When

missioners act in Christ's name more than the immediate agent are present subjects (Acts 15; 1 Corinthians 5).

6. *Generativity*: Antithetical to a theology of control, the leader is not measured by the scope of their personal influence over subordinates so much as their capacity to fan aflame the contributions of others (Ephesians 4:8–12).

7. *Volitionality*: The genius of the triune-shaped church is that it is not held together by rules policed by strict governance but cohered by fellowship with the head through discernment processes (Acts 15:28).

8. *Collegiality:* Leadership is never heroic or dramatic but mutually accountable and called into the foreground only by the presenting needs of the current landscape (1 Timothy 4:14, Acts 20:17, Galatians 2).

These are actually descriptions that could define a unique organisational culture.[21] This should not surprise us as the eternal Spirit knows no other cultural ideal than the triune reciprocity, generativity, volitionality, and mutuality in which the Spirit was and is eternally "socialised". The preconscious power of shared culture will either cooperate with the mindset of the Spirit, or, be co-opted by the preconscious phantasy agenda and these differences will be starkly obvious.

The change leader could focus their discernment upon four "vestiges" of trinitarian relating in particular. These four domains could also then be seen as spectra upon which the current culture can be located. The reason why these are selected is because they reflect cultural patterns that are incompatible with basic assumptions yet they are the very issues that have to be resolved for any culture to exist or have any permanence.[22] While these are distinct issues, these four cultural features should all be present in a consistently "triune" culture.

Domain #1: Means of Coordination: from resignation to empowerment

This dimension would reflect the degree to which persons are resigned to sponsoring the important clerics and professionals and become passive consumers of their care as a trade-off for compliance with their superiors, rather than being supplied with their own "transitional objects" or responsibilities to "sink their teeth into" on the road to personal reparation. There is a world of psychological difference between being held accountable to an alien strategic plan of a superior versus aiming to please the Giver of one's talents through creative self-expression.

Domain #2: Power Concentration: from monocentric asymmetry to polycentric symmetry

At one end of this domain, leaders have an automatic reflex to control ministry and shore up the legitimacy of their powers. Initiative flows downwards. At the renewed pole all are "in the know" and decision making is then a collaborative process in line with the Spirit's polycentric power disbursement. Trinitarian leaders don't so much give away power as recognise the power already resident within others.

Domain #3: Source of Coherence: from coercion to volition

At the carnal pole the *laos* instinctively senses that initiative must first be given permission, and leaders' first reflex is to construct policies or demand compliance to a procedure manual. Relationships are therefore contractual; compliance can be enforced. At the opposite pole, the synergy from shared vision or evolving from experimental learning produces outcomes greater than the sum of the individual capacities. In particular the trust which leaders enjoy as initiators is extended to similar initiatives of those they foster. In a way that a controlling manager cannot fathom, their role shifts from enforcing compliance to the sheer joy of generating ministry.[23]

Domain #4: Collegiality: from anxious enmeshment to robust relating

The leadership of a church is that group which is connected more than any other to the various systems and subcultures of any church. Any transformation that leaders desire for their churches has to commence in the essentials of communication within the colleagues entrusted to lead the church into the future. If relationships are anxious and enmeshed here, this anxiety cannot be contained within the team but will set the climate of the whole group. If all are genuinely heard and consensus is more than a democratic formality, this sub-culture will also permeate the whole community. Ironically, in the longer term a group where dissent is welcomed will achieve more in time than any covert politics to "push the agenda through" and without the psychodynamic side effects.

Given any culture change is always resisted and since the psychological expectation of a voluntary rational shift from a neurotic constellation to a healthy working culture is notably low,[24] when churches do take on the mandate of self-less, other-focused mission we have every reason to believe that a miracle of grace has occurred. The presence of the triune God is likely creating a culture that corresponds in some way to the eternal triune love.

Conclusion

Those who would love to see their church do what they espouse with regard to mission have two options in the process of attempting transformation of culture. One approach tends to act as if God is absent and utilises the construction processes of corporate culture. These inevitably focus upon establishing one's own powers within the culture or taming the primal forces within it. The problem is that such leaders have to marshal rhetoric for this power shift that comes from the carnal world to justify that coercive measures are godly in terms of being a means to a noble end, when disempowering measures contradict the imaging of the triune God. Such pragmatics has little impact upon the natural regressive tendencies of anxious groups, especially when they sense a culture change is brewing. Basic assumptions will surface, subverting the "real work" of mission. At best, committed/passive members become financial subscribers of imported professionals as substitutes for their own ministry responsibilities at the cost of their own healing and maturation. The total talent base of the church shrinks. A trinitarian vision trusts in the renewing, self-righting influence of a present triune God, building a cultural godliness through the aegis of his Spirit. But this is not to be confused with an apathy born of a naïve magical trust but a sacramental view of transformational leadership. Missional leaders prize the work of culture construction because God is at work in the multiple layers of inter- and intrapersonal complexity. It is, then, this renewed culture that becomes the seed-bed from which the unique creative local solutions and missional initiatives can take root and flourish without sabotage from the power of the preconscious. Then these potentialities that come in union with Christ through the baptism of the Spirit will orchestrate the redemptive engagement of this cultivation culture before the watching world, to the glory of God the Father.

Jeff Pugh is a practical theologian who has pastored several Baptist Churches in the 1980s and 1990s and since then has taught in Baptist seminaries in three states with roles as a denominational consultant in church development. In recent years his main role has been in developing the postgraduate research school with the Melbourne School of Theology. His research interests focus mainly upon organisational culture change and homiletics.

Giving Newcomers a Voice
What Newcomers Reveal about their Experience of Joining a Church

Ruth Powell

Through their own experiences, newcomers to church life can teach us about the process of discipleship. The National Church Life Survey gives a voice to thousands of people who have only started attending church in recent years. This chapter describes the demographic profile of newcomers and how they are spread across denominations. We learn about the significant people, activities, and events that help them come to faith. We find out how and why they joined their church. Do they go church-shopping? What triggered their decision to attend? The basis for this study is the main 2011 National Church Life Survey results as well as a series of random sample polls of church attenders. By testing our assumptions against the evidence, we can evaluate our practices and, perhaps, make it easier for more newcomers to find their way into faith communities.

Introduction

There are many people who are convicted of the need for "new wineskins" in Australian church life. To imagine and strive for new forms of church life is one way to strengthen the capacity of the people of Christ to contribute to God's ongoing mission. The challenge for those who attend churches is to determine what these new wineskins might look like in order to be effective vessels. What will improve connections with those who have little or no contact with the Christian community of faith? The Australian

National Church Life Survey (NCLS) can provide valuable information on this question drawn from people who are recent arrivals to church life — those we call "newcomers". We can give newcomers a voice so that we may learn about their experiences of both faith and church life. Long-termers or enthusiastic change agents may sometimes drown out the voices of newcomers. However, newcomers' views and experiences of coming to faith and finding a way into a church can provide a rich evidence base for the pursuit of the most helpful forms of new wineskins.

After first defining what we mean by "newcomers" in the National Church Life Survey, this chapter is organised into five parts:

- Part A: An overview of newcomers
- Part B: Coming to faith
- Part C: Finding a church
- Part D: Individual religious beliefs, practices, and experiences
- Part E: Becoming involved in local church life.

Defining newcomers in the National Church Life Survey

Australian National Church Life Surveys are multi-denominational projects that started in 1991. The primary aim of each NCLS is to provide information to congregations and parishes about the health or vitality of their church. In 2011, some 23 denominations and movements participated in the 2011 National Church Life Survey (2011 NCLS). This five-yearly national project occurs in the same year as the National Census of Population and Housing. The 2011 NCLS was the fifth time it has taken place in Australia.

This study is based on survey respondents who are "newcomers" to church life. Newcomers are defined as *those who have attended their present congregation for less than five years and previously were not regularly attending church.* They are made up of two groups: first-timers and returnees. First-timers are those who have attended church for less than five years and have no previous background of church involvement. Returnees are those who have returned to church life having not attended church for several years. In this chapter, we will not focus on differences between these subgroups.[1]

In National Church Life Surveys, newcomers are one category of church background and only one kind of "new arrival". The full array of possible church backgrounds is as follows:

- *Visitors:* Attenders who do not normally attend the congregation
- *New arrivals:* Attenders who have joined their present congregation in the last five years and are either:
  - *Transfers:* Previously attended a congregation of the same denomination
  - *Switchers:* Previously attended a congregation of a different denomination
  - *Newcomers:* Were not previously attending anywhere else
- *Long-term attenders:* Those who have attended their congregation for more than five years.

Part A: An overview of newcomers

Key finding 1: The level of newcomers to Australian churches remained static between 1996 and 2011 at 6%.

The overall level of newcomers to Australian churches has remained consistent over time. Some 5% of all church attenders were new in 1996, and 6% were new in 2001, 2006 and 2011.[2]

First-timers made up a third of these newcomers (2%), having never regularly attended a church in their life. Returnees made up two-thirds (4%): they have returned after a long absence from church life.

This balance between first-timers and returnees remained unchanged between 2001 and 2011.

Key finding 2: Newcomers were found in all denominations, although they made up higher proportions in Pentecostal, Salvation Army, Churches of Christ, Vineyard, and Anglican churches.

Table 1 lists the percentage of newcomers in the larger denominations that took part in the 2011 NCLS.

Pentecostal movements[3] had the highest proportion of newcomers (11%). Among this group, C3 Churches had the highest proportion overall with 14.5% newcomers. While it is true that part of the growth in this sector of Australian church life comes from attenders transferring or switching denominations, the inflow of newcomers should not be downplayed as another important component of their story of growth. These churches are successfully attracting people who have not been part of a church in the previous five years.

Other denominations with higher proportions of newcomers included the Salvation Army (10.6%), Churches of Christ (9.2%), Vineyard (8.3%), and Anglican churches (8.1%).

Table 1: Percentage of newcomers by denomination: 2011

Denomination	% in 2011
Anglican Church of Australia	8.1
Apostolic Church of Australia	10.5
Australian Christian Churches (Assemblies of God)	10.5
Baptist Churches	6.7
Catholic Church in Australia	3.4
C3 Church (was Christian City Church)	14.5
Christian Outreach Centre Australia	12.6
Christian Reformed Churches of Australia	1.3
CRC Churches International	8.5
Churches of Christ	9.2

Lutheran Church of Australia	3.7
Presbyterian Church of Australia	6.6
Pentecostal*	11.0
Seventh-Day Adventist Church	7.2
The Salvation Army	10.6
Uniting Church in Australia	5.9
Vineyard Churches Australia	8.3
Total	**5.8**

NB. *Some denominations are missing from data tables (e.g., Apostolic, Brethren, Christian Missionary Alliance and Foursquare, International Pentecostal Holiness Church, Grace Communion, Nazarene) because the sample of participating congregations was not sufficiently representative of the denomination.*

Pentecostal includes Apostolic Church, Australian Christian Churches (AOG), C3 Church, Christian Life Churches, Christian Outreach Centre, CRC Churches, Foursquare Church, International Pentecostal Holiness Church.

Key finding 3: Newcomers are more like the "average Australian" than other church attenders.

One way to learn about newcomers is to build a profile of their age, sex, education levels, ethnic background, and other demographic characteristics. There are numerous studies that have shown how different church attenders are from the "average Australian". National Church Life Surveys and other sources have shown that people who attend local congregations are much more likely to be female, older, married, and more highly educated than the wider population.[4] In contrast, on average, newcomers are more likely than other attenders to be younger, male, and separated or divorced. This brings them somewhat closer to representing the diverse mix of the Australian community.

The average age of a newcomer in 2011 was 43 years old. Figure 1 shows that newcomers were most likely to seek out the church in early to mid-adulthood (in their 20s to 40s). It also shows that, across all denominations, other new arrivals in the past five years were more likely to be younger on average: switchers (43 years) and transfers (47 years) compare with long-term attenders (59 years).

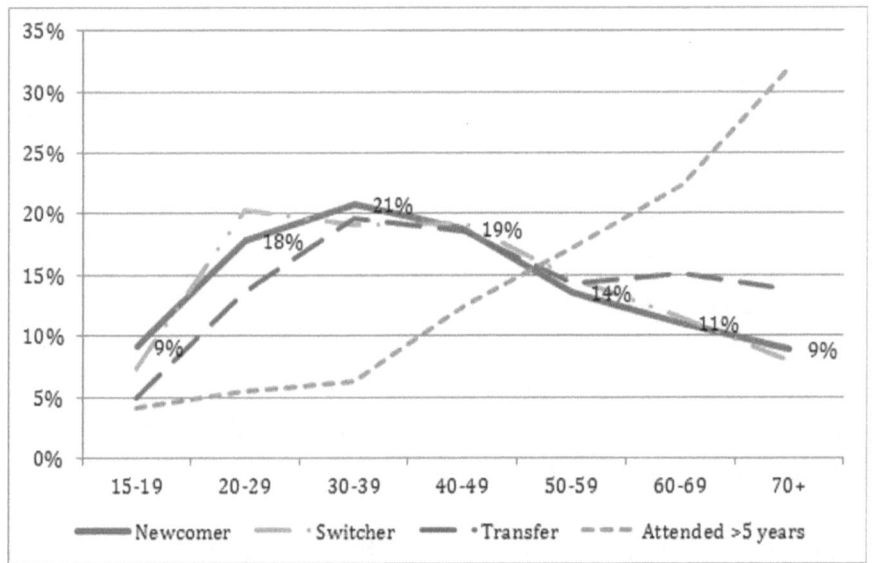

Figure 1: Age profile by church attender background

Source: 2011 National Church Life Survey — Attender Survey A (n = 216,373)

In terms of education levels, newcomers (32%) were similar to all attenders (33%) who had university degrees in 2011. This compares with 24% of the general Australian population in 2011. However, on closer inspection, newcomers differed from other new arrivals. They were less likely than switchers (40%) and transfers (47%) to be university educated. Further tests were conducted to check whether this difference was simply related to the fact that newcomers are younger on average and fewer have completed their tertiary-level education. However, the lower education levels of newcomers persisted even when controlled for age.

Figure 2 shows that compared with attenders with other church backgrounds, newcomers were:

- Slightly less likely to be female
- Among those most likely to be employed
- Most likely to be separated/divorced
- More likely than other new arrivals to be born in Australia.

While the demographic profile of church attenders continues to have large gaps when compared with the wider Australian population, newcomers are an important reference point, as they are the group that is closest to "normal" in terms of their age spread, gender balance, and marital status. Newcomers are not necessarily being drawn from Australia's recent migrant population, who are likely to have had some connection with church life in their country of origin.

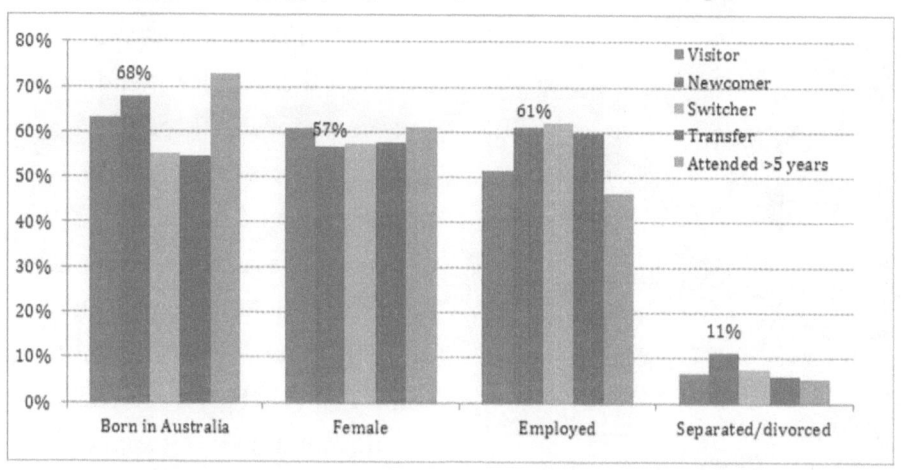

Figure 2: Demographic profile by church attender background

Source: 2011 National Church Life Survey — Attender Survey A (n = 216,373)

Part B: Coming to faith

In this part we explore newcomers' experience of coming to faith, learning who were among the most significant people in their faith journey, and what the most significant activities or experiences were.

The experience of coming to faith

Key finding 4: Nearly three out of ten newcomers have had a moment of decisive faith commitment, whereas 56% have had faith as long as they can remember, or have come to faith through a gradual process.

AS THE YEARS WENT BY, JEFFREY WOULD HAVE NO TROUBLE REMEMBERING HIS CONVERSION EXPERIENCE

Some people can identify a definite moment of commitment in their faith journey. Nearly three out of ten newcomers (29% vs. 31% overall) could identify a specific moment (or moments) of decisive faith commitment or Christian conversion. Yet, a larger group did not fit this convert profile. Newcomers were almost twice as likely as other regular attenders to have come to faith through a gradual process (35% vs. 17% overall). Around one in five (21%) of newcomers responded that they have had faith for as long as they can remember (vs. 46% overall). Some 15% said they do not know or that the question is not applicable (vs. 6% overall).

Attenders were asked if they could identify a particular age when they first became a Christian. Newcomers were less likely than all attenders to have been converted as a child (51% vs. 66% overall), and more likely to have been converted between the ages of 15 to 29 years old (34% vs. 23%) and 30 and over years old (9% vs. 7%).[5]

Significant people who showed what faith was about

Key finding 5: Mothers are most likely to be named as one of "the most significant people to show me what faith was about".

©Chris Morgan 1994   cxmedia.com

The role of mothers in the faith journey was important for newcomers (52%), as their role was for the majority of all church attenders (66%). Other family members who appear in the "top five" groups of significant people for newcomers were fathers (34%) and grandparents (17%). These results highlight the importance of close relationships in demonstrating a living faith. What more can be done to support families to explore and share faith with each other?

Newcomers were just as likely as all attenders to identify the minister as a significant person (28%). However, in contrast to all attenders, they were more likely to nominate peers/friends (23% vs. 11%) and other church attenders (12% vs. 5). (See Table 2).

Table 2: Most significant people for faith: newcomers vs. all attenders

"The most significant people to show me what faith was about…"	Newcomers %	All attenders %
Mother	52	66
Father	34	47
Minister	28	28
Peers/friends	23	11
Grandparents	17	14
Other church attenders	12	5
TV/radio evangelists	4	1
No-one in particular/don't know	6	1

Source: 2011 National Church Life Survey: Attender Survey B (n =1166).

Newcomers — including returnees — have had a different religious socialisation experience to those who perhaps have always been part of church life. Their parents were comparatively less involved in church, if at all, and their influence, while significant, was not as far-reaching. Around half of newcomers (46%) had either one or both parents attending church regularly before they were 12 years old, which is much lower than for other attenders (71%). The vital role of other close relationships, beyond the family, in helping people to engage questions of faith and life is confirmed by the experience of newcomers.

The most significant activities and experiences that help people come to faith

Key finding 6: Church worship services are the most significant event that newcomers recall in helping them come to faith.

Attenders could choose up to two options from a list of 13 activities that may have been significant to help people come to faith. The top seven significant activities for newcomers, in order, were:

1. Church/mass (62% vs. 60% overall)
2. Adult small group (17% vs. 10% overall)
3. Church camp (12% vs. 9% overall)
4. None of these (12% vs. 7% overall)
5. Confirmation (10% vs. 5% overall)
6. Sunday School (9% vs. 17% overall)
7. Youth group (9% vs. 15%).

Compared with other attenders, newcomers were less likely than average to name school Scripture (8% vs. 18%), mission group/organisations (5% vs. 3%), introductory series (4% vs. 3%), or major evangelistic events (0% vs. 5%). While these activities have their place in what has been described as "pre-evangelism", in this random sample they did not feature when newcomers were pressed to choose their top two significant activities.

It appears that the "ordinary" everyday activities of local churches must not be under-estimated in their role in nurturing people in their faith journeys. In particular, these results suggest that investing in the weekly worship service experience bears fruit for all.

Significant experiences in coming to faith

Attenders were also offered a list of possible experiences and asked which, if any, were most significant in their coming to faith. These included things such as the death of another person, serious health problems or injuries to self or others, financial hardship/job loss, getting married, the birth of a child, a change in relationship, a crisis or disaster, or a crime against your person or property.

The options provided in this question did not appear to resonate strongly with attenders as they recalled their own experience. Some 40% did not select any of the options, and 25% identified some other event. Of the listed events, newcomers were more likely than other attenders to name the death of another person (16% vs. 9%) or serious health problems/injuries to another person (8% vs. 4%). They were less likely than average to name getting married as one of their most significant events (3% vs. 10%). However, none of these differences between newcomers and others was statistically significantly different. Significant life events can trigger reflection on life's big questions that may lead to exploring Christian faith. Yet these results suggest they do not feature strongly as people recall their own faith journey.

Part C: Finding a church

Do newcomers shop around for churches? What triggers the first church attendance? What helped them stay? The questions we explore in this part are about joining and leaving churches and were included in a set of questions titled "why you came to *this church*".

©Chris Morgan 1994   cxmedia.com

Finding a church

Attenders were asked, "In the 12 months before you came to this local church for the first time, how many other local churches did you visit or attend regularly?"

Key finding 7: Newcomers do <u>not</u> shop around for churches.

In the 12 months before starting at their current church,

- 67% didn't visit or attend any other church.
- 19% visited/attended one other church and
- 6% visited/attended two or more other churches.

These results indicate that newcomers tend not go "church shopping". We cannot know from this study how many Australians tried to attend a church in the past 12 months and didn't continue. However, newcomers are dramatically different from other new arrivals: compared with two thirds of newcomers who now attend the first church they tried, only 11% denominational switchers and 17% of transfers did not shop around for churches.

What triggers the first church attendance?

Key finding 8: "Something was missing in my life" is the most common situation or event named by newcomers as most important in their decision to attend a local church again.

After a question that explored reasons why a person may have left a previous church, church attenders were asked, "When you *began attending a local church again,* what situation or event was most important in your decision to attend? (Mark one only)" Of course, for many attenders, this question is not applicable. However, it provides further important insights into how newcomers recall their own story, particularly those have returned to church after a long absence. Out of ten options (plus "not applicable"), the top five reasons for newcomers were as follows (compared with all attenders):

1. Thought something was missing in my life (24% vs. 7%)
2. Moved to a new area (10% vs. 24%)
3. Spouse invited me to attend/accompanied spouse (9% vs. 3%)
4. Had a conversion experience (9% vs. 2%)
5. Had a personal crisis (7% vs. 2%).

Other possible options included: wanted my children to have a religious upbringing, friend, family member, or other contact invited me, reasons related to my health, felt guilty about not attending, other reason/can't remember.

What helped newcomers stay at church?

Key finding 9: What is most important in helping newcomers stay in a church is the friendliness of the people/sense of community.

AFTER FINALLY CONVINCING HIS NEIGHBOUR TO COME TO CHURCH, STEVE STARTED QUESTIONING HIS PLAN.

Attenders were asked to think back to the time that they first became involved in "this local church" and identify how important various aspects were to starting to attend "here"? The proportion of newcomers who responded "very important/important" is shown in Table 3 (compared with all attenders).

Table 3: What is most important in helping people stay in a church: newcomers vs. all attenders

	Newcomers %	All attenders %
Friendliness of the people/sense of community	84	76
The quality of the preaching/teaching	77	73
Character/style of leader	76	74
Sense of God's presence	75	80
The stance of people on beliefs or values	67	65
Concern for wider community	62	67
Already having friends or acquaintances here	57	46
Being invited by an attender	51	33
Children/youth activities	43	50
Being invited here by my spouse or other relative	32	33

Source: 2011 National Church Life Survey — Attender Survey H (n = 1498).

When it comes to what helps people stay at a new church, some factors rise to the top for both newcomers and other attenders alike. That first experience of a friendly church community is vital for all. A second set of reasons seems to link with the worship experience. They are the quality of the preaching/teaching, the character/style of the leader, as well as a sense of God's presence. The presence of children/youth activities is also important to similar proportions of attenders from all backgrounds and highlights this important motivator.

Personal relationships are important for all attenders, however, they stand out as even more critical for helping newcomers to stay. Newcomers were more likely than other attenders to name such relationships as very important or important: already having friends or acquaintances here, being invited by an attender, or being invited here by a spouse or other relative.

In terms of intentional follow-up by the local church, a third of newcomers said there was no contact after their first visit and 19% said that an attender phoned them. Only around 6% to 13% could recall other intentional contacts, such as a visit, phone call, letter, or postcard from the minister/pastor/priest, a package of materials about the local church, a welcome gift, or an invitation to a program or activity for new people, or a meal in a home.

Views about worship services

Key finding 10: The most common reasons newcomers give for attending worship services are to experience God and learn about faith; most have grown in their faith in the previous 12 months.

When asked about their experience of the worship services, newcomers are second only to switchers in their positive experience of inspiration, joy, helpful preaching, growth in understanding about God, and challenge to action. They also reported having experienced much growth in faith in the past 12 months due to their congregation (40% vs. 24% overall).

A sample of attenders were able to choose two main reasons they attend worship services. The top three reasons newcomers gave for attending (compared with all attenders) were:

1. To worship/experience God (62% vs. 58%)
2. To learn more about the faith (32% vs. 12%)
3. For encouragement and inspiration (16% vs. 22%).

Similar proportions of newcomers named other motivators which, in a few instances, were significantly less important for them when compared with all attenders. They were:

- To share in Holy Communion/ Eucharist/ Lord's Supper (15% vs. 30%)
- I need a time of prayer or reflection (15% vs. 13%)

- To make sure my children are exposed to the faith (13% vs. 9%)
- To feel a sense of community (13% vs. 12%).

Newcomers were more likely than all attenders to favour worship that offers new experiences each week over consistent worship (44% vs. 36%) and to find sermons relevant (71% vs. 62%), educational (68% vs. 54%), inspirational (63% vs. 55%), comforting (62% vs. 48%), and challenging (52% vs. 48%). Yet, newcomers were less likely than other attenders to prefer a quiet, reflective worship style (32% vs. 42%). They were also less likely to agree that "music and singing is an important part of church worship for me" (47% vs. 68%).

How vital it is that worship services provide a nurturing space for visitors and new arrivals to worship God and learn about the Christian faith. How often do churches simply cater to the preferences of long-term attenders? Dealing with different cultural preferences in terms of worship style continues to be an ongoing challenge.

Part D: Individual religious beliefs, practices and experiences

Key finding 11: While newcomers are less likely to assent to orthodox beliefs, their views and experience of God are no different. They are most likely to have grown in their faith in the previous year.

When newcomers to church life were asked their beliefs about God, their responses were very similar to all attenders. Similar proportions of newcomers also claimed to definitely believe in heaven and hell. They were also just as likely to have had a significant religious experience of the presence of God. Similar to all attenders, they were more likely to take a contextual, rather than a literal view of the Bible.

©hris Morgan   1995   cxmedia.com

However, as Table 4 shows, they were less likely than all attenders to be definite in their acceptance of other Christian beliefs, such as those to do with Jesus Christ, life after death, and miracles. Further, fewer newcomers see God as one of the most important realities in their lives.

In terms of adopted various religious practices, newcomers were less likely to have adopted practices such as reading the Bible, regular private devotions, or saying grace at meals. On the other hand, they are no different from the average attender with regard to their involvement in prayer groups, practice of Christian meditation, or level of satisfaction with their private devotional life.

Joining a church can be a time of profound spiritual change for newcomers. Nearly one in five (18%) of newcomers said they had experienced one moment of decisive commitment or Christian conversion in the last five years (compared with only 4% of attenders generally). Previous work using National Church Life Survey results found that for most, the conversion experience occurred in the same year or after joining their present congregation.[6] However, in broad terms, this profile challenges any idea that there is a single clear moment, even at a definitive moment of conversion, when the whole "package" of Christian orthodox beliefs is adopted.

Of course, there is a variety of views about religious beliefs and practices across all attenders. Further, newcomers are in their first five years of being part of a local church — either returning after a long absence or as a first-timer — and it is possible their beliefs or practices will change over time. What is clear is that while belief in God is an uncontested foundation, beyond this, newcomers do not simply assent to a set of accepted Christian doctrines or beliefs.

Some caution also needs to be taken when making assumptions about the adoption of religious practices. While newcomers may adopt some recognised practices at a later stage, there is also evidence that they adopt other practices, which they claim at this stage in their faith journey to find just as satisfying.

It appears that many newcomers are in a stage of transition, taking on the beliefs of Christian faith and working through its implications for their lives. This is highlighted by the fact that newcomers are most likely to have experienced much growth in faith in the previous year and to say that the church was the source of their growth in faith "to a great extent".

Table 4: Religious beliefs, practices, and experience: newcomers vs. all attenders

	Newcomers %	All attenders %
Newcomers are <u>less likely</u> than all attenders to...		
Say that God is more important than almost anything else or the most important reality in my life	70	83
Agree Jesus was both fully God and fully human	87	93
Agree that Jesus' resurrection from the dead was an actual historical event	86	91
Definitely believe in life after death	70	75
Definitely believe in miracles	59	67
Believe the Bible is to be taken literally word for word	18	23
Have spent time in private devotions at least weekly	64	74
Read the Bible at least weekly	38	47
Say grace at meals every/most days	24	42
Pray as a family at least weekly	21	29
Have a shrine, altar, or a religious object on display	25	45
Newcomers are <u>no different</u> from all attenders in terms of...		
Belief in a trinitarian God	91	92
Using concepts of God, such as forgiving, loving, and merciful, in similar ways	98	98
Definitely believe in heaven	75	77
Definitely believe in hell	60	61

Having had an experience of God — "Suddenly and strongly are aware of God, sense that God is real, or sense God's presence or God's power"	83	85
Believe the Bible should be interpreted in light of its cultural and historical context	36	38
In prayer groups at least weekly	28	30
Practice Christian meditation at least weekly	25	20
Satisfaction with devotions	55	60
Newcomers are <u>more likely</u> than all attenders to...		
Experience much growth in faith in the previous year	57	42
Say the church was the source of their growth in faith to a great extent	46	39

Source: *2011 National Church Life Survey — Attender Survey A (n = 236,275), Attender Survey B (n = 1,365), Attender Survey C (n = 1,392), and Attender Survey J (n = 1,430).*

Part E: Becoming involved in local church life

Key Finding 12: While newcomers are less likely to be involved in formal church outreach and service activities or have ministry roles, they are most likely to be inviting others to church or informally helping others.

Previous National Church Life Survey results have revealed that, on many measures, newcomers are less involved in the activities of the churches. Contrasted with the image of the "starry-eyed enthusiast", the passage of newcomers into church life was described as sometimes tentative and slow.[7]

The 2011 NCLS results confirm again that newcomers were less frequent in worship attendance and less involved in congregational mission activities (see Table 5). Their sense of belonging to the institution, whether belonging to the local church, or to the denomination, was lower than for all attenders. They were less likely to have roles within congregational life, and less likely to have helped with parts of the service such as readings and prayers. Perhaps not surprisingly, they were also less involved in pastoral work (e.g., being an elder, visitation team). They were less likely to say that leaders have encouraged them to find and use their gifts and skills to a great or to some extent.

Yet, with the benefit of additional survey questions in the 2011 NCLS, there is more to add to this profile of how newcomers are involved in church life. On closer inspection, newcomers are no different from other attenders when it comes to how much they trust people at their church or their satisfaction with the closeness to their church friends. Further, they are no different in terms of the hours of voluntary time given to a congregation in ways to help people in need, or the number of important church projects they've been involved in.

Newcomers were also just as likely as other attenders to assist in running children's or youth programs. This is not simply because newcomers tended to be younger, as the results held after controlling for age. This result is in line with other findings that point to the motivation of some newcomers to provide a religious framework for their children.

In terms of mission engagement, newcomers actually stand out from attenders of other church backgrounds on some features. While they may not be part of the church's formal outreach activities, they are more likely overall to be willing to invite people to church and have actually done so in the past year. While they tend to be underrepresented in formal community service activities, newcomers are among those most likely to have been involved in informal helping actions, such as caring for or visiting the sick, lending/donating money or giving possessions, contacting parliamentarian/councillor on a public issue and so on. They are also more likely than average to want to prioritise social justice and aid in their church. Further, they are most likely to value social activities or meeting new people.

How do newcomers view leadership and directions for the future?

Key Finding 13: Newcomers are very positive about their local church leaders and are most confident about the church's capacity for innovation and achieving future goals.

Table 5: Involvement in church life: newcomers vs. all attenders

	Newcomers %	All attenders %
Newcomers are <u>less likely</u> than all attenders to…		
Attend church weekly or more often	69	82
Be involved in social groups within the congregation	26	31
Be involved in congregational mission activities	11	17
Feel at ease/mostly at ease talking about their faith	60	69
Be involved in community service activities	15	24
Say leaders encourage them to find and use their gifts and skills to a great or some extent	42	49
Have a ministry role	25	43
Help with parts of the service such as readings and prayers	19	29
Be involved in pastoral work (e.g., being an elder, visitation team)	1	8
Have a strong sense of belonging to the congregation	74	83

Have a strong sense of belonging to the denomination	78	85
Newcomers are <u>no different</u> from all attenders in terms of...		
How much they trust people at their church	93	92
Their satisfaction with the closeness to their church friends	81	78
Whether they give voluntary time to a congregation in ways to help people in need	50	50
Be involved in small groups within the congregation	29	30
Major involvement in one or more important church projects	14	18
Levels of assistance in running children's or youth programs	19	16
Always seeking out and welcoming new arrivals	14	15
Newcomers are <u>more likely</u> than all attenders to...		
Want to prioritise social justice and aid in their church	19	17
Be willing to invite people and done so in the past year	40	34
Most value social activities or meeting new people	18	12
Agree that leaders take into account people's ideas to a great extent	41	37
Agree that leaders inspire them to action	73	62
Agree that leaders keep them focused on the community	78	73
Agree that leaders in their church are strongly focused on future directions	78	73

Agree that leaders encourage innovation	73	65
Strongly agree that the church is always ready to try new things	22	17
Not to be aware of the church's vision	20	17
To be fully confident in the church achieving its vision	49	42

Source: 2011 National Church Life Survey — Attender Survey A (n = 236,275) and Attender Survey D (n = 1,440).

Newcomers tend to have very positive views of their local church leaders. When comparing attenders from different backgrounds, newcomers stand out as second only to switchers in their levels of positivity. They are among those most likely to agree that leaders inspire them to action, keep them focused on the community, communicate clearly/openly, encourage innovation, are strongly focused on future directions, and help the church build on its strengths.

Along with switchers who have joined from other denominations, newcomers have the highest proportions to agree that the church is always ready to try new things, that leaders encourage innovation and are strongly focused on future directions. While a subset of newcomers are not (yet) aware of the church's vision for the future (20% vs. 17% overall), a larger proportion are fully confident that the church will achieve its vision (49% vs. 42% overall).

Further analysis and reflection are needed to unpack these differences in how newcomers engage in church involvement. The differences may be quite subtle and, on the surface, the outcomes may look very similar. These results do suggest a form of commitment to the institutional church. However, perhaps this is not shaped by an overarching sense of duty and loyalty, but emerges out of a commitment to a set of supportive relationships between individuals, where trust is built. We need to better understand where and why newcomers do get involved. How much does self-interest, such as a commitment to the needs of their children, play a part, and how can this be harnessed? Do they get involved at the points where the opportunities are clearest or, perhaps, where they are allowed? In what ways do local churches unintentionally or intentionally exclude newcomers from participating, and thus potentially miss out on a fresh perspective? Newcomers may well be one of the strongest assets that a local church has for mission engagement. They are likely to have connections beyond the church, and tend, on average, to be motivated to get involved in social action and to share their experience of church and faith with others.

Summary

This chapter has provided a profile of newcomers to church life based on the results of the 2011 National Church Life Survey. The key findings from each part are summarised below.

An overview of newcomers

1. The level of newcomers to churches remained static between 1996 and 2011 at 6%.

2. Newcomers were found in all denominations, although they made up higher proportions in Pentecostal, Salvation Army, Churches of Christ, Vineyard, and Anglican churches.

3. Newcomers are more like the "average Australian" than other church attenders.

Coming to faith

4. Three out of ten newcomers have had a moment of decisive faith commitment, whereas around half have had faith as long as they can remember, or have come to faith through a gradual process.

5. Mothers are most likely to be named as one of "the most significant

people to show me what faith was about".

6. Church worship services are the most significant event that newcomers recall in helping them come to faith.

Finding a church

7. Newcomers do *not shop around for churches.*

8. *"Something was missing in my life"* is the most common situation or event named by newcomers as most important in their decision to attend a local church again.

9. What is most important in helping newcomers stay in a church is the friendliness of the people/sense of community.

10. The most common reasons newcomers give for attending worship services are to experience God and learn about faith; most have grown in their faith in the previous 12 months.

Individual religious beliefs, practices, and experiences

11. While newcomers are less likely to assent to some Christian beliefs, their views and experience of God are no different from other attenders. They are most likely to have grown in their faith in the previous year.

Becoming involved in local church life

12. While newcomers are less likely to be involved in formal church outreach and service activities or have ministry roles, they are most likely to be inviting others to church or informally helping others.

13. Newcomers are very positive about their local church leaders and are most confident about the church's capacity for innovation and achieving future goals.

By giving newcomers a voice we have learnt more about their experiences of both faith and church life. The evidence does not support the image of the "wild-eyed convert". Newcomers come to faith in a range of ways, often over time, with the help of close family and friends. They tend not to visit many churches, which makes it vital to keep them in mind for the normal activities of church life. While they do not necessarily adopt certain Christian beliefs or practices immediately, they are generally open to learning and growing in faith. Those who have managed to find their way into a faith community are among the most positive attenders, valuing the leadership and future directions, and getting involved in new and different ways. For those committed to supporting new followers of Christ, this is an encouraging profile of a group of people who have found some local churches to be places of welcome and nurture, and who can also make a valuable contribution to the church's ongoing mission.

Ruth Powell has been a part of the NCLS Research team since 1991, becoming Director in 2007. She has co-authored NCLS publications on church life such as Winds of Change, Shaping a Future, Taking Stock, Build My Church, Mission under the Microscope, and Enriching Church Life. Her doctoral thesis focused on age differences among church attenders and she is an Associate Professor with Australian Catholic University.

Copyright for cartoons in Chapter 13 is held by Chris Morgan. All cartoons were originally published in previous NCLS Research publications and permission has been granted for their reproduction in this publication.

A Contemporary Theology of Local Church Mission, in Global Perspective

Darren Cronshaw, David Chatelier, Brent Lyons-Lee, Ryan Smith and Anne Wilkinson-Hayes

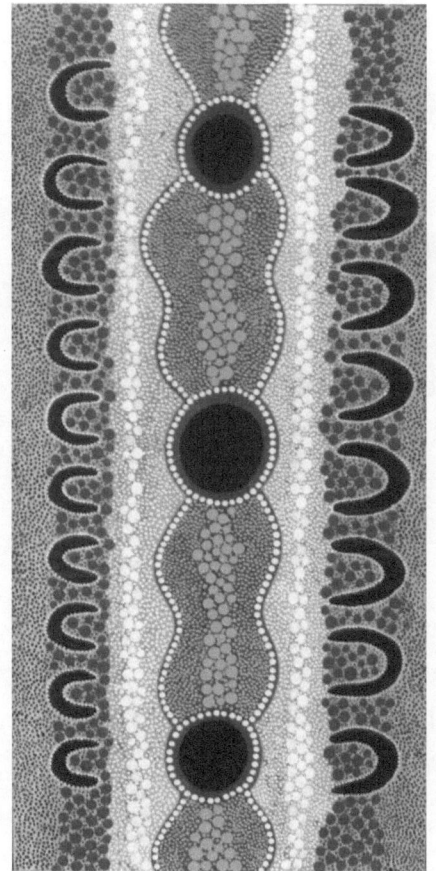

The Waters of Baptism by Robin (Goma) Conlon 2012.

The Baptist Union of Victoria (BUV), in common with many churches and denominations in the Western world, is realising it needs to revisit its purpose — what is its earthy use? Inspired by Micah 6:8, the BUV Mission Catalyst team has developed a contemporary theology of local church mission, in global perspective. Local church mission is firstly spiritual and starts with discipleship and listening to God (walking humbly with God). Second, local church mission is radically inclusive of people and groups across all sorts of boundaries and especially cultural diversity (loving kindness). Third, local church mission is transformational and fosters peace or shalom in our neighbourhoods and our world (committed to doing justice). The local church in mission ought to be good news and caring for individuals, communities, society, and the environment.

A recent radio talkback episode explored the question "of what earthly use is the church?"[1] We might ask that question with more focus, "of what earthly use is our church?" or "What is our particular contribution to our neighbourhoods and to our world?" We like to ask this of our churches. What would be your response?

Goma's painting: *The Waters of Baptism*

What do you see when you look at this image of Robin (Goma) Conlon's painting "The Waters of Baptism"? Maybe just shapes, dots and wavy lines?

Perhaps the title helps you to see the river running down the centre of the picture? Humans, in indigenous artwork, are depicted by curved crescent shapes, which reflect the pattern a man or woman makes when they sit in the sand. On the right hand side the shapes are slightly larger — reflecting the elders in a community. Men and women of faith and wisdom are calling others to leave the darkness of the world (the smallest black edging dots) and, washed in the blood of Jesus (the red dots which surround the crescents), they should commit themselves to a new life following Jesus, mediated by the Holy Spirit (the white dots) by coming through the waters of baptism (the central river of blue) and joining the community of faith. The large black circles are the traditional symbols of initiation so the three circles show being baptised and starting a new life in the name of the Three — Father, Son, and Holy Spirit.

This is an image of the mission of the church. The people of God call others to turn around and start a new allegiance and live new values. We are to transform the darkness of life and bring light, love, and healing in Christ, and so build a new community of grace and peace.

This is the earthly use of the church. This is the earthly use of our Baptist tribe of churches. This is, firstly and foundationally, a spiritual activity — it can only take place in partnership with the living God. David Tacey writes that, in contemporary postcolonial Australia, spirituality is entering our life from below, and the feet play a more important role than the intellect. Tacey quotes Barbara Blackman as saying that if we want to "under-stand" spirituality in this country we have to "stand-under" our habitual logic and our usual perceptions, since that is the vantage point from which the spirit is found. Understanding calls us away from our conscious conventions.[2]

It is also, secondly, an inclusive activity, for all are called into God's kingdom and the life of Jesus must be accessible to all.

It is also, ultimately, a transformational activity because change is at the heart of the good news of Jesus. Tacey encourages us to learn from Indigenous Australians:

> We are witnessing the rebirth of an ancient experience of the spirit. The spirit is holistic, embodied, mystical, and immanental rather than transcendental. And while the process has only just begun, and will take a great deal more time to be realised, Australia could provide important spiritual leadership to the Western world, because what we are undergoing here is a transformation that all Western nations will eventually have to undergo if civilisation is to recover a creative relationship with the earth.[3]

We are changed, and the world around us is changed, when we accept the call and allow God's love to work in and through us.

Our Theology of Mission is thus encapsulated in this lovely image — we encourage churches to use it to imagine and tell their story of call and transformation.

Reimagining the BUV

Just over 350,000 people or 1.64% of the population identified as Baptist in the 2011 Australian Census. Of that number, 60 percent participate in church monthly or more, which equates to 1 percent of the Australian population participating in Baptist churches. In Victoria our Baptist church started in 1837. Since 1862 Baptist churches have associated and resourced one another as the Baptist Union of Victoria. In 2014 our tribe of Victorian churches numbers 216, with about 15,000 formal members and 30,000 participating. And we are growing although mainly through immigration. Compared with other denominations, Baptists are going okay, but these figures are disappointing given the "greatest cause" in the world we have to share.

A recent re-imagining process for the BUV identified mission as the key organising principle for the church. A missionary is not only someone who is sent overseas. We are all missionaries. Michael Frost writes that mission is the unstoppable program of God's unfurling kingdom on earth; both the *announcement* and the *demonstration* of the reign and rule of the triune God.[4] Our goal is to alert people to God's reign by demonstrating (justice, love, reconciliation) and announcing (heralding, worship, evangelism) that reign.

We read of this invitation in Micah 6:8:

> He has told you, O mortal, what is good;
> and what does the Lord require of you
> but to do justice [be transformational],
> and to love kindness [be inclusive],
> and to walk humbly with your God [be spiritual]?
>
> (NRSV)

Or in the words of an Australian paraphrase:

> Come on people! God has told us what is good.
> We know what the LORD wants from us:
> To make sure everybody gets a fair go;
> To be passionate about caring for others;
> And to stay on track with God without getting full of ourselves.
>
> (Nathan Nettleton LaughingBird.net©2002)

We love this verse and how it shows the earthly use of the church in all different directions. Does your church tend to focus on one or two of these, rather than all three? Sometimes we focus more on wanting to demonstrate care with mercy, or changing the world for justice, or personally relating to God and helping others do that. Yet they are all equally important and necessary expressions of the church showing the dream of God.

Historically there has been an unhealthy tension between the "announcing" and the "demonstrating" of the kingdom because it has been reduced to singular concepts of "evangelism" and "social action". Many Christians believed that evangelism was more important than social action. Frost helpfully points out that evangelism and social involvement are so entwined that you can't unravel them. They are both equally important and necessary expressions of alerting people to the reign of God: "We feed the hungry because in the world to come there will be no such thing as starvation. We share Christ because in the world to come there will be no such thing as unbelief."[5]

Mission is everything God is doing in the world to restore the world to God's dream. Thus mission is the overarching purpose of God, which includes evangelism, mercy, advocating for justice, and caring for creation. According to David Bosch mission is a larger, more expansive, all-encompassing enterprise of which there are many subsets including evangelism and social action.[6] This is important to understand in order to transform the Christian mindset to be kingdom orientated.

In announcing and demonstrating the kingdom we need to reflect God's justice. Understanding the justice of God and the call of the local congregation is best demonstrated as "shalom": the fullness of life and delight and wholeness that come with God's kingdom. Our template is shown in Jeremiah 29 and Isaiah 65 which hold up the hope of a whole new world of peace, fulfilment, and belonging. The people of God are continually called and *sent* to fulfil this agenda of God's, and to cooperate in its fulfilment.

Thus, the key question for the church is not *what can we do for God? It is what is God already doing and sending us into?* Where do we see evidence of God already at work? Our goal and desire are to join with and enhance what God is doing in the world.

Let us explore three principles to help us identify kingdom living and what it means in terms of mission in local church(es). Like a three-legged stool, we need all three legs to be useful and balanced. Yet we need to begin by realising that as churches we are of earthly use when we are most authentically spiritual.

A. Local church mission is spiritual

The invitation of a loving God is to walk humbly with God. John wrote: "*We love, because God first loved us*" (1 John 4:19). This is the starting point of mission. Our voluntary joining in with all that God is doing in the world is first and foremost a response of gratitude to the generosity of God. If our lives are not filled with the enormity of all that God has done for us in Christ, then any attempt at "doing mission" will be an awkward addition to church life — yet another "should" or "ought" on our agenda. Paul had this in mind when he admitted:

> If I speak in the tongues of mortals and of angels, but do not have love, I am a noisy gong or a clanging cymbal. And if I have prophetic powers, and understand all mysteries and all knowledge, and if I have all faith, so as to remove mountains, but do not have love, I am nothing. If I give away all my possessions, and if I hand over my body so that I may boast, but do not have love, I gain nothing.
>
> (1 Corinthians 13:1–3, NRSV)

If mission does not naturally flow from our life in Christ, then we should stop thinking about mission and start thinking about prayer and discipleship.

Mike Breen, who founded 3DM as a movement to refocus on discipleship and mission, comments:

> People want to create missional churches or missional programs or missional small groups. The problem is that we don't have a "missional" problem in the Western church. We have a discipleship problem. If you know how to disciple people well, you will always get mission. Always.[7]

Our experience confirms Breen's observation. We need to invest in our spiritual lives and the spiritual lives of our people. A church that loses its soul will be unable to conduct effective mission. Recent literature about revitalising churches and helping them recover a mission-focused ministry tells us that it starts with people rediscovering a passion for Jesus, and a fresh encounter with God. Let's honestly ask, are we running on empty as far as relationship with God is concerned? When we tell our testimonies are they all about events that happened years or decades ago, or are we telling stories of what we are experiencing God doing this week?

The 3DM questions for accountability groups are, "What am I hearing God saying?" and "What am I going to do about it?" These questions are a good starting point for renewing discipleship for mission by starting with God. Local church mission is essentially spiritual. We therefore need to be spiritually renewed before we can begin to do effective mission in God's way.

Simply making time to stop is a key issue in our busy lives. Jesus regularly withdrew to be on his own with God. In Matthew 14, Jesus heard John the Baptist was murdered and he "withdrew … to a solitary place" (v.13) until 5000 people needed feeding and healing. He sent the disciples on in a boat and "went up on a mountainside to pray" (v.23) till the disciples' boat needed help from a storm. Jesus was in demand but he needed to get away regularly for prayer and solitude. It was obviously difficult for Jesus as the crowds tended to follow him and people were constantly interrupting his retreats, but it was still a clear aim. If it was important for Jesus, how much more do we need to make space to hear God?

In what ways can we cultivate a closer attentiveness to what God is saying to us, and cultivate mission that is spiritual?

Spending just ten minutes a day being still and silent — slowing your breathing, listening to the birdsong, noticing the hum of the house or street outside and simply being present to God — can begin a new journey. Most of us have grown up being told that prayer meetings are good for us, but for many, reciting the round-robin shopping list of needs is no longer a satisfying and life-giving experience. The wordiness of prayer meets our needs in the early days of our faith journey, and it's important as a congregation to pray for one another and the world around us, but God often invites into an intimacy with God that goes beyond words. The invitation is to move beyond "communication" into "communion".[8]

Others are finding new life in various spiritual disciplines. The traditional "quiet-time" can be life-giving for some, but others are finding disciplines from the monastic traditions, including alternative ways to prayerfully read Scripture, to be helpful — lectio divina (slow contemplative reading), the examen (asking what is life-giving and life-draining), and fasting are just a few examples.

Often it is hard to begin new rhythms alone. Deliberately meeting with a couple of others can be valuable. Being silent with others can help the discipline, and being accountable to each other for how we act on what God is teaching us can be key spurs to testing out hunches and taking small steps of faith.

Telling the stories of what God is doing in people's lives can also be deeply encouraging. Let's do more to promote and publicise stories of faith, answers to prayer, and the transforming effects of God's initiatives amongst us. This is where our family of churches can be really helpful. It may seem as if God is not moving amongst us, but once we hear what God is doing in other places it begins to heighten our awareness of divine activity on our own doorstep.

Another factor to consider is our environment. When we survey people and ask when do they most frequently encounter God, the top answer is usually "in the natural world — mountains, beaches, forests". Creating the opportunity for people to be in the most appropriate setting, at retreats or camps, or inviting people to wonder about God while we walk bike paths or parks, may be really important for our community's spiritual life.

Many churches are finding that doing prayer walks in the wider community is a great way to get to know your area better and is yet another way to broaden spiritual life and open our eyes and hearts to what God is doing and saying in our neighbourhood.

Balwyn Baptist had always been a place that relied on prayer. The pastor, Gayle Hill, acknowledged that the church's emphasis on the leading of the Holy Spirit for mission could become more focused if they included prayer walking during their evening prayer meetings. She was concerned that none of the new people coming to church were local — they were all driving across suburbs to come to the church. So a small group began prayer walking the neighbourhood around the church: being attentive to what was happening, noticing the people they encountered, and discovering new things about the immediate streets around the church. This they did once a week over twelve months at night (so no-one would see this strange mob at night in the dark!). All the time they lifted the people, places, and their sense of what was happening before God and prayed God's blessing on their neighbours. The following year Gayle and others suddenly realised that the new people who had come to church over the last few months were all local. Something had changed — praise God!

Some honest questions about our spirituality, followed by a willingness to experiment with new ways of discerning where God is at work, might be the beginning of fresh missional transformation for our church(es).

Ideas for discussion and action

1. What examples could you add from your own experience at church or from other places about where local church mission is spiritual?
2. Talk to a sample of 5–10 people in your congregation. Ask them to tell you honestly about their prayers — What works for them? What is a struggle? Do they mainly talk or listen? What do they long for in their prayer life?
3. Could you find two or three people prepared to experiment with different methods of prayer and listening together?

The second principle is that we are of earthly use as local churches when we are inclusive.

B. Local church mission is inclusive

Micah 6:8 invites us to walk humbly with our God and love mercy, and one implication of this is that our community needs to be inclusive, like Jesus. During his inaugural sermon at Nazareth, Jesus outlined his mission manifesto:

> "The Spirit of the Lord is upon me,
> because he has anointed me
> to bring good news to the poor.
> He has sent me to proclaim release to the captives
> and recovery of sight to the blind,
> to let the oppressed go free,
> to proclaim the year of the Lord's favor."
>
> (Luke 4:18–19 NRSV)

Jesus came not merely to stretch popular boundaries of who was acceptable in the community of God — he came to remove those boundaries altogether. The kingdom Jesus proclaimed would be radically inclusive. We use categories like goodness, education, occupation, social status, politics, ethnicity, ability, and physicality to draw boundaries around who is in and out. Jesus made it clear that the kingdom was an open invitation to all. His announcement was to *the poor, the prisoners, the blind, and the oppressed*, and it was good news. Everyone who would come is welcome at Jesus' table.

Jesus not only announced a kingdom of radical inclusion — he demonstrated it. He recruited a band of disciples, not from the religious elite, but from those of the "out-crowd" — Galilean fishermen, tax-collectors, and extreme zealots. He travelled with women, ate with tax-collectors and sinners, touched and healed the unclean. Jesus upset Jewish conventions of who "made the grade" within the Jewish community. This was the main reason they crucified him — he messed with their carefully constructed definitions of righteousness.

But Jesus went further and confronted ethnic and religious boundaries. He initiated conversation with a Samaritan woman of questionable morals. He healed Samaritan lepers. He told a story which cast a Samaritan man, not merely in a sympathetic light, but as the hero! To the Jewish lawyer whose question, "Who is my neighbour?" prompted that story, Jesus made it clear that, in the economy of God, no-one is excluded on the basis of ethnicity. Jesus allowed a Gentile, Syro-Phonecian woman to catalyse a deeper understanding of his calling. He sent the twelve to the tribes of Israel, but he sent the seventy to the nations. Jesus' mission was radically inclusive. Sara Miles suggests: "When you let the wrong people in, the promise of change could finally come true".[9] The kingdom Jesus came to establish challenged socially exclusive boxes. To say, "All are welcome at the table" was Jesus' practice.

Beyond middle-class Bible studies

Ryan Smith belonged to a small group that modelled inclusiveness. He was the designated leader, but through the influence of a young woman whose heart was clearly shaped by kingdom values, it included a diverse array of people. There were two men with acquired brain injuries who come in wheelchairs and so it was an exercise transporting them and getting them into the house. There was a single mother with four children from multiple fathers, a financial planner, an older man with severe and chronic bipolar disorder who could be both delightful and also massively inappropriate, and a few professional people. And then there were the not infrequent guests who accompanied them. Ryan recalls it was chaotic, fun, and completely unpredictable. They frequently had to throw out the agenda and deal with spontaneous issues. Yet God was there, often in surprising and unexpected ways, and the group loved and connected with each other. They prayed, sang, read Scripture, laughed, and cried together.

They once hosted a celebration meal to conclude a term together. They had a guest, a foreign doctor, who, unable to practise yet in our country, was working as a carer in the home of one of the brain injured men. After the meal, which was punctuated by frequent near-choking episodes from this same man, and no doubt caused the doctor some concern, they gathered in their usual circle. Ryan asked a question, "How have you grown through our group this term?" The answers were varied, and often not related to the question at all! But this didn't matter, they were listening to each other. When they came to the doctor, Ryan politely offered him an out, recognising that the question was not so relevant for him. "But feel free … if there is anything you'd like to say?" He paused for a second, and then simply said, "What is this?"

There followed a moment of laughter as it dawned on the group what this doctor had landed himself in that night. The doctor had got a glimpse of the welcoming kingdom of God.

The kingdom of God is radically inclusive — Jesus welcomes all who would come. But by its very nature, it is counter-cultural and confronting. It challenges our neatly constructed boxes. For Jesus that meant standing up against those who drew boundaries around the community of God, and who by doing so, found themselves excluded: the religious elite opposed to Jesus (Matt 23:13–15), the proud who wouldn't humble themselves (Mark 10:14–15), and the rich (Mark 10:17–31). It seems that while all are welcome, some are not able to accept the terms of a radically inclusive kingdom.

Propelled beyond borders

Our picture of an inclusive community of God demonstrated by Jesus inspires our missionary venture. This was so in the early church where the disciples, inspired and propelled by the Spirit of Jesus, saw the influence of the kingdom spread from Jerusalem and Judea, to Samaria, out to the ends of the earth (following Acts 1:8). Exclusive Jewish boxes had been blown apart through Jesus, and Paul was able to proclaim:

> For in Christ Jesus you are all children of God through faith. As many of you as were baptized into Christ have clothed yourselves with Christ. There is no longer Jew or Greek, there is no longer slave or free, there is no longer male and female; for all of you are one in Christ Jesus. (Galatians 3:26–28 NRSV)

Inclusion in the kingdom of God was now defined, not by race, religion, social status, gender, or whatever else we might use to box people, but by simple faith in Jesus Christ. As Australian Baptists, we are compelled by this same mission conviction that in Jesus, all are welcome. Jesus described the kingdom of God as being like a great banquet or wedding feast (Luke 14:15–24; Matthew 22:1–14). The only ones excluded are those who reject the invitation. The hospitality of God offers a place to the poor, crippled, blind, and lame but more than that, we are to go out into the "highways" and "byways" seeking those on the margins of society who don't yet know they are welcome. There is an outward dynamic to kingdom activity: like the refrain from the Narnia books, *further on and further in.*

This hospitality of God has inspired some Victorian Baptists to move out from their conventional meeting places and offer hospitality in the name of Jesus in varying and interesting ways. One community started an alternate "gathering" in a local pizza restaurant which they called "Banquet" based on this parable. It included food, storytelling, celebration, prayers, teaching — many of the same elements familiar in a conventional church service, but "delivered" in a way which is inclusive in a post-Christian context.

Inclusion of cultural diversity

In what areas do you and your church most want to stretch with being inclusive?

One area all our churches need to grapple with is inclusion of cultural diversity. The main reason — and almost the only reason — Baptist churches have grown over the last decade, 2001–2011, is from immigration: 42,430 immigrants have come to Australia who have then identified as Baptists. On the Census figures, this is 98 percent of our growth as Baptists over the last decade! If not for immigration, we would be well below population growth. This underlines how important it is to welcome and celebrate the contribution of newcomers from other cultures. Today 29.8% of Australian Baptists were born overseas, and we need to give fresh thought to helping shape church to welcome and include them. Moreover, the fact that most of our growth (and a lot of our youth and most committed members) comes from immigration strongly suggests we need to give fresh attention to how we include and nurture the faith of our children and youth, many of whom don't make the step into an adult faith and church involvement. And it shows the importance of giving fresh focus to reaching and including other Australian-born people. The immigration growth masks the fact that we are not connecting so well with "average Aussies" and younger generations.[10]

But how well are we doing in including people of diverse cultures, as well as diverse ages, and people with diverse or no experience of church?

Jesus was largely crucified for his inclusion of those whom others excluded. We are called to follow him and be like him. Would they crucify our churches for their radical inclusion?

Ideas for discussion and action

1. If the parable of the great banquet in Luke 14 is a picture of the inclusiveness of the kingdom of God, who are those in the highways and byways in our communities?
2. What patterns and structures can you identify in your own community that knowingly or unknowingly exclude people from exploring or entering the hospitality of God?
3. In what ways can we challenge and move out of our exclusionary boxes?

C. Local church mission is transformational

We are convinced that local church mission is firstly spiritual — founded in love. Secondly it is inclusive — embodying the practices of Jesus. And finally we as local churches will be of earthly use when we are transformational — resulting in peace, or *shalom*.

Transformation is one of those huge, all-inclusive terms. It touches every aspect of our lives: from personal renewal and restoration of our relationships with God and with others, to changing communities, social structures, and cultures; indeed, to the re-creation of creation itself. Transformation is implicit in everything that changes by being touched by the Spirit of God, and yet, in its purest form, the word *transformation* is rarely found in the Scriptures: in the transfiguration of Jesus, in the command to "be continually transformed by the renewing of your minds" (Romans 12:2) [literally, "keep being metamorphosed"], and finally in 2 Corinthians 3:18 where the veil of the old covenant is lifted and set aside in Christ, through the Spirit.

If the term "transformation" is so wide that it applies to everything that changes or so narrow that it applies only to the renewal of our minds, how may we more easily embrace the vision of *Mission as Transformation*? Perhaps one way to do this is to centre on the word "peace"; not just the Greek word from which we get the term "eirenical", but the Hebrew word that encompasses all of our lives, our relationships, and our surroundings: "shalom". Shalom is the vision of wholeness that enables us to enjoy all of our relationships. As Nicholas Wolterstorff says, "Shalom is the human being dwelling at peace in all his or her relationships… to dwell in shalom is to *enjoy* living before God, to *enjoy* living in one's physical surroundings, to *enjoy* living with one's fellows, to *enjoy* life with oneself".[11]

What does "the good life" look like? Plato saw it in terms of *order or orderliness;* Aristotle saw it as *happiness;* and the Enlightenment placed emphasis upon *freedom.* More recently social researcher Hugh Mackay postulated that the good life is encapsulated in Jesus' golden rule, "Do unto others as you would have them do unto you" (Luke 6:31).[12] There is truth in all this. But the biblical vision of transformation that comes closest is captured in the concept of shalom/wholeness/peace.

If mission is transformational, then mission brings *shalom,* or complete peace:

- Peace with God
- Peace with self
- Peace with my neighbour; my enemy; peace in all my relationships
- Peace in our structures
- Peace with creation

The biblical record begins with a perfect creation and ends with a perfectly restored creation. But we live in in-between times, times of tension, disharmony, brokenness, and sin. We have a foretaste of what can be through Jesus, our Prince of Peace, and through the prophets glimpse a tantalising vision of what a transformed creation looks like: when the lion lies down with the lamb, when swords are beaten into ploughshares, when God wipes tears from eyes, and death, mourning, crying, and pain will be no more (Isaiah 65).

Is this view of mission as transformation so distant and utopian that we either dismiss it as a dream or, with Woody Allen, turn it into satire: "the lion shall lie down with the lamb, but the lamb will get no sleep"? Or will we be captivated by the hope that comes from Jesus, that the kingdom of God is like that smallest of all seeds, a mustard seed, that grows ... or like seed that a farmer sows that, even while the farmer is passively asleep, sprouts, and begins its growth towards harvest? Will the struggles of life, around us and within us, squeeze the hope of peace out of us, or will we sing with the angels, "peace on earth" and proclaim with the Apostle Paul that Jesus himself is our peace; that he has broken down the dividing wall of hostility and made peace through the cross?

The dividing wall that separated and that is now broken down in Jesus calls us to an inclusive community where we live out the truth that we are all one in Christ Jesus. Paul framed this in the dividing categories of his day: Jew/Gentile; male/female; slave/free. How might you and I express that in categories that are relevant today as we seek an inclusive community that welcomes all who are held in the embrace of God?

Transforming neighbourhoods and beyond

Several years ago, Indian students studying in Australia did not feel safe travelling outside at night. A local Anglican church, St Columbs in Hawthorn, was not content to sit and let this be the case. They took action and remodelled their church hall, turning it into a cricket pitch. They formed a couple of teams to play against each other, put out a sign, and put out the word that hospitality and welcome were on offer to Indian and other students. Today, the St Columbs Premier League (SPL) has grown dramatically with 400 players in 33 teams. Our AuburnLife Baptist Church is partnering with St Columbs in fielding teams and helping run the program.[13]

Our vision of local church mission as transformation has terrifically good news for individuals, but also for our neighbourhoods and society, for nations and the environment. How broad do you see the transformational influence of the gospel reaching?

As the BUV Mission Catalyst team, we have reflected on the transformation that came to us as individuals when we came to faith at different ages and stages. We recall the transformation that occurred and the peace that came when we first placed our hope in Jesus. We recall how it transformed our relationships with our family and with our work colleagues. It transformed the way we lived our lives and the choices that we made with money and time. With more maturity, we recall how it transformed our view of nations and nationalism, of artificial boundaries and landmarks that we set up to divide people. It transformed our views of war and peace. It transformed us and the environment around us.

Sadly, one of the transformations that did not occur early in our faith for many of us was an ecological transformation in our view of creation. Some of us held a false theology that this world did not matter because it was going to be destroyed by fire. Our more recent transformation is the way in which we see ourselves and others being called to be stewards, caretakers, and curators of creation.

The Micah Challenge states:

> In integral mission our proclamation has social consequences as we call people to love and repentance in all areas of life. And our social involvement has evangelistic consequences as we bear witness to the transforming grace of Jesus Christ.[14]

Our theology informs our minds, actions, and emotions. When we see mission as transformation, and are captivated by the biblical image of peace as the restoration of all creation, we see ourselves, others, our culture, society, and world in a whole new light.

Mission as transformation impels, cajoles, and prompts us towards the hope of wholeness, a shalom bought by Jesus, and empowered by the Spirit, for the glory of God. We dare not give up on this hope as we pray, "Your kingdom come, your will be done" and as we live out our mustard-seed faith.

Ideas for discussion and action

1. What does mission as transformation mean as we learn to love and accept our self, and live in the peace that God gives us?

2. What does mission as transformation mean as we choose to be at peace with others, praying, "forgive us our sins as we forgive those who sin against us"?

3. In what ways can local church mission transform our neighbourhood? And our world?

4. What does mission as transformation mean as we seek to live as stewards of creation, transforming the brokenness resulting from selfishness and sin?

Conclusion

John Hus was a priest and martyr of the fifteenth-century reforms, precursor to the Protestant Reformation. Hus served in the Bethlehem chapel in Prague. Legend has it that prostitutes and swindlers spoiled the local water source, in part from making it a place for unwanted babies. It was a horrific loss of life and loss of good water. The church was compelled to respond to this very real local need. They dug a well near the pulpit inside the church, added a side door for access, and it was even available for locals to use during worship services. They also arranged for art to adorn the chapel walls, commemorating the lost local children and other local scenes.[15]

The response of Hus and that chapel in Prague urges us to ask where are we at our best in local church mission in responding to local and global needs? What is our well? Where is God inviting us to engage in local church mission that is transformative, inclusive, and spiritual?

> He has told you, O mortal, what is good;
> and what does the Lord require of you
> but to do justice [be transformational],
> and to love kindness [be inclusive],
> and to walk humbly with your God [be spiritual]?
>
> (Micah 6:8, NRSV)

This chapter is a collaborative effort of the Baptist Union of Victoria Mission Catalyst team:

Rev. A/Prof Darren Cronshaw is Mission Catalyst — Researcher

Rev. David Chatelier is Mission Catalyst — New Churches

Rev. Brent Lyons-Lee is Mission Catalyst — Community Engagement

Rev. Ryan Smith is Director of Global Interaction — Victoria

Rev. Anne Wilkinson-Hayes is Mission team leader and Catalyst for Revitalisation.

Conclusion
Does the Future Have a Church?

Darrell Jackson

My earliest memories of attending church are as a three-year-old. I was taken by my parents to a parish church, named for St Francis, in the north-west of England. My memories of the church building are vague and impressionistic but they are nevertheless real.

Over the last twenty-five years I have been a member of four Baptist churches. Each of these has had a vision for their future and in each of them I was invited to become a part of imagining what that future might be. In each instance this has involved trying to discern the mind of God's Spirit for the congregation. Perhaps unsurprisingly, the conclusions drawn have typically been somewhat vague and impressionistic, but the vision that has emerged in each instance has nevertheless been real.

It seems to me that memories and imagination are closely related. Each is a way of creating mental maps of reality; of the past and of the future, respectively. We pour our energies, time, resources, as well as prayer, into shaping a future that gives concrete expression to our shared hopes and aspirations concerning the coming of God's kingdom "on earth as in heaven" (Matthew 6:10). Jesus taught his disciples about the coming kingdom using parables and metaphor. In doing so, he was teaching them the centrality of imagination as a way of anticipating God's future purposes. John's apocalyptic vision in the book of Revelation is arguably an indication that Jesus was successful in imparting this practice to his disciples.

Imagination is central to Gerard Delanty's account of the nature and formation of contemporary community. Delanty is a sociologist with several very helpful insights concerning the value, formation, vitality, and sustainability of community. He argues that the "vitality of community is above all due to its imagined capacity ... in the search and desire for it. Community ... has to be imagined and does not simply reproduce meaning but is productive of meaning ..." He concludes with the claim that "community is more likely to be expressed in an active search to achieve belonging than in preserving boundaries."[1]

For Delanty the vitality of any community, including a church community, reflects the degree to which it has developed the capacity for imagination. Secondly, vitality is dependent on the degree to which the discursive activity of its members can generate new possibilities and alternative futures. Discursive activity, for Delanty, is the activity through which members of a community talk, write, or otherwise publicly express their collective history, identity, and aspirations. We could say that the church cannot become what it cannot imagine. Of course, we might immediately want to add that theological imagination and theological vision do not have their sole origins in the collective activity of a community of God's people. It should also properly reflect Christian theological tradition and history and, ultimately, the revealed will of God through the Scriptures.

It should come as no surprise then that Darren Cronshaw, in his co-editor's foreword to this volume, highlights the need for imagination and advocacy when considering the topicality and urgency of congregational transformation and change. His concern is clearly shared by the many practitioners, researchers, and theologians who gathered in March 2014 as part of the *New Wineskins Symposium* at Whitley College, Melbourne. That we did so in an atmosphere of prayerful devotion and attentive listening to the word of God is an indication that to engage in the theological task in the absence of spiritual Christian practices is to run the risk of secularising our practices of mission and ministry.

On re-reading their papers, one is struck by their frequent use of metaphor and image as a way of trying to express the realities of congregational life and transformation that they are so eagerly pressing towards. Indeed, and most obviously, the use of the imagery of "new wineskins" is itself an attempt to hint at imaginative practices that are located in the teaching ministry of Jesus, practices which retain their capacity for capturing key insights about the contemporary social and cultural realities of our churches. The chapters of this book prove that the new wineskins imagery has stimulated and provoked thinking and reflection in a way that is timely, topical, and urgent. The Baptist community which identifies closely with *Crossover Australia* is faced yet again with fresh questions about its preparedness to receive the new wine of God's future. The March 2014 *Symposium* was a step along the way in engaging researchers and missional strategists to imagine God's future for the Baptist churches of Australia and the neighbourhoods and people that they are called to serve in the name of Jesus.

Of course, as with any metaphor, there is always the danger of it being over-used. Familiarity can, and does, breed contempt. Avoiding this danger requires us to ponder what Jesus meant when he first used the metaphor of old and new wineskins (Matthew 9:17). We also have to consider the extent to which it is valid to equate "new wineskins" with "Baptist church life". Finally, we may also be left wondering what we are to understand as the "new wine" of our contemporary situation.

Careful exegesis of Matthew chapter nine (and its synoptic parallels) will provide some answers to the questions posed here, but it will only take us so far. Even though Jesus may have been referring to his own teaching as the new wine, is it then automatically invalid to use the metaphor to say something about the significance of other phenomena in our own time and place? The authors in our volume seem to think it is highly relevant to apply the words of Jesus in this way. The constant question on many of their lips has been, "What does the 'new wine' of new members, new ideas, and new missional patterns, for example, have to say about the current state of the wineskins of the Baptist community in Australia?" They have learned to talk respectfully yet honestly about the wineskins that they have inherited. They have discovered inadequacies in them but have learnt to appreciate the past as providing wineskins that were wholly appropriate for an earlier time. The questions addressed here reflect the need to investigate whether these have now lost their relevancy or potency. In reviewing their wonderfully diverse and rich contributions I have been struck by the wide variety of ways in which the metaphors of new wine as well as of new wineskins have been given life and expression.

I have noticed a common and underlying conviction that the search for congregational transformation is always directed to the end of spotlighting God's reign and the accompanying *shalom* thereby promised to the wider community. In the contribution from the Baptist Union of Victoria, for example, the team of writers demonstrates that the transformational, spiritual, and inclusive nature of local mission is directed towards seeking the increase of God's *shalom* in the neighbourhood and surrounding community. In other chapters I can see that the need to change church cultures is anticipated as a necessary prior step towards becoming a more intentionally missional and incarnational presence in the community.

Of course, changing church culture is likely to occur at the junction where our collective memories of the past intersect with our congregational imagining of the future. Several of our authors have discussed church consultancy in a way that shows that memories and aspirations can become entwined with congregational identity and vision. Understanding the impact and orientation of both memories and aspirations is central to the practices of intentional interim ministries, for example, in its focus on history (especially of conflict) and identity, as well as upon the need to commit collectively to imagining and working towards a shared future.

In some of the discussion underway within this volume, the new wine is readily associated with the presence of new arrivals within a Baptist congregation. Their presence raises questions about the extent to which a congregation is resourcing them to relate their newly found faith to family members and friends. Research presented here shows that new arrivals in a congregation are far more likely to have existing friendships with people outside the church than are longer-standing members of the church. Of equal significance for congregations located in culturally diverse suburbs across metropolitan Australia is the reality that numerical growth has often been due to new ethnic minority groups joining existing Baptist congregations instead of forming their own ethnically distinct congregations.

Some sociologists (and some practical theologians) appear dismissive of church growth due to the influx of newer church members from diverse ethnic backgrounds. The impression is sometimes conveyed that this kind of growth is, at best, like winning the consolation prize in a church-growth competition. For more critical commentators, it is manifestly a sign of the failure of the church in the West. It seems to me that such claims are highly problematic. Firstly, they devalue the emphasis that Baptist congregations have always placed on locality and neighbourhood, an emphasis that is illustrated superbly throughout this volume. In a suburb with a significant ethnic Chinese population, one might hope to see that reflected in the life of a local Baptist congregation. Secondly, they fail to comprehend the rapidly changing nature of global Christianity on the move. The move towards becoming more authentically integrated and ethnically inclusive requires imagination and advocacy in moving towards a greater fulfilment and anticipation of the biblical vision of "every tongue and tribe" worshipping together in the kingdom of God.

This typical Baptist commitment to locality and local mission is also evident in understanding the need for new wineskins and new patterns of congregational presence at the urban margins, particularly among the vulnerable and exploited. Some authors press this further, arguing that authentic communities of the kingdom will live out a commitment to advocacy that at times brings them into conflict with political and other forms of authority that appear to be hindering the purposes of God's kingdom reign. This commitment to advocacy serves as a test of the extent to which congregational vision is authentically an imagining of the coming kingdom of God.

In sum, what has been presented here in this volume should not be taken as merely a series of case studies which provides principles for activists who are desperate to repeat the alleged success of others. Instead, what this volume has set out to do is to build on the biblical insight that it is the Saviour himself who has taken the responsibility of establishing his church (Matthew 16:18). To this extent, the congregational activity, transformation, and missional activity that we have been describing here is actually an extension of Jesus' mission. Of course, his mission should also be seen as an expression of the *missio Dei* (or mission of God). Only after these primary missional movements is it the case that we are then sent into *this* mission. In taking up their (metaphorical) pens, each of these authors shows that they are wrestling with the same issue of how best to respond to the realities of changing social and cultural contexts in a way that reflects faithfulness to the teaching of Jesus and to the missional nature of the church that he is establishing.

The diversity of views and practices outlined here reflects the extent to which reading the biblical texts of Matthew chapter nine is always under negotiation. Our practices both shape, and are shaped by, our understanding of the teachings of Jesus, particularly where these are expressed in parable and imaginative metaphor. The value of the current volume rests in the degree to which it will foster your own imagination, and that of the congregations of which you are a part, and lend wings to the ideas nested here. If these things happen, they will stand as a fitting testimony to the originators and sponsors of the *New Wineskins Symposium* and the ongoing research, practice, experimentation, and missional imagination that they will continue to encourage.

Darrell Jackson has served in pastoral ministry, regional youth ministry, and was the National Mission Advisor to the Baptist Union of Great Britain. He was the Executive Researcher for the Conference of European Churches, Geneva, and the founding Director of the Nova Research Centre, Redcliffe College, England. Since 2012 he has been the Senior Lecturer in Missiology at Morling College. He is a Mission Commission Associate of the WEA, the Chair of the Lausanne International Researchers Network, a member of the Editorial Board of Lausanne Global Analysis, and a member of the International Board of European Christian Mission International.

Endnotes

Foreword
1. Philip Hughes, *Launch of Baptists in Australia*, Melbourne, 2013.
2. Personal correspondence with Director of NCLS Research, Dr Ruth Powell, April 2015.

Introduction
1. Kenneth J. Cable, "Johnson, Richard (1753-1827)", in *Australian Dictionary of Biography*, Volume 2: 1788-1850, I-Z, ed. A. G. L. Shaw and C. M. H. Clark (London: Melbourne University Press, 1967), 17-19; Darren Cronshaw, *Credible Witness: Companions, Prophets, Hosts and Other Australian Mission Models* (Melbourne: Urban Neighbours of Hope, 2006), 45.
2. Simon Holt, *Eating Heaven: Spirituality at the Table* (Brunswick East: Acorn, 2013).
3. Kim Hammond and Darren Cronshaw, *Sentness: Six Postures of Missional Christians* (Downers Grove, IL: IVP, 2014), 181-182.

It Started with a Parable
1. John Dominic Crossan, *The Dark Interval: Towards a Theology of Story* (Sonoma, California: Polebridge, 1988).
2. Cited in John C. Hoffman, *Law, Freedom and Story: The Role of Narrative in Therapy, Society, and Faith* (Waterloo, Canada: Wilfrid Laurier University Press, 1986), 78.
3. Victor Turner, *Drama, Fields, and Metaphors* (Ithaca: Cornell University Press, 1974), 33.
4. Hoffman, *Law, Freedom and Story*, 90.
5. Hoffman, *Law, Freedom and Story*, 90.
6. Turner, *Drama, Fields, and Metaphors*, 273.
7. Hoffman, *Law, Freedom and Story*, 93.
8. Hoffman, *Law, Freedom and Story*.
9. Turner, *Drama, Fields, and Metaphors*, 298.

Education as a Community-Creating Missional Platform
1. He actually said, "If you build it, he will come".
2. For example, Mark McCrindle claims that in 1976 Australia had a population of 13.9 million, of whom 3.9 million attended church, whilst in 2014, with a population of 23.3 million, the number of church attendees has declined to 3.5 million. McCrindle also claims that as a percentage of population, Christianity has declined by 22% in this period, while church attendance has declined by 48%. Mark McCrindle, "Australian Social Trends and Implications for Churches," in *Crossover Consultation* (Brisbane: 2014).
3. Carey Community Baptist Church and Carey Baptist College. With the launch of the second campus in 2016, the original campus will be called Carey Harrisdale, and the newer campus, Carey Forrestdale.

4. David J. Bosch, *Witness to the World: The Christian Mission in Theological Perspective* (London: Marshall, Morgan and Scott, 1980).
5. http://www.oxforddictionaries.com/us/definition/american_english/mission, accessed 3 September, 2014.
6. "Mission has to do with the crossing of frontiers. It describes the total task which God set the Church for the salvation of the world." Bosch, *Witness to the World*, 17.

Missional Rejuvenation of Historic Inner-City Churches

1. "Inner City Development", http://www.abs.gov.au/Ausstats/abs@.nsf/90a12181d877a6a6ca2568 b5007b861c/460a9505966480c2ca256cc1008131fe!OpenDocument. Accessed 18 January 2013.
2. "Historic Inner-City Churches" are defined as those which have retained a physical presence within their inner-city precincts for at least 100 years.
3. Trevor Archer, "London Calling", http://www.fiec.org.uk/news/article/london-calling. Accessed 27 November 2012.
4. Philip Hughes, "Using Census Data Locally", *Christian Reseach Association: Pointers* 22, no. 3 (2012), 11.
5. Mark R. Gornik, *To Live in Peace: Biblical Faith and the Changing Inner City* (Grand Rapids, Michigan: Eerdmans, 2002), 12.
6. James Hopewell, *Congregation: Stories and Structures* (Philadelphia: Fortress, 1987).
7. Scott L. Thumma, "Methods of Congregational Study", in *Studying Congregations: A New Handbook*, ed. Jackson Carroll Nancy Ammerman, Carl Dudley and William McKinney (Nashville: Abingdon, 1998), 196–239,
8. Thom S. Rainer, *Autopsy of a Deceased Church* (Nashville: B&H, 2014), 17–23.
9. Hopewell, *Congregation*.
10. Penny Becker, *Congregations in Conflict: Cultural Models of Local Religious Life* (New York: Cambridge University Press, 1999), 13.
11. "Pray for us too, that God may open a door for our message, so that we may proclaim the mystery of Christ, for which I am in chains. Pray that I may proclaim it clearly, as I should." (Colossians 4:3–5 NIV)

Life in Community

1. Manuel Castells, *The Rise of the Network Society* (Malden: Blackwell, 2008), 187.
2. Dwight Zscheile brings this concept to a new vision of denominational systems, also inspired by scholars such as Manuel Castells and Rodney Starks: Dwight Zscheile, "Social Networking and Church Systems," *Word & World* 30, no. 3 (2010), 247–255.
3. Ann Morisy, *Journeying Out: A New Approach to Christian Mission* (London: Morehouse, 2004), 17.
4. Darren Cronshaw, "Mission and Spirituality at Solace Emerging Missional Church", *Australian Journal of Mission Studies* 2, no. 2 (2008), 38.
5. Athol Gill, *The Fringes of Freedom: Following Jesus, Living Together, Working for Justice* (Homebush West: Lancet, 1990), 87.
6. "Items of Interest – West Moreland Baptist Church", The Argus, 31 January 1922, 8, accessible at

http://trove.nla.gov.au/ndp/del/article/4708628
7. Robert Morsillo, "On Church as Community", Greenshoots (August 1987).
8. Michael Frost and Alan Hirsch, The Shaping of Things to Come: Innovation and Mission for the 21st-Century Church (Grand Rapids: Baker Books, 2003, revised and updated 2013), 79.
9. Morisy, Journeying Out, 197.
10. Frost and Hirsch, The Shaping of Things to Come, 67.
11. Morisy, Journeying out, x.
12. Morisy, Journeying out, 3.
13. Morisy, Journeying out, 57.
14. Cf. Robert Morsillo, "Introduction to Worship at Moreland", (1985), retrieved 23 May 2014 from http://www.morelandbaptistchurch.org.au/MBC/Stuff_files/MBC%20Worship.pdf.
15. Cronshaw, "Mission and Spirituality at Solace".
16. Quote from a young member of the church.
17. Morisy, Journeying Out, 188 (original emphasis).
18. Frost and Hirsch, The Shaping of Things to Come, 23.
19. Mara Einstein, Brands of Faith: Marketing Religion in a Commercial Age (London & New York: Routledge, 2008), 8.
20. Peter Horsfield, "Editorial: Re-placing Religion", Australian Journal of Communication 39, no. 1 (2012): h-i.
21. Rodney Stark, The Rise of Christianity: A Sociologist Reconsiders History (Princeton: Princeton University Press, 1996), 20.
22. Castells, The Rise of the Network Society, 187.
23. Mary Grey, "Where Does the Wild Goose Fly To? Seeking a New Theology of Spirit for Feminist Theology", New Blackfriars 72, no. 846 (1991), 92.
24. Mary Grey, The Outrageous Pursuit of Hope: Prophetic Dreams for the Twenty-First Century (London: Darton, Longman & Todd, 2000), 79.
25. Cheryl Peterson, "Spirit and Body: A Lutheran Feminist Conversation", in Transformative Lutheran Theologies: Feminist, Womanist and Mujerista Perspectives, ed. M. J. Streufert (Minneapolis: Fortress, 2010), 162.
26. Gary Bouma, Being Faithful in Diversity: Religions and Social Policy in Multifaith Society (Adelaide: ATF, 2011), 2, 67, 104.
27. Morisy, Journeying Out, 110.
28. Mario Vargas Llosa, "The Sign of the Cross" in The Language of Passion: Selected Commentary Trans. Natasha Wimmer (New York: Picador, 2000, 2003), 85.

Encounter Baptist Church's Journey with 3DM Discipleship and Mission

1. Mike Breen and Steve Cockram, Building a Discipling Culture: How to Release a Missional Movement by Discipling People Like Jesus Did (USA: 3DM, 2011).
2. Mike Breen, Leading Kingdom Movements: The "Everyman" Notebook on How to Change the World (Pawleys Island, SC: 3 Dimension Ministries, 2013).

3. Mike Breen, *Multiplying Missional Leaders: From Half-Hearted Volunteers to a Mobilized Kingdom Force* (Pawleys Island: 3DM, 2012); Mike Breen, *Leading Missional Communities: Rediscovering the Power of Living on Mission Together* (Pawleys Island: 3DM, 2013); Mike Breen and Alex Absalom, *Launching Missional Communities: A Field Guide* (USA: 3DM; Sheriar, 2010).

A Joining of the Ways

1. Faith Communities Today Survey 2005 as reported in Jim Tomberlin and Warren Bird, *Better Together: Making Church Mergers Work* (San Francisco: John Wiley & Sons, 2012).
2. Tomberlin and Bird, *Better Together*, 4–5.
3. Miroslav Volf, *After Our Likeness: The Church as the Image of the Trinity* (Grand Rapids: Eerdmans, 1998).
4. David Stevens, *God's New Humanity: A Biblical Theology of Multiethnicity for the Church* (Eugene, Or: Wipf & Stock, 2012).
5. Peter L. Berger, *The Sacred Canopy: Elements of a Sociological Theory of Religion* (Garden City, NY: Anchor Doubleday, 1967).
6. Lyle E. Schaller, *Reflections of a Contrarian: Second Thoughts on the Parish Ministry* (Nashville: Abingdon, 1989), 148.
7. Tomberlin and Bird, *Better Together*, 18.
8. Dan Reiland, "Mergers and Turnarounds", *The Pastor's Coach* (2013), http://globalchristiancenter.com/church-leadership/mergers-and-turnarounds.html.
9. Reiland, "Mergers and Turnarounds".
10. John P. Kotter, *Leading Change* (Harvard: Harvard Business Press, 1996).

The Swan Island Peace Convergence

1. Brian Toohey and William Pinwill, *Oyster: The Story of the Australian Secret Intelligence Service* (Port Melbourne: Heinemann, 1989), 64–65.
2. Rafael Epstein and Dylan Welch, "Secret SAS squadron sent to spy in Africa", T*he Sydney Morning Herald*, Sydney, 2012, http://www.smh.com.au/federal-politics/political-news/secret-sas-squadron-sent-to-spy-in-africa-20120312-1uwjs.html, (accessed February 26 2014).
3. G. Sharp, *The Politics of Nonviolent Action: Part Two: The Methods of Nonviolent Action* (Boston: Extending Horizons Books, 2005), 114.
4. "But before all this occurs, they will arrest you and persecute you; they will hand you over to synagogues and prisons, and you will be brought before kings and governors because of my name. This will give you an opportunity to testify. So make up your minds not to prepare your defence in advance; for I will give you words and a wisdom that none of your opponents will be able to withstand or contradict." (Luke 21:12–15)
5. "Seriously — the intelligence, articulacy [sic] and commitment evident in these was hugely inspiring. It was also heartening that the judge was obviously genuinely influenced by them. I'm all for diversity of tactics — but if all activists had their shit together anything like these people do, then The Revolution would be totally a done deal already." – Facebook comment from a secular activist in response to our court appearance16 April 2014.
6. John H. Yoder, *The Politics of Jesus: Vicit Agnus Noster* (Michigan: Eerdmans, 1972), 132.
7. Ephesians 3:20.

Imagining a Renewed Story at AuburnLife

1. This material was originally presented at AuburnLife, 11 May 2014; at a Uniting Church Presbytery of Yarra Yarra conference 12 September 2014; and co-presented with AuburnLife Sunday Stuff co-coordinator Beth Barnett at the "This is My/Our Story: Narrative and Mission in Contemporary Contexts", British and Irish Association of Practical Theology conference, Edinburgh, 15-17 July 2014. Conference travel was supported with a University of Divinity grant, and the research is part of a broader Baptist Union of Victoria project on church revitalisation supported by a Collier Charitable Grant.
2. John Green, *The Fault in Our Stars* (New York: Penguin, 2012), 32-33; and https://www.youtube.com/watch?v=9ItBvH5J6ss
3. J. R. Woodward, *Creating a Missional Culture: Equipping the Church for the Sake of the World* (Downers Grove, IL: IVP Books, 2012), 37-38.
4. Woodward, *Creating a Missional Culture*, 37-38. Other consultants who similarly urge churches to explore their stories from different angles include: James Hopewell, *Congregations: Stories and Structures* (Philadelphia: Fortress, 1987); Nancy Tatom Ammerman et al., eds., *Studying Congregations: A New Handbook* (Nashville: Abingdon, 1998), 40-62; Gil Rendle and Alice Mann, *Holy Conversations: Strategic Planning as a Spiritual Practice for Congregations* (Bethesda, MD: Alban Institute, 2003), 113-115,127-128; David Dadswell, *Consultancy Skills for Mission and Ministry* (London: SCM, 2011); Barry Harvey, *Can These Bones Live? A Catholic Baptist Engagement with Ecclesiology, Hermeneutics, and Social Theory* (Grand Rapids, MI: Brazos, 2008), 131-164; Alan J. Roxburgh, *Missional Map-Making: Skills for Leading in Times of Transition* (San Francisco: Wiley, 2010); Matthew Floding, ed. *Welcome to Theological Field Education! Reflective Practice* (Herndon, VA: Alban Institute, 2011), 79-80.
5. Hopewell, *Congregations*; Rendle and Mann, *Holy Conversations*, 113.
6. Darren Cronshaw, "Revitalisation Consultancy Models: Australian Church Case Studies", *International Journal of Practical Theology* (forthcoming).
7. Cf. Paul S. Fiddes, ed. *Faith in the Centre: Christianity and Culture* (Oxford: Regent's Park College, 2001).
8. Mark Lou Branson, *Memories, Hopes and Conversations: Appreciative Inquiry and Congregational Change* (Herndon: Alban Institute, 2004); Dadswell, *Consultancy Skills*.
9. Rendle and Mann, *Holy Conversations*, 113-115, 127-128; drawing on Ammerman et al., *Studying Congregations*, 40-62.
10. Ross Morgan, "Historical Summary", in Auburn Baptist Church Centenary Order of Service, 14 February 1988; David Hughes and Joanna Hughes, "Auburn Baptist Church History", Interview with author, 30 April 2014.
11. Morgan, "Historical Summary".
12. Ken Edmonds, "One Hundred and Fifty Years of Changing Architecture among Victorian Baptists", A paper presented to the Victorian Baptist Historical Society by architect Ken Edmonds, 8 March 2012, and published in *Our Yesterdays*; Ken Edmonds, Interview with author (27 May 2014).
13. Morgan, "Historical Summary"; Hughes and Hughes, "Auburn Baptist Church History".
14. Edmonds, Interview with author.
15. Morgan, "Historical Summary"; Hughes and Hughes, "Auburn Baptist Church History".
16. Ken R. Manley, "Mission Policy and Leadership at Home, 1958-1983", in *From Five Barley Loaves: Australian Baptists in Global Mission 1864-2010*, ed. Tony Cupit, Ros Gooden, and Ken

Manley (Preston Vic: Moasic, 2013), 431.

17. Hughes and Hughes, "Auburn Baptist Church History"; Ross Morgan, email to author, 26 August 2014.
18. Manley, "Mission Policy and Leadership at Home, 1958–1983", 431.
19. Edmonds, interview with author.
20. Ian G. Charles, *A First Biography of Rev. Hedley J. Sutton* (2-7-1876 — 6-2-1946) (AuburnLife Baptist Church archives, 1983), 26, 28; Gerald B. Ball, "India — Searching for an Identity", in *From Five Barley Loaves: Australian Baptists in Global Mission 1864–2010*, ed. Tony Cupit, Ros Gooden, and Ken Manley (Preston Vic: Moasic, 2013), 21–22; Elsie Sutton, Clause 3 of Will of Elsie Sutton, On file at Baptist Union of Victoria (27 January 1950).
21. Ball, "India — Bengali Disappointments", 77–78; Manley, "Mission Policy and Leadership at Home, 1913–1957", 187–191.
22. Ross Morgan, "Auburn Baptist Church History", interview with author, 12 May 2014; Hughes and Hughes, "Auburn Baptist Church History".
23. Keith Pickett, "Auburn Baptist Church History", interview with author, 12 May 2014.
24. There were ten leaders when the church was averaging 38 on a Sunday in mid-2012, though at the time of writing in May 2014 the team was back to five leaders with Sundays averaging 24.
25. Darren Cronshaw, "Being Church for Curious Visitors", *Witness: The Voice of Victorian Baptists* 91: 6 (August 2011), 8.
26. See the St. Columb's Premier League website: http://www.spltwenty20.com; Darren Cronshaw, "A Dream for Our World — including Auburn", *Witness* (3 September 2013), http://www.buv.com.au/witness-2/entry/a-dream-for-our-world-including-auburn
27. http://garamministry.weebly.com/about-us.html
28. Woodward, *Creating a Missional Culture*, 37–38.
29. Joseph Myers, *Organic Community: Creating a Place Where People Naturally Connect* (Grand Rapids: Baker, 2003), 80.
30. Expanded from Morgan, "Historical Summary".

Four Questions To Ask when Leading a Church into Change

1. Different perspectives on the social phenomena behind this change — both inside and outside of the church — can be found in Michael Riddell, *Threshold of the Future: Reforming the Church in the Post-Christian West* (London: SPCK, 1998) 1–16;Alan Roxburgh, *The Sky is Falling: Leaders Lost in Transition* (Eagle, Idaho: ACI, 2005), 19–27; Alan Hirsch, *The Forgotten Ways: Reactivating the Missional Church* (Grand Rapids: Brazos, 2006); Tom Sine, The New Conspirators: Creating the Future *One Mustard Seed at a Time* (Downers Grove IL: IVP, 2008), 17–28.
2. Stevens and Collins conceive the pastor–people relationship using the metaphor of marriage. R. Paul Stephens and P. Collins, *The Equipping Pastor* (New York: Alban Institute, 1993), 2.
3. Eugene Peterson affirms this aspect of the pastoral role in times of crisis, yet one might ask, why only in such circumstances? Eugene H. Peterson, *Five Smooth Stones for Pastoral Work* (Atlanta: JohnKnox, 1980), 93. Patton reminds us to be aware of the "normative horizon" which underpins our approach to pastoral care, and shapes our beliefs about proper outcomes. John Patton, *Pastoral Care in Context: An Introduction to Pastoral Care* (Louisville, Kentucky: Westminster/John Knox, 1993), 59.

4. A fundamental aspect of pastoral care is that of listening —honouring the history of the church is, in reality, listening to its story. In listening to the church's story, we will hear invitations to care and shape the future. James D. Whitehead and Evelyn Eaton Whitehead, *Shadows of the Heart: A Spirituality of Painful Emotions* (New York: Crossroad, 1996), 180.
5. For a good introduction to metaphors for organisational structures, see G. Morgan, *Images of Organisation* (London: Sage, 2006).
6. A good overview of the contextual approach in an inner-urban environment is explored by Simon Holt, *God Next Door: Spirituality & Mission in the Neighbourhood* (Blackburn South: Acorn, 2007). For a broader perspective, Leonard Sweet, *Soul Tsunami: Sink or Swim in the Millennium Culture* (Grand Rapids, MI: Zondervan, 1999) provides helpful questions for reflection and discussion.
7. Government statistics and local council web sites are good avenues for broad demographic data. In the Australian context, census data is broken down into smaller localities to assist in mapping the information for your own area. These are called Socio-Economic Indexes for Areas (SEIFA) and can be found at http://www.abs.gov.au/websitedbs/censushome.nsf/home/seifa. The various publications of the National Church Life Survey (ncls.org.au) are also helpful.
8. The theology and biblical metaphors available here are rich. Robert Banks, *Paul's Idea of Community: The Early House Churches in their Historical Setting* (Homebush West: ANZEA, 1988), 33–70 offers insights from the Pauline canon. Hans Kung, *The Church* (New York: Image Books, 1977), 147–313 reflects on broader theological themes.
9. This is a term I first encountered in the works of J.E. LesslieNewbigin, *The Household of God: Lectures on the Nature of the Church* (London: SCM, 1953) but has since fallen into disuse. This work was republished in 2002 by Paternoster.
10. See Edward Said's excellent essay on the experience of exile: "Reflections on Exile" in Edward W. Said, *Reflections on Exile and Other Literary and Cultural Essays* (London: Granta, 2000), 173-186.
11. Charles V. Gerkin, *An Introduction to Pastoral Care* (Nashville: Abingdon, 1997), 113, and Edward Farley, "Interpreting Situations: An Inquiry into the Nature of Practical Theology", in *The Blackwell Reader in Pastoral and Practical Theology*, ed. James Woodward and Stephen Pattison (Oxford: Blackwell, 2000), 11.
12. Windquist talks of "imaginariums" to fund this creativity: in Andrew D. Lester, *Hope in Pastoral Care and Counseling* (Louisville: John Knox, 1995), 109f.
13. The first of three stages identified in leading across cultural difference identified by Lago and Thompson: C.Lago and J. Thompson, *Race, Culture and Counselling* (Buckingham: Open University, 1996).
14. For an alternative approach which reframes the challenge, see Robert Kegan and L. L. Lahey, *Immunity to Change: How to Overcome It and Unlock the Potential in Yourself and Your Organization* (Boston: Harvard Business Press, 2009), 11–30.
15. Cameron refers to this in the context of positive relationships, linking positive social relationships in a context to the positive outcomes for an organisation: K. Cameron, *Positive Leadership: Strategies for Extraordinary Performance* (San Francisoc: Berret Kohler, 2012), 45–64.
16. Emmanuel Y.Lartey, *In Living Color: An Intercultural Approach to Pastoral Care and Counseling* (London: Jessica Kingsley, 2003), 62.

When the Wineskins Burst

1. Joshua 9:13; Matthew 9:17; Mark 2:22. It would be surprising if wine was not also stored in jars similar to the water jars of John 2:6, but smaller in size.
2. There are other reasons for IIM pastors to be called to fractured churches, but this is one of the most significant reasons.
3. Michael D. Watkins, *The First Ninety Days: Proven Strategies for Getting Up to Speed Faster and Smarter* (Boston: Harvard Business Review), 72.
4. Loren B. Mead, *Intentional Interim Ministry: A Training Conference for Interim Ministers*, Australian Edition (Brisbane: Transitional Ministries of Australia, 2002).
5. Many social commentators, such as Alan Kirby in Digimodernism: *How New Technologies Dismantle the Postmodern and Reconfigure Our Culture*, assert that post-postmodernism has arrived.
6. Carver Governance uses a hierarchical model in which the owners have the ultimate authority within an organisation (www.policygovernance.com; FAQ 9). A movement in the Western World applies this principle to churches in which the senior pastor is accorded ultimate authority. A Baptist church nearby my residence moved to this interpretation. The church's 350 Sunday morning attendance collapsed to 50, with the Board citing the "Carver Model" as the cause.
7. Cited in Rebecca Huntley, T*he World According To Y: Inside the New Adult Generation* (Crows Nest: Allen & Unwin, 2006), 9.
8. Rebecca Huntley, *The World According To Y: Inside the New Adult Generation* (Crows Nest: Allen & Unwin, 2006).
9. Based on Watkins, *First Ninety Days*, 59.
10. Kerry Patterson, Joseph Grenny, David Maxfield, Ron McMillan and Al Switzler, Influencer: The Power to Change Anything (New York: McGraw-Hill, 2008).
11. John Bevere, The Bait of Satan, DVD (Palmer Lake: Messenger International, 2006).
12. Kenneth Quick, "Attachment Disorder Churches: If Your People Won't Follow, It May Be the Result of Past Abandonment", *Leadership Journal* Vol XXIX, No 4 (2008), 88. One can understand how this would happen as the children wouldn't want to be hurt again.
13. John Woodley, "Developing a Leadership Structure for North-east Baptist Church", Nundah: North-east Baptist Church Board Meeting, June, 2012.
14. Watkins, *The First Ninety Days*.
15. Watkins, *The First Ninety Days*.
16. Peter Van Donge, "Decision-Making Model for a Teams-Based Church", Nundah: North-east Baptist Church Board Meeting, June, 2012.
17. Based on Kim S. Cameron, and Robert E. Quinn, *Diagnosing and Changing Organizational Culture: Competing Values Framework* (San Francisco: Jossey-Bass), 38.
18. Kim S. Cameron and Robert E. Quinn. *Diagnosing and Changing Organizational Culture: Competing Values Framework* (San Francisco: Jossey-Bass), 53.
19. Adapted from Cameron and Quinn, *Diagnosing and Changing Organizational Culture*, 53.
20. The original OCAI virtually sought percentages that were decided in each segment. When the level of ministry is so low, I believed that it was better to place where ministry was occurring and then move out from there.
21. Based on Cameron and Quinn, *Diagnosing and Changing Organizational Culture*, 88.

22. Based on Cameron and Quinn, *Diagnosing and Changing Organizational Culture*, 98.
23. Based on Carl S. Dudley and Nancy T. Ammerman, *Congregations in Transition: A Guide for Analyzing, Assessing, and Adapting in Changing Communities* (San Francisco: Jossey Bass), 39.
24. John 15:1–5.
25. Australian Broadcast Commission News, Channel 2, 7.00 p.m. AET, 1/1/2000.
26. Craig S. Watkins, *The Young and the Digital: What the Migration to Social-Networking Sites, Games, and Anytime, Anywhere Media Means for Our Future* (Boston: Beacon, 2009), ix.
27. David Meerman Scott, *The New Rules of Marketing & PR: How to Use Social Media, Online Video, Mobile Applications, Blogs, News Releases, & Viral Marketing to Reach Buyers Directly* (Hoboken: Wiley, 2013), 282–283.
28. Ram Charan, "Ending the CEO Succession Crisis", *Harvard Business Review* February (2005).
29. Rosabeth Moss Kanter, "Leadership and the Psychology of Turnarounds", *Harvard Business Review* June (2003), 3–11.
30. Kanter, "Leadership and the Psychology of Turnarounds", 3–11.

From Stuck to Growing

1. Peter L. Steinke, *Healthy Congregations: A Systems Approach* (Bethesda: Alban Institute, 1996), 17–18.
2. Les Scarborough, Scott Pilgrim, and Peter Davies, editors, *Church Consultancy Manual* (Epping, NSW: Baptist Churches of NSW and ACT, 2007 (revised)), 1.
3. Marjatte Maula and Flemming Poulfelt, Knowledge *Transfer, Consulting Modes and Learning: Do the Codes of Conduct and Ethics Reflect Reality in Management Consulting?* Working Papers (Copenhagen Business School, Department of Management, Politics and Philosophy, 2000), 7–8.
4. Edgar H. Schein, *Process Consultation. Volume II: Lessons for Managers and Consultants*, Addison-Wesley Series on Organization Development. (Reading: Addison-Wesley, 1987), 22–35.
5. Different types of church consultancies are expanded on in Duncum, "Explore the Impact", along with literature surveys and theologies of church health, church growth, and church consultancy. Other statistical analyses, including cross-tabulations, descriptives, and ANOVA tables are also included in the thesis.
6. Seeking to discern God's call together — and in so doing advancing God's kingdom within and beyond the church — is one of the significant differences of church consultancy from business consultancy.
7. John J Scherer, Gina Lavery, Roland Sullivan, Ginger Whitson, and Elizabeth Vales, "Whole System Transformation — The Consultant's Role in Creating Sustainable Results", in *Consultation for Organizational Change*, Anthony F. Buono and David W. Jamieson, eds., Research in Management Consulting Series (Charlotte, NC: Information Age Pub., 2010), 58–59.
8. Anthony F Buono and Kenneth W. Kerber, "Intervention and Organizational Change: Building Organizational Change Capacity", in Consultation for Organizational Change, Anthony F. Buono and David W Jamieson, eds., Research in Management Consulting Series (Charlotte, NC: Information Age, 2010), 82–83.
9. Warren Bennis and Robert Townsend, *Reinventing Leadership: Strategies to Empower the*

Organization (New York: Morrow, 1995); Louis Carter, et al., *Best Practices in Leadership Development and Organization Change: How the Best Companies Ensure Meaningful Change and Sustainable Leadership* (San Francisco: Pfeiffer, 2005); Kurt Lewin, *The Complete Social Scientist: A Kurt Lewin Reader*, ed. Martin Gold (Washington, DC: American Psychological Association, 1999); George Lovell, *Consultancy Modes and Models* (Calver: Cliff College, 2005); William J. Rothwell and Roland Sullivan, eds, *Practicing Organization Development: A Guide for Consultants* (San Francisco: Pfeiffer, 2005); Peter M. Senge, *The Fifth Discipline: The Art and Practice of the Learning Organization* (New York: Doubleday/Currency, 1990).

10. Peter Davies, "Consultancy Master List Numerical 070919 (Version 2). Xls", Excel sheet of all church consultancies to date, Baptist Churches of NSW/ACT Church Consultancy Team (Epping, NSW, 2007), 1.

11. Alice Mann, *The In-Between Church: Navigating Size Transitions in Congregations* (Bethesda: Alban Institute, 1998); Alice Mann, *Raising the Roof: The Pastoral-to-Program Size Transition* (Bethesda: Alban Institute, 2001).

12. NCLS Research has isolated the following nine core qualities of healthy and vital churches: an alive and growing faith, vital and nurturing worship, strong and growing belonging, a clear and owned vision, inspiring and empowering leadership, open and flexible innovation, practical and diverse service, willing and effective faith-sharing, and intentional and welcoming inclusion. Additionally, NCLS has identified three quantitative measures of the missional impact of churches: young adult retention — the proportion of the children of attenders still attending a church: newcomers — the percentage of newcomers at a church; and attendance change — patterns of growth or decline in the number of people attending a church over time.

13. Pastor of Church C, Interview Transcript, (Sydney, 2009), 2; Pastor of Church F, Interview Transcript, (Sydney, 2009), 2; Pastor of Church H, Interview Transcript, (Sydney, 2010), 2; Pastor of Church I, Interview Transcript (Sydney, 2009), 2.

14. Pastor of Church C, Interview Transcript, 3; Pastor of Church F, Interview Transcript, 3; Pastor of Church I, Interview Transcript, 3.

15. Pastor of Church F, Interview Transcript, 3.

16. Pastor of Church F, Interview Transcript, 3.

17. Pastor of Church C, Interview Transcript, 2.

18. Pastor of Church C, Interview Transcript, 2.

19. John Bellamy, Bryan Cussen, Sam Sterland, Keith Castle, Ruth Powell, and Peter Kaldor, *Enriching Church Life: A Practical Guide for Local Churches*, (Adelaide, South Australia: NCLS, 2006),10–29.

20. There are some missing values in attendance data for all churches. However, membership data, which is more robust, confirms the small change in attendance patterns of all churches over this time period: membership in all NSW/ACT Baptist churches increased from 20705 in 2001 to 20776 in 2006, an increase of 0.3%. Again in this instance research is hampered by the small number of consultancy churches in gaining statistical significance of p<0.05.Alan Soden, *NSW and ACT Baptist Churches Handbook 2001–2002*, 217; Alan Soden, *NSW and ACT Baptist Churches Handbook 2006–2007*, 287. The figures are as at 30 June, 2001 and 30 June 2006 respectively.

21. Summaries of the Church Consultancy Reports incorporating objectives that were set by the various leadership groups of those churches and recommendations made by the consultants regarding each objective are contained in Appendices AA to JJ in Duncum, "Explore the Impact".

22. NCLS Research, Church Life Profile — Church D Baptist Church (Sydney South: NCLS

Research, 2006), 23.
23. ABS Census of Population and Housing, *Suburb Profiles — Demographics*.
24. Baptist Churches of NSW and ACT Church Consultancy Team, "Church D Baptist Church Consultancy Report" (Epping NSW, 2001), 4.
25. Baptist Churches, "Church D Consultancy Report", 6.
26. NCLS Research, Church Life Profile — Church D Baptist Church, 6.
27. NCLS Research, Church Life Profile — Church D Baptist Church, 23.
28. NCLS Research, Church Life Profile — Church F Baptist Church (Sydney South, NSW: NCLS Research, 2006), 23.
29. NCLS Research, Church Life Profile — Church F Baptist Church, 24.
30. NCLS Research, Regional Church Life Profile — Baptist Church NSW/ACT (Sydney South, NSW: NCLS Research, 2006), 24.
31. ABS Census of Population and Housing, *Suburb Profiles — Demographics*.
32. Baptist Churches of NSW and ACT Church Consultancy Team, "Church F Baptist Church Consultancy Report" (Epping NSW, 2001), 4.
33. Pastor of Church F, Interview Transcript, 1.
34. Pastor of Church F, Interview Transcript, 2.
35. NCLS Research, Church Life Profile — Church F Baptist Church, 24–25.
36. NCLS Research, Church Life Profile — Church F Baptist Church, 6, 23–24.
37. Pastor of Church A, Interview Transcript, 2; Pastor of Church C, Interview Transcript, 3; Pastor of Church F, Interview Transcript, 3; Pastor of Church H, Interview Transcript, 3; Pastor of Church I, Interview Transcript, 2.
38. Kaldor, Bellamy, and Powell, *Shaping a Future: Characteristics of Vital Congregations*, (Adelaide: Openbook, 1997), 196–99.
39. Pastor of Church F, Interview Transcript, 1.
40. Paul D. Borden, *Direct Hit: Aiming Real Leaders at the Mission Field* (Nashville: Abingdon, 2006).

The Work of Transformation

1. J. D. Zizioulis, *Being as Communion: Studies in Personhood and the Church* (Crestwood, St Vladimir's Seminary Press, 1985); L. Boff, *Holy Trinity Perfect Community* (Maryknoll, Orbis, 2000); Jurgen Moltmann, *The Church in the Power of the Spirit: A Contribution to Messianic Ecclesiology* (San Francisco, Harper Collins,1977, 1991); Catherine La Cugna God for Us (New York Harper Collins, 1991); Miroslav Volf, *After Our Likeness: The Church as the Image of the Trinity* (Grand Rapids, Eerdmans, 1998); Stanley Grenz *The Social God and the Relational Self*, Louisville (Westminster, John Knox, 2001).
2. J. Moltmann, *The Spirit of Life: A Universal Human Affirmation* (Minneapolis, Fortress, 1992), 309.
3. Volf, *After Our Likeness*, 217.
4. Moltmann, *Church in the Power of the Spirit*, 299.
5. Volf, *After Our Likeness*, 236. It is difficult to conceive of situations 2 and 3.
6. Manfred Kets De Vries, *The Leadership Mystique: A User's Manual for the Human Enterprise*

(London, Prentice Hall, 2001), 4–5.

7. This is my own research experience. See J. Pugh, *Fantasyland Faith: The Redemptive Role of Ethical Leaders in Neurotic Church Systems* (Saabrucken, VDM Verlag, 2007), 431–445.

8. For examples see K. B. Lyon, "Paranoid Schizoid Phenomena in Congregational Conflict: Some Dilemmas of Reconciliation", *Pastoral Psychology*, 47, 273–293, and M. J. Moran, "Curing Group Paralysis", *Human Development*, 18 No. 2, 16–21.

9. The unusual spelling from "fantasies" is used to distinguish these preconscious group contagions about the role of the leader or the group that stem from shared infancy issues, from conscious and explicit pictures of current reality that are somewhat inaccurate or delusional.

10. W. R. Bion, *Experiences in Groups and Other Papers*, (New York, Balantyne, 1961).

11. This is the most dangerous of the basic assumptions for pastoral health as any good aspects of the pastor are dismissed in the powerful infantile actions of splitting and projection deployed during the primal paranoid stage of development against the less-than-perfect mother. As with the mother so the threatening pastor is depersonalised as a non-feeling half-object.

12. D. J. Louw, "God as Friend: Metaphoric Theology in Pastoral Care", *Pastoral Psychology* 46 (1998) 233–242.

13. In recent times Manfred Kets De Vries has expanded Bion's categories. To Bion's classifications he adds the following finer distinctions: *The Dramatic Organisation, Suspicious Organisation, Compulsive Organisation, Detached Organisation, Depressive Organisation*. See Manfred F. R. Kets de Vries, *The Leader on the Couch: A Clinical Approach to Changing People and Organizations* (Milton: John Wiley/Jossey Bass, 2006), 322–330.

14. Manfred F. R. Kets De Vries and Danny Miller, *The Neurotic Organization* (San Francisco, Jossey Bass, 1984), 147f & 168f: also, A. Zalezenik, "The Mythological Structure of Organizations and its Impact", in L. Hirschhon and C. Barnett (eds.) *The Psychodynamics of Organizations* (Philadelphia: Temple University Press, 1993), 179–190; M. Kets De Vries, *Leader on the Couch*, specially, 219f.

15. L. F. Stapley, *The Personality of the Organization: A Psychodynamic Explanation of Culture and Change* (London, Free Association Books, 1996), and L. Hirschhorn, *The Workplace Within: The Psychodynamics of Organizational Life* (Cambridge, MIT, 1988).

16. Stapley, *The Personality of the Organization*, 176.

17. Hirschhorn, *The Workplace Within*, 219.

18. Meissner is the first theologian to think through the implications of object relations theory within a Christian church setting. He also lists other readily available transitional objects such as well designed, God-centred liturgy, teaching people the basis of petitionary prayer, and faith itself. See W.W. Meissner SJ, *Psychoanalysis and Religious Experience* (London, Yale University Press, 1984). For a secular equivalent see W. Van Buskirk, "Organizational Cultures as Holding Environments: A Psychodynamic Look at Organizational Symbolism", *Human Relations* 52: 6 (1999), 805–832.

19. Gk *katatismon*

20. For the most compelling of critiques see Kathryn Tanner, *Christ the Key* (Oxford University Press, 2010). Tanner cautions against Volf's identification of trinitarian and ecclesial communion, in particular reminding us of the great distinction between created persons and the eternal infinite God. Likewise there is no way that humans can co-inhere each other as with the Trinity, and she sees that, while we are called to model Christ, we are never explicitly called to model the Trinity. See especially her fifth chapter and also S. Hunt, "Trinity and Church Explorations in Ecclesiology from a Trinitarian Perspective", *St Marks Review* No. 1

(2005), 32–44. While Tanner's cautions are salutary it could be also noted that, just as trinitarian formulation is in process in the New Testament period, the formulas of later eras do not and cannot serve the basis of ecclesial agendas. However, the assumptions of the writers reflect remarkable political and structural parallels repeatedly across the whole New Testament corpus while we are not called explicitly to model our life upon the life of the Trinity. However, the apostles never condone a cultural arrangement that moves in a direction in tension with the revelation of the triune nature either revealed in the relating of the Son to the Father in his incarnate life or in explicitly doctrinal formulae.

21. This vision is very similar to what is technically termed a "cultivation" or "possibility-personal" culture. These culture types value the development of persons *through* their labours and their orientation is toward future possibilities rather than present actualities. They are people-driven and open-minded in their decision making and emphasise ideals, beliefs aspirations, and creative achievements in contrast to pragmatic "corporate" (hierarchical), "competitive", or personalist "collaborative" (communal) types. William E. Schneider, *The Re-engineering Alternative* (New York: McGraw Hill, 2000), 112 ff.
22. E. Schein, *Organizational Culture and Leadership* (San Francisco: Jossey Bass, 1992), 70,71.
23. A "cultivation" culture depends upon internal sources of motivation rather than external constraint. The cohesive centripetal force is "… *the magnetism caused essentially by the level of commitment that its people can attain … Decisions hinge upon content and processes that exist within people*". Schneider, *The Reengineering Alternative*, 122.
24. Kets De Vries and Miller, *The Neurotic Organization*, 168ff.

Giving Newcomers a Voice

1. This study draws on a range of small sample surveys from the 2011 NCLS. For responses on some questions, the sample sizes may be too small to be reliable if we split newcomer results into both first-timers (2%) and returnees (4%).
2. Peter Kaldor, [computer file], 1996 NCLS Attender Survey (Sydney, Australia: NCLS Research, 1996); Keith Castle, [computer file], 2001 NCLS Attender Survey (Sydney: NCLS Research, 2001): Keith Castle, [computer file], 2006 NCLS Attender Survey (Sydney: NCLS Research, 2006): Ruth Powell, [computer file], 2011 NCLS Attender Survey (Sydney: NCLS Research, 2011).
3. 'Pentecostal' includes Apostolic Church, Australian Christian Churches (AOG), C3 Church, Christian Life Churches, Christian Outreach Centre, CRC Churches, Foursquare Church, and International Pentecostal Holiness Movement.
4. E.g., Ruth Powell, John Bellamy, Sam Sterland, Kathy Jacka, Miriam Pepper and Michael Brady, *Enriching Church Life* (2nd ed) (Adelaide: Mirrabooka, 2012).
5. All cartoons are ©cxmedia. See www.cxmedia.com
6. Peter Kaldor, John Bellamy, Sandra Moore, Ruth Powell, Keith Castle, and Merilyn Correy, *Mission under the Microscope: Keys to Effective and Sustainable Mission* (Adelaide, Openbook. 1995), 132.
7. Peter Kaldor and John Bellamy, "Fresh through the Door: Newcomers to Church Life in Australia", in *Joining and Leaving Religion: Research Perspectives*, ed. L. Francis, and Y. Katz (Herefordshire, UK: Gracewing, 2002).

A Contemporary Theology of Local Church Mission, in Global Perspective

1. "The Issue: Of what earthly use is the church?", Panel discussion, Sunday Nights with John Cleary, ABC Radio (Sunday 2 June 2013), http://www.abc.net.au/sundaynights/stories/s3772783.htm; and related reflection: Darren Cronshaw, "Of What Earthly Use Is The Church?" Witness (5 June 2013), http://www.buv.com.au/witness/entry/of-what-earthly-use-is-the-church
2. David Tacey, *Re-enchantment: A New Australian Spirituality* (Sydney: Harper Collins, 2000), 97.
3. Tacey, *Re-enchantment*, 99–100.
4. Michael Frost, *The Road to Missional: Journey to the Center of the Church* (Grand Rapids: Baker, 2011).
5. Frost, *Road to Missional*, 28.
6. David J. Bosch, *Transforming Mission: Paradigm Shifts in Theology of Mission* (Maryknoll: Orbis, 1991).
7. Mike Breen and Steve Cockram, *Building a Discipling Culture: How to Release a Missional Movement by Discipling People Like Jesus Did* (USA: 3DM, 2011).
8. Ruth Haley Barton, *Sacred Rhythms — Arranging Our Lives for Spiritual Transformation* (Downers Grove: IVP, 2006), 64.
9. Sara Miles, *Take This Bread: A Radical Conversion* (New York: Ballantine, 2007), 241.
10. Philip Hughes and Darren Cronshaw, *Baptists in Australia: A Church with a Heritage and a Future* (Melbourne: Christian Research Association, 2013), 74–78.
11. Nicholas Wolterstorff, *Until Justice and Peace Embrace: The Kuyper Lectures for 1981 Delivered at the Free University of Amsterdam* (Grand Rapids: Eerdmans, 1983), 69–70.
12. Hugh Mackay, *The Good Life: What Makes a Life Worth Living* (Melbourne: Pan Macmillan, 2013).
13. Darren Cronshaw, "A Dream for Our World — including Auburn," Witness (2013), http://www.buv.com.au/witness-2/entry/a-dream-for-our-world-including-auburn; St Columb's Premier League, http://www.spltwenty20.com.
14. http://www.micahnetwork.org/integral-mission
15. Will Mancini, *Church Unique: How Missional Leaders Cast Vision, Capture Culture, and Create Movement* (San Francisco: Jossey-Bass, 2008), 86.

Conclusion

1. Delanty, Gerard, Community, (2nd edition) Abingdon, UK: Routledge, 2009, 186–189.

www.ingramcontent.com/pod-product-compliance
Lightning Source LLC
Chambersburg PA
CBHW032029290426
44110CB00012B/726